# vegetarian *times*

# PLANT-POWERED PROTEIN

## COOKBOOK

Over 200 Healthy & Delicious
Whole-Food Dishes

Mary Margaret Chappell
and
the editors at *Vegetarian Times*

### Globe Pequot

GUILFORD, CONNECTICUT

# Globe Pequot

An imprint of The Rowman & Littlefield Publishing Group, Inc.
4501 Forbes Blvd., Ste. 200
Lanham, MD 20706
www.rowman.com

Distributed by NATIONAL BOOK NETWORK

ACTIVE INTEREST MEDIA

British Library Cataloguing in Publication Information Available

**Library of Congress Cataloging-in-Publication Data Available**

ISBN 978-1-4930-3097-2 (hardback)
ISBN 978-1-4930-5044-4 (paperback)
ISBN 978-1-4930-3098-9 (e-book)

**Photo Credits**

Photos by *Vegetarian Times* except for the following: p. ii: Photography: Darren Kemper, Food Styling: Terry Schacht; p.viii: Antonina Vlasova/SHUTTERSTOCK.com; p. ix: phive2015/istockphoto.com; p. x: Lukas Gojda/SHUTTERSTOCK.com; p. 6: Kiian Oksana/SHUTTERSTOCK.com; p.7: janecocoa/SHUTTERSTOCK.com; p. 8: monticello/SHUTTERSTOCK.com; p. 12: Nattika/SHUTTERSTOCK.com; p. 38: Kate Kosaya; p. 40: Photography Ronald Tsang, Food Styling: Bernadette Ammar; p. 56: Photography: Darren Kemper, Food Styling: Terry Schacht; p. 93: Kate Kosaya; p.120: By Natalia Livingston/SHUTTERSTOCK.com; p. 149 TorryPhoto; p. 154: Artichokes levkr/istockphoto.com; Asparagus esanbanhao/istockphoto.com; Bean Sprouts photohunter/SHUTTERSTOCK; Beets bergamont/istockphoto.com; Broccoli rimglow/istockphoto.com; Brussels Sprouts tpzijl/istockphoto.com; Peas ValentynVolkov/istockphoto.com; Fennel IngridHS/istockphoto.com; Leafy Greens sarsmis/SHUTTERSTOCK; Lima Bean Fengjin/istockphoto.com; Edamame nipapornnan/istockphoto.com; Sweet potatoesegal/istockphoto.com; p. 191: Kate Kosaya; p. 221 Bowls of beans barmalini/istockphoto.com; p. 254 eAlisa/istockphoto.com; p. 255 lily_rochha/istockphoto.com; p.340: Kate Kosaya; p. 369: Kate Kosaya

# CONTENTS

# INTRODUCTION

**Food fads come and go** (Remember the kale craze?), but your body's needs remain the same. Protein is one of those primary needs. Long before protein attained the food sensation status that it now enjoys, *Vegetarian Times* was paying close attention to the essential nutrient and making sure our recipes had enough of it. We had to. New vegetarians were constantly asking us, "Will I get enough protein?" (Yes!) Longtime vegetarians and vegans regularly turned to us for wholesome, delicious dishes that they could incorporate into a balanced diet. And, the nutritional information we've always included with our recipes meant there was no way to ignore protein counts any more than we could ignore fat or calories.

Now, at long last, what *Vegetarian Times* has known for nearly fifty years has become part of the mainstream health message: Vegetarian protein sources are important for everyone, everywhere, regardless of age, lifestyle, or diet. Author and activist Michael Pollan sums it up in his three simple food rules: "Eat food. Not too much. Mostly plants." These rules echo the number one health recommendation from the World Health Organization, to "eat a variety of foods mainly from plants, rather than animals." There are signs that Americans are heeding this advice, with meat consumption falling 19 percent between 2005 and 2014. Favoring plant-based proteins in your diet is also critical for the environment. Animal agriculture remains one of the lead causes of climate change; the livestock industry produces more greenhouse gases than does transportation. Understanding how to make the most of the plant-based proteins means you can do your part to save the planet while ensuring a healthy lifestyle for yourself.

With this cookbook, *Vegetarian Times* hopes to take the meat-free protein message one step further. We want to show how to integrate protein-rich recipes into everyday home cooking for optimum wellness and maximum satisfaction. The 200 recipes that follow are ample proof of how easy it is to make tasty, nourishing, satisfying, protein-rich dishes for any occasion.

## THE BENEFITS OF A PROTEIN-RICH DIET

Health care professionals, nutritionists, fitness coaches, and diet experts all agree: Getting enough protein is the key to reaching wellness goals. Need to lose weight? Protein helps curb hunger pangs and keeps you satisfied on your diet. Looking to get in better shape? Protein provides the building blocks for muscle mass and sustains energy levels. Want to stave off chronic disease? Diets rich in healthy proteins have been shown to reduce the risk of cardiovascular disease, type 2 diabetes, and certain cancers. Trying to balance your meals to avoid the ping-pong hunger effect that leads to snacking and sluggishness? Again, paying attention to protein can help. But, protein isn't a dietary supplement or a lab compound. Protein is found in foods (even those high-protein powders used in fitness shakes are derived from something edible). The goal, then, isn't to pursue Protein with a capital "P," but to seek out protein-rich foods and recipes that nourish and satisfy while delivering key nutrients as well.

## NUTRIENT-DENSE PROTEINS

In this cookbook, we'll focus on nutrient-dense, protein-rich foods, how they fit into delicious vegetarian and vegan dishes, and how to make them a part of your cooking routine. We've chosen the term "nutrient-dense" over "vegetarian" for a couple of reasons. First, this book isn't just for vegetarians. Nutrient-dense, protein-rich diets are recommended and beneficial for everyone. The term also allows us to single out protein-rich foods that are high in other essential nutrients such as fiber, vitamins, minerals, and antioxidants. And it lets us exclude nutrient-poor, high-protein options that may still be vegetarian or plant-based. Take processed "fake meats" found in most supermarkets today. These may be free of animal products and they can be tasty, but aside from protein, they offer very little in the way of other nutrients. (They can also contain hidden sugars and high levels of sodium, which are best avoided.)

## EGGS AND DAIRY

Eggs and low-fat dairy are included among our nutrient-dense protein foods because they offer unique nutritional profiles that can benefit a vegetarian diet. Both provide excellent sources of vitamins and minerals like vitamins D and $B_{12}$ that are not available from plant-based protein options. But don't let the inclusion of eggs and dairy put you off if you're following a plant-based/vegan diet. The majority of the recipes in this book are VEGAN or can be veganized with suggested changes and substitutions. There are sections devoted to egg and dairy substitutes as well.

## THE FAB FIVE

There are five superstar foods that are excellent sources of protein and consistently deliver vitamins, minerals, and essential micronutrients. You'll see them again and again in this cookbook as they are the building blocks of a healthy, protein-rich diet.

**BEANS AND LEGUMES**  Easy-to-prepare, inexpensive, and ultra-versatile, beans and legumes (also called pulses) can be the cornerstone of protein-rich recipes or a last-minute addition to up the protein count of a dish.

**WHOLE GRAINS**  These complex carbohydrates complement protein-rich foods while boasting more key nutrients than their refined counterparts like white rice and all-purpose flour. Some, like quinoa, buckwheat, and millet, are good sources of protein themselves.

**NUTS AND SEEDS**  These tasty nuggets are also excellent sources of healthy fats and fiber.

**SOY AND SEITAN**  Tofu, tempeh, and edamame (fresh soybeans) offer excellent main-dish options for protein, as does seitan, a meat substitute made from wheat gluten. Tofu can even be blended to a creamy consistency and used in sauces and desserts.

**EGGS AND DAIRY**  These two often get put into the same category because they are both animal products suitable for vegetarians, but not vegans. They offer many of the same nutritional benefits, including being excellent sources of vitamins D and $B_{12}$.

## THE POWER OF PROTEIN

An interesting thing happens when you focus on incorporating nutrient-dense protein sources from the Fab Five into your meals and snacks: Everything else starts to fall into place nutritionally. Beans, lentils, and legumes are the best examples of this phenomenon. One cup of cooked legumes delivers between 8 to 16 grams of protein along with iron, vitamins, minerals, and up to 12 grams of fiber. Bam! Just like that, with just one ingredient, you attain most of the nutrition goals set for a meal. From there, you can add on to your heart's content, using nuts or seeds for good fats and extra-fiber vegetables galore for vitamins and antioxidants, whole grains for complex carbohydrates and more protein...the possibilities are endless, and endlessly delicious.

Increased satisfaction is another benefit to including nutrient-dense protein sources every time you eat. Nutrient-dense, protein-rich foods keep you feeling fuller longer, slow down digestion to prevent sugar spikes and crashes, and help sustain energy levels. That translates into fewer mid-morning snacks needed to tide you over between meals, and snacks that really do their job satisfying hunger pangs and keeping you energized.

## PROTEIN-POWERED COOKING

This book is not a diet manual. Nor is it a collection of recipes crammed with high-protein ingredients with the sole aim of getting more protein. We set no strict protein guidelines for each recipe (except for a minimum of 4 grams for everything but sauces and condiments). Instead, The 200 recipes in this book use nutrient-dense, protein-rich foods as a gateway to healthy eating. It's a comprehensive cookbook that stands on its own delicious merits with recipes that naturally balance protein and other nutrients and promote long-lasting healthy eating habits.

# UNDERSTANDING PROTEIN & YOUR DIETARY NEEDS

Protein is one of the three crucial macronutrients your body requires in large amounts, along with carbohydrates and fat. One gram of protein contains the same number of calories as 1 gram of carbohydrates (fat contains 9 calories per gram), but your body processes protein differently, prioritizing its use for other healthy body functions besides energy. (It's only when you haven't consumed enough carbohydrates or fat that your body will turn to protein for energy.) Your body breaks protein down into amino acids that can then be used to build new proteins that perform specific functions, such as building and repairing cells, producing hormones and enzymes, and fighting illness and disease.

The recommended dietary allowance of protein in the United States is 46 grams of protein for women and 56 for men. That's about 15 to 20 grams of protein per meal.

Pregnant and breastfeeding women should increase their protein intake by 10 to 15 grams per day. The Harvard Institute of Medicine calculates recommended allowances in a different way and sets a wide range for protein intake—10 to 35 percent of the calories consumed each day

Nearly all foods contain some protein, even fruits and vegetables. But not all proteins are created equal. A 3-ounce beef steak may contain a whopping 20 grams of protein, but it's also super-high in cholesterol and saturated fat. Steak also scores really low in all but a few essential vitamins and minerals, and it has zero fiber. Compare that to the same amount of cooked beans, which delivers an average of 9 grams of protein and 8 grams of fiber, are a good source of vitamins and minerals, and contain zero saturated fat or cholesterol. Then, compare the steak and beans to a cup of low-fat Greek yogurt with 20 grams of protein and just 1 gram of saturated fat. Greek yogurt may not contain fiber, but it is rich in vitamins and minerals like calcium and has a higher protein digestibility rating than steak or beans.

The key when incorporating protein into a healthy diet is to choose nutrient-dense options from plant-based sources as well as eggs and low-fat dairy.

# ESSENTIAL AMINO ACIDS

Protein is made up of amino acids that are strung together in long chains. Of the 20 amino acids found in food protein, 9 are considered essential because the body cannot synthesize them on its own and so they must be consumed from other sources. "Complete" proteins are those that contain all 9 essential amino acids. Animal products are sources of all 9 essential amino acids. Most plant-based protein sources are not complete proteins and lack one or more of the essential amino acids.

But that's not a problem! It was once thought that you needed to consume all 9 essential amino acids in the same meal in order for your body to utilize the molecular building blocks. Nutrition professionals even went so far as to recommend specific combinations of foods in order to ensure all 9 essential amino acids were present in a meal. That belief and practice have been completely disproven. You do need and should aim to get all the essential amino acids from protein sources in a day. Doing so is easy: Simply eat a variety of foods including nutrient-dense, protein-rich items like nuts, seeds, beans, whole grains, and soy.

# PROTEIN AND YOUR DIET

If you practice healthy eating habits, you're probably getting plenty of protein. But to turn those eating habits into a healthy lifestyle, you may need to focus on what types of protein you choose—and when you eat them. Recent studies show that the right protein consumption can help control appetite, promote weight loss, improve energy levels, and reduce the risk of certain chronic diseases.

In August 2016, the *Journal of the American Medical Association* published the following recommendation: "Substitution of plant protein for animal protein...may confer substantial health benefit. Therefore, public health recommendations should focus on improvement of protein sources." Ten years prior, the *New England Journal of Medicine* cited a 20-year study of over 80,000 women and found that those who ate low-carbohydrate diets that were high in vegetable sources of fat and protein had a 30 percent lower risk of heart disease compared with women who ate high-carbohydrate, low-fat diets. Consuming more plant protein has also been linked to a 12 percent lower risk of cardiovascular death and a 10 percent lower risk of death from all causes.

In a 2014 study published in the *American Journal of Clinical Nutrition*, researchers found that replacing red meat with one serving of nuts, low-fat dairy, or whole grains each day reduced the risk of developing type 2 diabetes by 16 to 35 percent. Another study that same year in the *International Journal of Cancer* concluded choosing protein sources other than red meat in adolescence may decrease premenopausal breast cancer risk.

According to the Harvard School of Public Health, "the same high-protein foods that are good choices for disease prevention may also help with weight control," citing a study published in 2014 that showed that eating one serving of beans or legumes per day can increase feelings of fullness. Previous studies showed that increasing dietary protein, even when all other factors remained the same, may help with weight loss by increasing satiety levels. The top weight-loss diets, including the DASH diet, the Mediterranean diet, and Weight Watcher's, all focus on including healthy protein as a way to slow digestion, sustain energy levels, and curb hunger.

## PROTEINS AND FIBER

One of the biggest benefits of following a vegetarian or vegan diet is that plant-based protein sources are usually high in other nutrients, including fiber. Fiber is an indigestible carbohydrate found in foods that helps slow down digestion, which in turn helps regulate your body's blood sugar levels and keeps you feeling full and satiated. Like protein, fiber can help control appetite, promote weight loss, improve energy levels, and reduce the risk of certain chronic diseases.

Most people get enough protein in their diets, but fiber is another story. In general, Americans only get 15 grams of fiber per day, while their bodies need at least 20 to 30 grams. Many nutrient-dense proteins furnish the body with both protein and fiber, making that 20- to 30-gram recommendation easy to reach. As mentioned before, a serving of beans can furnish 8 or more grams of fiber along with protein and other nutrients. And high-fiber carbohydrates (complex carbohydrates) work the other way around, delivering higher levels of protein than their refined, simple carbohydrate counterparts. Whole grains offer a good example of this: Whole grain brown rice is almost 25 percent higher in protein than white rice.

## PROTEIN AND ENERGY

You may have read statements like "protein gives you energy" or seen energy-boosting protein shakes marketed to athletes. Strictly speaking, protein does not usually provide our bodies with energy. That role falls to carbohydrates and fats. Protein and carbohydrates both have 4 calories per gram, fat has 9 calories per gram, but our bodies process them in different ways. Carbohydrates are broken down into simple sugars that travel through the bloodstream to feed and provide energy to cells. Fat is broken down into fatty acids that cells feed on for energy as well. Protein, on the other hand, is broken down into compounds that the body then uses to build new proteins with specific functions in the body. Because of this distinction, we avoid saying "protein gives you energy," preferring the more accurate "protein makes you feel energized" or "protein improves energy levels."

## BEYOND PROTEIN

A balanced, varied, vegetarian diet that focuses on nutrient-dense protein foods will pretty much guarantee you're getting the recommended allowances of essential micronutrients (vitamins and minerals) and macronutrients (protein, carbohydrates, and fat). There are a handful of these essential nutrients so vital to good health for everyone that they are worth extra attention when making food choices.

### VITAMIN $B_{12}$

Everyone should be concerned about getting enough $B_{12}$. This vitamin is needed by the body for DNA synthesis, blood cell production, and nerve cell maintenance. For vegetarians and vegans, vitamin $B_{12}$ is considered a nutrient of concern because the only natural sources of the nutrient are in animal-derived foods. As we get older, our bodies have a harder time processing vitamin $B_{12}$, which increases the dietary amounts needed.

**Sources:** Eggs, dairy, fortified foods including nondairy milk, nutritional yeast, cereal, and soy products

### VITAMIN D

From building bones and enhancing calcium absorption to reducing the risk of dementia, depression, and certain chronic diseases, vitamin D plays an important role in long-term well-being. The body can synthesize vitamin D from sunlight, but most people's main source of vitamin D comes from fortified foods like milk and cereal

**Sources:** Egg yolks, mushrooms, fortified dairy and nondairy products, fortified cereals

## IRON

Iron is an essential mineral the body uses to produce hemoglobin, the red blood cells that transport oxygen to the body's organs and tissues, and myoglobin, the cells that distribute oxygen to muscles. Inadequate iron consumption may lead to iron depletion or deficiency characterized by feelings of lethargy, shortness of breath, and fatigue, or anemia.

**Sources:** Soy products, beans and legumes, whole grains, nuts and seeds, leafy greens, peas, beets, tomatoes, cabbage

## VITAMIN C

The water-soluble vitamin (meaning your body can absorb it directly and quickly) best known for its immune-boosting properties is also a potent antioxidant and enhances your body's ability to absorb iron.

**Sources:** Leafy greens, bell peppers, fruits, citrus, broccoli, berries

## CALCIUM

Bone, muscle, and nerve cells all require calcium to function properly. When the body is calcium-deficient, it will start leveraging the calcium stored in bone cells for other functions, which increases the risk of osteoporosis.

**Sources:** Dairy products, leafy greens, white beans, edamame, broccoli, fortified foods including tofu, nondairy milks, and cereals

## OMEGA-3 FATTY ACIDS

There are three types of Omega-3 fatty acids. DHA (docosahexaenoic acid) and EPA (eicosapentaenoic acid) are found in animal products, like fish oil, while ALA (alpha-linolenic acid) comes from plant-based sources including seeds and nuts. These acids play a role in brain health, fight inflammation, and have been shown to reduce the risk of cardiovascular disease and other chronic health issues. Our bodies have the ability to convert ALA to EPA and DHA, but to help the body attain recommended levels of omega-3s using plant-based sources, you should reduce omega-6 fatty acid intake by decreasing consumption of processed and fried foods.

**Sources:** Walnuts, flaxseeds, chia seeds, hemp seeds, seaweed, leafy greens.

# YOUR PROTEIN-RICH PANTRY

This list of ingredients covers the essentials of what you will need to produce nutrient-dense, protein-rich, delicious meals on a regular basis, whether you follow the recipes in this book or improvise with your own. In some places, we've given representative recommendations rather than cover every single legume, grain, pasta, or vegetable variety. The list includes nutrition information so you can build your understanding of nutrient-dense protein foods and make informed choices when balancing your meals.

## BEANS, LENTILS, AND LEGUMES

**CHICKPEAS (1 CUP COOKED)**
Calories 269
Protein 14 g
Fiber 12 g
Fat 4 g

**LENTILS (1 CUP COOKED)**
Calories 230
Protein 17 g
Fiber 15 g
Fat <1 g

**SPLIT PEAS (1 CUP COOKED)**
Calories 231
Protein 16 g
Fiber 8 g
Fat <1 g

**WHITE BEANS (1 CUP COOKED)**
Calories 120
Protein 8 g
Fiber 10 g
Fat <1 g

## WHOLE GRAINS

**QUINOA (1 CUP COOKED)**
Calories 222
Protein 8 g
Fiber 5 g
Fat 3 g

**BROWN RICE (1 CUP COOKED)**
Calories 248
Protein 6 g
Fiber 3 g
Fat 2 g

**FARRO (1 CUP COOKED)**
Calories 280
Protein 12 g
Fiber 6 g
Fat <1 g

**MILLET (1 CUP COOKED)**
Calories 207
Protein 6 g
Fiber 2 g
Fat <1 g

**OATS (1 CUP COOKED)**
Calories 196
Protein 6 g
Fiber 4 g
Fat <1 g

**SORGHUM (1 CUP COOKED)**
Calories 316
Protein 10 g
Fiber 7 g
Fat 2 g

**WHEAT BERRIES (1 CUP COOKED)**
Calories 300
Protein 12 g
Fiber 12 g
Fat <1 g

**WILD RICE (1 CUP COOKED)**
Calories 166
Protein 7 g
Fiber 3 g
Fat <1 g

**SPELT FLOUR (¼ CUP)**
Calories 120
Protein 4 g
Fiber 4 g
Fat <1 g

**WHOLE-WHEAT FLOUR (¼ CUP)**
Calories 102
Protein 4 g
Fiber 3 g
Fat <1 g

**WHOLE-GRAIN PASTA (1 CUP COOKED)**
Calories 154
Protein 6 g
Fiber 5 g
Fat 1 g

**WHOLE-WHEAT PASTA (1 CUP COOKED)**
Calories 145
Protein 6 g
Fiber 4 g
Fat 2 g

**QUINOA PASTA (1 CUP COOKED)**
Calories 200
Protein 4 g
Fiber 1 g
Fat <1 g

## NUTS, NUT BUTTERS, AND SEEDS

**CASHEWS (1 OZ.)**
Calories 157
Protein 5 g
Fiber 1 g
Fat 12 g

**WALNUTS (1 OZ.)**
Calories 185
Protein 4 g
Fiber 2 g
Fat 18 g

**SMOOTH PEANUT BUTTER (1 TBS.)**
Calories 86
Protein 4 g
Fiber 1 g
Fat 8 g

**ALMOND BUTTER (1 TBS.)**
Calories 98
Protein 3 g
Fiber 1 g
Fat 9 g

**PUMPKIN SEEDS (1 OZ.)**
Calories 163
Protein 8 g
Fiber 2 g
Fat 14 g

**FLAXSEEDS, GROUND (1 TBS.)**
Calories 37
Protein 1 g
Fiber 2 g
Fat 4 g

**HEMPSEEDS, HULLED (1 TBS.)**
Calories 55
Protein 3 g
Fiber <1 g
Fat 5 g

**CHIA SEEDS**
Calories 45
Protein 2 g
Fiber 3 g
Fat 4 g

## SOY AND SEITAN

**FIRM TOFU (3.5 OZ.)**
Calories 78
Protein 9 g
Fiber 1 g
Fat 4 g

**TEMPEH (3.5 OZ.)**
Calories 167
Protein 19 g
Fiber 8 g
Fat 5 g

**SEITAN (3.5 OZ.)**
Calories 141
Protein 25 g
Fiber 1 g
Fat 2g

**EDAMAME (1 CUP COOKED)**
Calories 188
Protein 18 g
Fiber 8 g
Fat 8 g

## EGGS, DAIRY, AND DAIRY SUBSTITUTES

**LARGE EGG**
Calories 72
Protein 6 g
Fiber 0 g
Fat 5 g

**LOW-FAT (1%) MILK (1 CUP)**
Calories 102
Protein 8 g
Fiber 0 g
Fat 2 g

**UNSWEETENED ALMOND MILK (1 CUP)**
Calories 39
Protein 2 g
Fiber 0 g
Fat 3 g

**UNSWEETENED SOY MILK (1 CUP)**
Calories 79
Protein 7 g
Fiber 1 g
Fat 4 g

**FULL-FAT COCONUT MILK (¼ CUP)**
Calories 112
Protein 1 g
Fiber 1 g
Fat 12 g

**LOW-FAT COTTAGE CHEESE (1 CUP)**
Calories 186
Protein 28 g
Fiber 0 g
Fat 1 g

**PLAIN LOW-FAT GREEK YOGURT (7 OZ.)**
Calories 167
Protein 20 g
Fiber 0 g
Fat 4 g

**PLAIN SOY YOGURT (6 OZ.)**
Calories 160
Protein 6 g
Fiber 2 g
Fat 4 g

**PLAIN COCONUT YOGURT (5 OZ.)**
Calories 121
Protein 0 g
Fiber 2 g
Fat 4 g

**PLAIN LOW-FAT YOGURT (1 CUP)**
Calories 154
Protein 13 g
Fiber 0 g
Fat 4 g

**PART-SKIM MOZZARELLA (1 OZ.)**
Calories 72
Protein 7 g
Fiber 0 g
Fat 5 g

**FRESH/SOFT GOAT CHEESE (1 OZ.)**
Calories 75
Protein 5 g
Fiber 0 g
Fat 6 g

**LOW-FAT RICOTTA CHEESE (½ CUP)**
Calories 120
Protein 14 g
Fiber 0 g
Fat 6 g

**FETA CHEESE (¼ CUP)**
Calories 99
Protein 5 g
Fiber 0 g
Fat 8

## FRESH VEGETABLES

**ARTICHOKE (1 WHOLE)**
Calories 64
Protein 3 g
Fiber 7 g
Fat <1 g

**ASPARAGUS (1 CUP COOKED)**
Calories 40
Protein 4 g
Fiber 4 g
Fat <1 g

**AVOCADO (½)**
Calories 161
Protein 2 g
Fiber 7 g
Fat 15 g

**BEAN SPROUTS (1 CUP)**
Calories 50
Protein 6 g
Fiber 4 g
Fat 1 g

**BEETS (1 CUP COOKED)**
Calories 74
Protein 3 g
Fiber 2 g
Fat <1 g

**BROCCOLI (1 CUP COOKED)**
Calories 54
Protein 4 g
Fiber 5 g
Fat <1 g

**BRUSSELS SPROUTS (1 CUP COOKED)**
Calories 56
Protein 4 g
Fiber 4 g
Fat <1 g

**BUTTERNUT SQUASH (1 CUP COOKED)**
Calories 82
Protein 2 g
Fiber 7 g
Fat <1 g

## (CONTINUED) FRESH VEGETABLES

**FENNEL, BULB (1 WHOLE)**
Calories 73
Protein 3 g
Fiber 7 g
Fat <1 g

**KALE (2 CUPS RAW)**
Calories 16
Protein 1 g
Fiber 1 g
Fat <1 g

**LIMA BEANS (1 CUP COOKED)**
Calories 209
Protein 12 g
Fiber 10 g
Fat <1 g

**MUSHROOMS, WHITE OR BUTTON (1 CUP)**
Calories 21
Protein 3 g
Fiber 1 g
Fat <1 g

**PEAS (1 CUP COOKED)**
Calories 67
Protein 5 g
Fiber 5 g
Fat <1 g

**SPINACH (1 CUP COOKED)**
Calories 41
Protein 5 g
Fiber 4 g
Fat <1 g

**SWEET POTATO (1 CUP COOKED)**
Calories 180
Protein 4 g
Fiber 7 g
Fat <1 g

**TOMATO (1 LARGE)**
Calories 33
Protein 2 g
Fiber 2 g
Fat <1 g

## FRUITS

**APPLE (1 MEDIUM)**
Calories 95
Protein <1 g
Fiber 4 g
Fat <1 g

**BANANA (1 MEDIUM)**
Calories 105
Protein 1 g
Fiber 3 g
Fat <1 g

**GRAPES (1 CUP)**
Calories 104
Protein 1 g
Fiber 1 g
Fat <1 g

**KIWI (1 MEDIUM)**
Calories 42
Protein 1 g
Fiber 2 g
Fat <1 g

**ORANGE (1 LARGE)**
Calories 45
Protein 1 g
Fiber 2 g
Fat <1 g

**RAISINS (1 OZ.)**
Calories 85
Protein 1 g
Fiber 1 g
Fat <1 g

**DRIED FIGS (1 OZ.)**
Calories 83
Protein 1 g
Fiber 3 g
Fat <1 g

## FATS AND OILS

**OLIVE OIL (1 TBS.)**
Calories 120
Fat 14 g
Saturated Fat 1 g
Cholesterol 0

**CANOLA OIL (1 TBS.)**
Calories 120
Fat 14 g
Saturated Fat 1 g
Cholesterol 0

**COCONUT OIL (1 TBS.)**
Calories 120
Fat 14 g
Saturated Fat 12 g
Cholesterol 0

**UNSALTED BUTTER (1 TBS.)**
Calories 102
Fat 12 g
Saturated Fat 7 g
Cholesterol 31 mg

Fats and oils are culinary and nutritional essentials, but they contain zero protein.

*Source: USDA Food Composition Databases

# LOCAL, SEASONAL, ORGANIC, SUSTAINABLE, HUMANE

ENVIRONMENTAL, SOCIAL, AND ANIMAL WELFARE CAUSES GO HAND IN HAND
WITH VEGETARIANISM. MAKE THESE FIVE FOOD CHOICES YOUR
MANTRA WHEN YOU GO SHOPPING.
HERE'S THE DIFFERENCE YOU MAKE WHEN YOU DO:

## LOCAL

Buying locally sourced ingredients supports your community and its businesses
and reduces the impact on the environment. It also guarantees you're getting
the freshest, tastiest fruits and vegetables: Most of the produce shipped to the
supermarket was picked four to seven days before it makes it to your grocery cart.

## SEASONAL

Better flavor, lower cost, smaller carbon footprint...and the list goes on for why you
should choose recipes that feature fruits and vegetables that are in season.

## ORGANIC

Free of chemicals and pesticides and produced with respect for animal
welfare and the environment, certified organic or organically grown foods
are worth seeking out. Even when they have been mass-produced, their
purchase sends the message to growers, distributors, and manufacturers
that consumers prefer healthier choices for food.

## SUSTAINABLE

Sound environmental practices, social and economic equality, and fair and profitable
business practices are the three tenets of sustainable agriculture. Together, their goal
is to ensure a healthy, uncompromised food system for future generations.

## HUMANE

If you include eggs and dairy in your diet and are concerned about the welfare of
the animals that produce them, choose Certified Humane products or investigate
how the animals are treated and raised by the producers you buy from.

# SMOOTHIES, SCRAMBLES & BREAKFAST CEREALS

Whether your breakfast of choice is a thick, lightly sweet smoothie you can take on the go or a sit-down affair involving cereal or a scramble, protein should play a big part in your morning meal. Studies show that high-protein breakfasts help you feel full longer and may curb the brain activity that can trigger food cravings. Now that's a wake-up call for those of us who find ourselves fighting snack attacks around 10:00 a.m. or experiencing the afternoon munchies.

The secret to sticking to a high-protein breakfast routine on the weekdays is simplicity. Blend-and-go smoothies, make-ahead cereals, and speedy scrambles are the foods you'll return to again and again. And for those weekend breakfasts? Making them special with a pretty presentation or a tasty garnish is key so that they win out over nutrient-poor (if tasty) waffles and pancakes!

# BLUEBERRY PIE SMOOTHIE

YIELD: SERVES 4

**1 cup plain, fat-free yogurt**

**1½ cups skim milk or nondairy milk**

**1½ cups fresh or frozen blueberries**

**½ cup cooked diced beets**

**⅓ cup quick oats**

**¼ cup (4 scoops) unflavored or vanilla whey protein**

**¼ cup ground flaxseeds**

**2 Tbs. blueberry preserves**

Flaxseeds and oats add thickness and extra fiber to this super-satisfying, calcium-packed smoothie. Beets lend it a deep-purple color, plus iron and antioxidants. If you don't have cooked beets on hand, you can skip them—the smoothie's flavor won't suffer.

Blend all ingredients in blender until smooth.

GLUTEN-FREE

30 MINUTES OR LESS

MAKE IT VEGAN **Use nondairy yogurt and milk and a vegan protein powder.**

MIX THINGS UP **by substituting frozen sweet cherries for the blueberries and cherry jam for the blueberry preserves.**

## NUTRITION INFORMATION

Calories: 216
Protein: 14 g
Total Fat: 4 g
Saturated Fat: <1 g
Carbohydrates: 33 g
Cholesterol: 11 mg
Sodium: 115 mg
Fiber: 4 g
Sugar: 23 g

# SUPER SEEDS CHOCOLATE SMOOTHIE

**YIELD: SERVES 4**

¼ cup chia seeds

4 cups plain, vanilla, or chocolate almond milk

1 large banana

¼ cup hemp seeds

¼ cup (4 scoops) unflavored or vanilla hemp protein

2 Tbs. unsweetened cocoa powder or raw cacao powder

2 tsp. vanilla extract

1 Tbs. cacao nibs, optional

1 Tbs. coconut sugar, optional

Chia and hemp seeds add omega-3 fats, protein, and fiber to this rich, chocolaty treat. Chia is also the secret to keeping the smoothie thick, even at room temperature. For best results, grind the chia ahead of time in a clean coffee grinder or spice mill. If you can't find cacao nibs, substitute chocolate chips, or add 1 Tbs. finely ground espresso for an extra boost.

Grind chia seeds to fine powder in coffee grinder or spice mill. Transfer to blender, and add almond milk, banana, hemp seeds, protein powder, cocoa powder, and vanilla, and blend until creamy. Add cacao nibs and sugar, if desired, and process to desired consistency.

VEGAN

GLUTEN-FREE

30 MINUTES OR LESS

NUTRITION INFORMATION

Calories: 245
Protein: 14 g
Total Fat: 12 g
Saturated Fat: 1 g
Carbohydrates: 21 g
Cholesterol: 0 mg
Sodium: 185 mg
Fiber: 9 g
Sugar: 5 g

# FRUIT FORWARD YOGURT SMOOTHIE

**YIELD: SERVES 1**

½ **cup orange juice**

½ **cup low-fat vanilla or plain yogurt**

½ **frozen banana**

6 **frozen straw-berries, hulled**

2 **peeled, frozen peach quarters**

⅓ **cup frozen blueberries**

3 **Tbs. soy protein powder or hemp protein powder**

3 **ice cubes**

1 **tsp. honey, optional**

If you're constantly crunched for time in the morning, this is the smoothie for you. Simply pack the frozen fruit into individual servings in resealable plastic bags, pull one out of the freezer in the morning, blend the contents with the other ingredients, and you're ready for the day.

Put all ingredients in blender, and purée until smooth.

GLUTEN-FREE

30 MINUTES OR LESS

NUTRITION INFORMATION

Calories: 386
Protein: 33 g
Total Fat: 3 g
Saturated Fat: 1 g
Carbohydrates: 60 g
Cholesterol: 6 mg
Sodium: 84 mg
Fiber: 5 g
Sugar: 47 g

# GOJI BERRY SUNRISE SMOOTHIE

**YIELD: SERVES 4**

**2 15-oz. cans light coconut milk**

**2½ cups fresh or frozen pineapple chunks**

**¾ cup fresh or frozen mango cubes**

**¼ cup (4 scoops) unflavored or vanilla pea-protein powder**

**¼ cup goji berries**

**1 Tbs. agave nectar, optional**

This island-inspired smoothie is made with coconut milk and loaded with fruit for a flavor reminiscent of a favorite tropical beverage. Goji berries add antioxidants and a lovely peach blush. If you can't find goji berries, substitute ¼ cup fresh or frozen raspberries or cherries.

Blend all ingredients in blender until smooth.

VEGAN

GLUTEN-FREE

30 MINUTES OR LESS

## NUTRITION INFORMATION

Calories: 276
Protein: 12 g
Total Fat: 14 g
Saturated Fat: 13 g
Carbohydrates: 27 g
Cholesterol: 0 mg
Sodium: 127 mg
Fiber: 2 g
Sugar: 22 g

# BERRY GREEN SMOOTHIE

YIELD: SERVES 1

**4 cups baby spinach leaves**

**½ cup low-fat milk or plain nondairy milk**

**1¼ cups frozen blueberries**

**½ cup firm tofu cubes**

**2 Tbs. hemp seeds**

**2 tsp. agave nectar (optional)**

**⅛ tsp. ground allspice (optional)**

Ramp up your vitamin and mineral intake with only 28 calories when you add baby spinach to a lightly sweet fruit smoothie. Feel free to substitute your favorite fruit for the blueberries.

Purée spinach leaves with milk in blender. Add blueberries, tofu, hemp seeds, agave nectar (if using), and allspice (if using); blend until smooth.

GLUTEN-FREE

30 MINUTES OR LESS

## NUTRITION INFORMATION

Calories: 348
Protein: 20 g
Total Fat: 14 g
Saturated Fat: 1 g
Carbohydrates: 42 g
Cholesterol: 0 mg
Sodium: 223 mg
Fiber: 15 g
Sugar: 19 g

# ARUGULA-RICOTTA OMELET FOR ONE

YIELD: SERVES 1

**1 egg plus 2 egg whites, or 2 whole eggs**

**1 small shallot, chopped (2 Tbs.)**

**1 oil-packed sun-dried tomato, finely chopped, plus ½ tsp. oil from jar**

**1 cup arugula**

**1 Tbs. low-fat ricotta cheese**

Here's an easy breakfast or brunch option that can be made with ingredients straight from the fridge. The recipe serves one, but can easily be quadrupled and made in a large skillet to serve four people.

**1.** Whisk egg and egg whites with 1 Tbs. water in small bowl. Season with salt and pepper, and set aside.

**2.** Place shallot, sun-dried tomato, and reserved oil in small nonstick skillet, and heat over medium heat. Sauté 2 to 3 minutes, or until shallot is softened. Add arugula, and sauté 2 to 3 minutes, or until leaves are wilted.

**3.** Pour in egg mixture, stirring to distribute arugula and tomato bits evenly. Reduce heat to medium-low, and cook 2 minutes, or until omelet begins to set. Dollop ricotta cheese on one side, and cook 1 to 2 minutes more, or until omelet is set. Fold over omelet to cover cheese and form half-circle shape.

GLUTEN-FREE

30 MINUTES OR LESS

## NUTRITION INFORMATION

Calories: 167
Protein: 16 g
Total Fat: 6 g
Saturated Fat: 3 g
Carbohydrates: 6 g
Cholesterol: 191 mg
Sodium: 234 mg
Fiber: <1 g
Sugar: 2 g

# GREEN EGGS & YAM TOASTS

This fun dish falls somewhere between an omelet and an open-faced sandwich.

YIELD: SERVES 4

1 cup plus 2 Tbs. plain nonfat yogurt, divided

4 Tbs. chopped fresh mint, divided

2½ tsp. white balsamic vinegar

8 long whole-grain baguette slices

4 ¼-inch-thick round slices peeled yam

1 pinch salt

2 Tbs. butter, divided

2 green onions, chopped (¼ cup)

2 oz. packed chopped mustard greens (2 cups)

6 large eggs

**1.** Preheat oven to 350°F.

**2.** Whisk together 1 cup yogurt, 3 Tbs. mint, and vinegar in small bowl. Season with salt and pepper, if desired; set aside.

**3.** Coat bread slices on both sides with cooking spray, season with salt and pepper (if desired), and arrange on baking sheet. Bake 8 minutes, or until crisp. Cool.

**4.** Meanwhile, stack yam slices, and cut crosswise into ½-inch-wide sticks. Coat nonstick skillet with cooking spray, and add yam, ¾ cup water, and salt. Bring to a simmer over medium heat. Cover, and cook 8 to 10 minutes, or until yam is tender. Transfer yam to small bowl using slotted spoon; boil off any remaining water.

**5.** Melt 1½ tsp. butter in same skillet over medium heat. Add green onions and remaining 1 Tbs. mint, and sauté 1 minute. Mix in mustard greens, and sauté 2 minutes, or until greens are tender. Add to bowl with yams.

**6.** Whisk together eggs and remaining 2 Tbs. yogurt in medium bowl; season with salt and pepper, if desired.

**7.** Melt remaining 1½ Tbs. butter in same skillet over medium heat. Pour butter into egg mixture, and whisk to combine. Spread vegetables evenly on bottom of skillet, and pour egg mixture over top. Cook undisturbed 30 to 40 seconds. As sections of top edge become opaque and begin to set, push each set section toward center using heat-proof spatula. Continue to push eggs from edge toward center 2 minutes, or until eggs are mostly set but still very moist. Remove from heat. Stir, and let sit a few seconds.

**8.** Spoon 1 cup egg mixture over each toast, pressing lightly to adhere. Drizzle ¼ cup yogurt sauce over each serving.

## NUTRITION INFORMATION

| | |
|---|---|
| Calories: 360 | Cholesterol: 296 mg |
| Protein: 19 g | Sodium: 548 mg |
| Total Fat: 15 g | Fiber: 4 g |
| Saturated Fat: 6 g | Sugar: 8 g |
| Carbohydrates: 40 g | |

# NUTRITIONAL YEAST

This non-active yeast is sold as flakes or a powder and has a cheesy-nutty flavor. Nutritional yeast is also a good source of B vitamins (including $B_{12}$), protein, folic acid, and zinc.

# BREAKFAST TACOS
## WITH CHEESY SCRAMBLED TOFU

Rich in protein and minerals, these hearty tacos offer a delectable cheesy flavor thanks to the combination of nutritional yeast and hemp seeds.

**YIELD: SERVES 6**

**1 14-oz. pkg. superfirm tofu, drained**

**2 Tbs. tahini paste**

**½ cup nutritional yeast**

**1½ tsp. onion powder**

**1 Tbs. coconut oil**

**½ cup hemp seeds**

**12 4½-inch organic corn tortillas, warmed**

**1 cup thinly sliced green onions**

**1 cup cilantro leaves**

**4 limes, cut into wedges**

**Hot sauce for drizzling**

**1.** Mash tofu into scrambled-egg-like crumbles in medium bowl. Stir in tahini, nutritional yeast, and onion powder; season with salt and pepper, if desired.

**2.** Heat coconut oil in nonstick skillet over medium-high heat. Add tofu mixture, and cook 5 minutes, mixing occasionally. Turn off heat, add hemp seeds to pan, and mix well. Transfer to serving bowl.

**3.** Generously fill each tortilla with tofu mixture. Serve with bowls of green onions, cilantro, lime wedges, and hot sauce for individual assembly.

VEGAN

GLUTEN-FREE

30 MINUTES OR LESS

## NUTRITION INFORMATION

Calories: 322
Protein: 21 g
Total Fat: 16 g
Saturated Fat: 4 g
Carbohydrates: 27 g
Cholesterol: 0 mg
Sodium: 164 mg
Fiber: 6 g
Sugar: 2 g

# SOUTHWESTERN TOFU SCRAMBLE

YIELD: SERVES 6

The vibrant colors of this simple scramble make it especially appetizing. Ground turmeric gives it a golden hue. Leftovers (if any) make a great sandwich filling.

1 medium red bell pepper, diced (about 1 cup)

1 small carrot, diced (about ½ cup)

4 green onions, chopped (about ½ cup)

1 clove garlic, minced (about 1 tsp.)

½ tsp. ground cumin

¼ tsp. ground turmeric

1 14-oz. pkg. extra-firm tofu, drained and crumbled

½ tsp. hot sauce

2 Tbs. chopped cilantro

Heat large nonstick skillet over medium heat and coat with cooking spray. Add bell pepper and carrot, and cook 7 minutes, or until just tender. Stir in green onions, garlic, cumin, and turmeric, and cook 1 minute more. Add tofu and hot sauce, and cook 5 minutes, or until heated through and all liquid has cooked off. Stir in cilantro.

VEGAN

GLUTEN-FREE

30 MINUTES OR LESS

## NUTRITION INFORMATION

Calories: 113
Protein: 11 g
Total Fat: 6 g
Saturated Fat: 1 g
Carbohydrates: 6 g
Cholesterol: 0 mg
Sodium: 32 mg
Fiber: 3 g
Sugar: 2 g

### 5 More Savory Scramble Options

Want to take your breakfast flavors in a different direction? Omit the cumin, hot sauce, and cilantro and replace them with:

**Spanish:** smoked paprika, olive oil, and fresh parsley

**French:** herbes de Provence, black pepper, and 1 tsp. dried tarragon

**Cajun:** fresh or dried parsley, Cajun seasoning, and chopped green onion

**Asian:** grated fresh ginger, toasted sesame oil, and chopped green onion

**Italian:** Italian seasoning, extra garlic, and chopped fresh basil

# TOFU SCRAMBLES 101

For the best tofu scrambles, choose extra-firm tofu, and press it between two paper towels for 10 to 15 minutes to remove excess moisture. Crumble the tofu into a bowl, then toss with seasonings. Ground turmeric will give your scramble a golden hue. Nutritional yeast and a few dashes of tamari or soy sauce add flavor. (You can also add the seasonings directly to the pan if you're pressed for time.) If adding vegetables, sauté them first, then add the tofu to the skillet and cook 5 to 7 minutes, or until tofu is firm and curd-like.

# BAKED OATMEAL
## WITH BLUEBERRIES, ALMONDS & COCONUT MILK

With a lightly crunchy, granola-like layer on top and a doughy, coconut-saturated center, this baked oatmeal is hearty and comforting. Serve warm or at room temperature.

**1 large egg**

**2 cups light coconut milk, whisked, if necessary**

**2 Tbs. honey, plus more for serving**

**¼ tsp. kosher salt**

**⅛ tsp. ground cinnamon**

**3 cups rolled oats**

**¼ cup plus 2 Tbs. brown sugar**

**1 heaping cup fresh blueberries, plus more for sprinkling**

**5 Tbs. sliced almonds, plus more for sprinkling**

**1.** Preheat oven to 375°F. Coat 8-inch-square glass baking dish with cooking spray.

**2.** Beat egg until lightly frothy in medium bowl. Whisk in coconut milk, honey, salt, and cinnamon.

**3.** Toss oats with brown sugar in large bowl. Pour coconut mixture over oat mixture, and toss to coat. Stir in blueberries and almonds.

**4.** Spread oatmeal mixture in prepared baking dish, and sprinkle with rest of blueberries and almonds. Bake 25 to 30 minutes, or until lightly golden on top and cooked throughout.

**5.** Serve warm or at room temperature, and drizzle lightly with honey.

### NUTRITION INFORMATION

Calories: 255
Protein: 7 g
Total Fat: 9 g
Saturated Fat: 4 g
Carbohydrates: 40 g
Cholesterol: 23 mg
Sodium: 77 mg
Fiber: 4 g
Sugar: 19 g

# CHIA BIRCHER MUESLI

As simple as combining a few ingredients in a bowl and refrigerating overnight, Bircher muesli is the go-to choice for a nutritious, quick-and-delicious breakfast.

YIELD: SERVES 2

¾ cup regular rolled oats

¾ cup almond milk, plus more for serving

⅓ cup freshly squeezed orange juice

½ cup (packed) grated apple

2 Tbs. golden raisins

1 Tbs. chia seeds

½ cup fresh berries or sliced summer fruit

2 Tbs. chopped walnuts

Pure maple syrup, optional

**1.** Stir together oats, ¾ cup almond milk, orange juice, apple, and raisins in medium bowl. Fold in chia seeds. Cover, and refrigerate overnight.

**2.** Serve topped with berries and walnuts, and drizzled with almond milk and maple syrup (if using).

VEGAN

GLUTEN-FREE

## NUTRITION INFORMATION

Calories: 293
Protein: 9 g
Total Fat: 10 g
Saturated Fat: <1 g
Carbohydrates: 46 g
Cholesterol: 0 mg
Sodium: 71 mg
Fiber: 8 g
Sugar: 16 g

# MIXED-GRAIN HOT CEREAL

YIELD: 2 SERVINGS

**⅓ cup quinoa, rinsed and drained**

**⅓ cup millet, rinsed and drained**

**⅓ cup amaranth, rinsed and drained**

**2 cups low-fat milk or vegetable milk**

**⅓ tsp. salt**

Equal parts quinoa, millet, and amaranth yield a rich, creamy hot cereal that has endless possibilities. Doctor it up with the flavor suggestions, or make it ahead for reheat-and-serve breakfast ease on busy mornings. The ratio used in this basic recipe is 1 cup (total) grains to 4 cups liquid. To make a batch that stays smooth and creamy for 4 days in the fridge, increase the grain-to-liquid ratio to 1 to 5, or 1 cup grains to 2½ cups milk plus 2½ cups water.

Heat quinoa and millet in large saucepan over medium heat 5 minutes, or until fragrant and toasted, swirling often. Stir in amaranth, then milk or vegetable milk, salt, and 2 cups water. Cover, and bring to a boil. Reduce heat to medium-low, and simmer 30 to 40 minutes, or until most of the liquid is absorbed and cereal is creamy. Serve with plain Greek yogurt and your favorite sweetener.

GLUTEN-FREE

## NUTRITION INFORMATION

Calories: 22
Protein: 10 g
Total Fat: 4 g
Saturated Fat: <1 g
Carbohydrates: 39 g
Cholesterol: 6 mg
Sodium: 218 mg
Fiber: 4 g
Sugar: 6 g

# SWEETEN THE DEAL

IF YOU'VE EVER BEEN TEMPTED BY PREPARED HOT CEREALS THAT SOUND MORE LIKE DESSERT THAN A HEALTHY BREAKFAST, THEN YOU'LL LOVE THESE WAYS TO CUSTOMIZE YOUR OWN MORNING PORRIDGE WITH TREAT-INSPIRED ADD-INS:

### BLUEBERRY MUFFIN

Stir in 1 to 2 tsp. vanilla sugar, and sprinkle with ½ cup fresh or frozen blueberries. Add a dollop of plain yogurt or sour cream.

### CINNAMON ROLL

Stir together ¼ cup dark brown sugar and 1 Tbs. ground cinnamon. Sprinkle 1 to 2 Tbs. cinnamon-sugar and then 1 to 2 Tbs. chopped pecans over cereal. Garnish with dollop (1 Tbs.) whipped cream cheese.

### CHOCOLATE-CHIP BANANA

Stir ¼ cup mashed banana into hot cereal. Sprinkle with 1 to 2 Tbs. chocolate chips.

### PIÑA COLADA

Sweeten cereal with your favorite sweetener, then top with ¼ cup diced fresh pineapple and 1 to 2 Tbs. shredded coconut.

# MILLET PORRIDGE PANCAKES

Cooked millet is the base for these light, tender pancakes that are naturally sweetened with apple juice and grated apple. The batter can be made a day ahead to save time in the morning, and will keep up to 48 hours. Serve with fresh fruit.

**YIELD: SERVES 5 (3 PANCAKES EACH)**

2 cups unsweetened apple juice

⅓ cup millet

1 large Granny Smith apple, peeled and grated

1 cup white whole-wheat flour or all-purpose flour

1 Tbs. baking powder

1 tsp. salt

3 large egg whites or 2 whole eggs

1 cup fat-free milk or buttermilk

2 Tbs. butter or margarine, melted

vegetable oil, for greasing pan

1. Bring apple juice to a boil in small saucepan. Stir in millet, cover, reduce heat to medium-low, and simmer 35 to 40 minutes, or until texture is like creamy oatmeal. Remove from heat, let stand, covered, 5 minutes. Transfer to large bowl, and cool 15 minutes.

2. Stir grated apple into millet.

3. Whisk together flour, baking powder, and salt in separate bowl. Stir flour mixture into millet mixture.

4. Whisk together egg whites or eggs, milk or buttermilk, and butter or margarine in small bowl. Fold egg mixture into millet mixture.

5. Heat large skillet over medium heat, and coat lightly with oil. Ladle ¼ cup batter for each pancake into skillet. Cook pancakes 3 minutes per side, or until golden brown. Transfer to plate, and repeat with remaining batter.

## NUTRITION INFORMATION

Calories: 283
Protein: 8 g
Total Fat: 6 g
Saturated Fat: 1 g
Carbohydrates: 50 g
Cholesterol: 1 mg
Sodium: 571 mg
Fiber: 3 g
Sugar: 18 g

# SNACKS & FINGER FOODS

So many snack foods—even homemade ones—are chock-full of fat and loaded with "empty" calories and that's no way to start a meal or stave off hunger.

While you don't have to make sure that every nibble you pop in your mouth is a protein bomb, the right balance of protein, fiber, and good fats can keep you energized long after you're done noshing or offer satisfaction levels that keep you from overindulging before you sit down to eat. In fact, some of the recipes in this chapter are so satisfying, they could be served as a light meal all on their own.

# (ALMOST) INSTANT APPETIZERS

HERE ARE SIX SIMPLE NOSHES TO
SERVE WITH DRINKS THAT CAN
BE WHIPPED UP IN NO TIME.

### FLAVORED GOAT LOG

Roll large log of goat cheese in 2 tsp.
dried herbs (try za'atar or a blend
of dried rosemary and thyme).
Drizzle with 3 Tbs. olive oil, and
serve with multigrain pita chips.

### CHILE NUTS

Toss 2 cups nuts with 1 tsp. olive oil,
½ tsp. salt, and ¼ tsp. chipotle or
ancho chile powder. Roast on baking
sheet in 325°F oven for 10 minutes
or in cast iron skillet. Cool.

### PARMESAN CRISPS

Spread circles of grated Parmesan cheese
on a silicone mat–lined baking sheet.
Bake 5 minutes at 400°F. Cool on mat,
then carefully remove with spatula.

### WASABI DEVILED EGGS

Mash yolks of 6 hard-boiled eggs with
3 Tbs. mayonnaise and 1 tsp. wasabi
paste. Fill egg halves with yolk mixture;
garnish with minced green onions.

### CREAMY BEAN DIP

Blend one 15-oz. can beans or chickpeas
(rinsed and drained) with ¼ cup water,
2 Tbs. lemon juice, 2 Tbs. olive oil,
and 2 tsp. minced garlic.

### MINI MOZZARELLA BRUSCHETTA

Toss 2 cups bocconcini (mini mozzarella
balls) with 1 cup sun-dried tomato pesto.
Arrange on baguette slices, and broil
1 minute, or until cheese has melted.

# CRISPY KALE CHIPS

**YIELD: SERVES 4**

**1 Tbs. olive oil**

**1 12-oz. bunch curly kale, tough stems removed and torn into large pieces**

**⅓ cup nutritional yeast**

This will become your go-to kale chip recipe. Nutritional yeast gives the crisped leaves a cheesy flavor along with a hit of protein, iron, and vitamin $B_{12}$. To give them a spicy kick, sprinkle with your favorite seasoning blend just before baking.

**1.** Preheat oven to 350°F.

**2.** Rub oil into kale until well coated and shiny. Add nutritional yeast, and toss to coat. Divide kale between 2 baking sheets. Bake 5 minutes, or until leaves look shrunken. Flip and move kale leaves with tongs. Bake 5 to 10 minutes more, or until kale is crispy. Sprinkle with salt, if desired.

VEGAN

GLUTEN-FREE

30 MINUTES OR LESS

NUTRITION INFORMATION

Calories: 91
Protein: 7 g
Total Fat: 4 g
Saturated Fat: <1 g
Carbohydrates: 9 g
Cholesterol: 0 mg
Sodium: 28 mg
Fiber: 4 g
Sugar: 0 g

# SPANAKOPITA STRUDEL

YIELD: SERVES 6

The beloved Greek casserole gets an appetizing makeover when it's rolled into a strudel instead of layered in a pan. Each bite is packed with spinach and tangy cheese wrapped in light, crispy phyllo pastry.

**2 leeks, white and light green parts thinly sliced (about 1 cup)**

**1 small onion, diced (about ¾ cup)**

**2 cloves garlic, minced (about 2 tsp.)**

**¼ tsp. ground nutmeg**

**2 10-oz. pkg. frozen chopped spinach, thawed**

**1 Tbs. fresh lemon juice**

**2 eggs, lightly beaten**

**4 oz. low-fat feta cheese, crumbled (½ cup)**

**¼ cup grated Romano cheese**

**12 phyllo sheets, thawed**

**1.** Coat large nonstick skillet with cooking spray, and heat over medium heat. Add leeks, onion, and garlic, and cook 5 to 7 minutes, or until soft. Stir in nutmeg, and cook 1 minute more. Add spinach, and cook 5 minutes. Remove from heat, season with salt and pepper, if desired, and stir in lemon juice. Transfer to colander, and let cool.

**2.** Preheat oven to 375°F. Coat baking sheet with cooking spray. Squeeze all liquid out of spinach mixture. Transfer spinach to bowl, and stir in eggs, feta, and Romano.

**3.** Spray 1 phyllo sheet with cooking spray. Stack second sheet of phyllo on top. Repeat spraying and stacking until you have 6 layers.

**4.** Shape half of spinach filling into log on phyllo stack, leaving 1½-inch border around edges. Fold short edges over filling, then roll lengthwise into tight log. Place seam-side down on prepared baking sheet, and spray with cooking spray. Cut slashes 1 inch apart on top of strudel with sharp knife. Repeat with remaining phyllo and filling. Bake 40 to 45 minutes, or until golden brown. Cool 10 minutes before slicing and serving.

MAKE IT VEGAN **Substitute 1 cup crumbled firm tofu for the feta cheese and eggs in the filling and replace the Romano cheese with ¼ cup nutritional yeast.**

## NUTRITION INFORMATION

| | |
|---|---|
| Calories: 256 | Cholesterol: 84 mg |
| Protein: 15 g | Sodium: 711 mg |
| Total Fat: 10 g | Fiber: 4 g |
| Saturated Fat: 3 g | Sugar: 3 g |
| Carbohydrates: 30 g | |

# SRIRACHA TOFU LETTUCE WRAPS

YIELD: MAKES
16 WRAPS

**2 tsp. vegetable oil**

**1 medium onion,
chopped (1½ cups)**

**1 Tbs. minced fresh
ginger**

**1 Tbs. minced
lemongrass**

**2 cloves garlic,
minced (2 tsp.)**

**1 lb. extra-firm
tofu, drained and
crumbled**

**1 8-oz. can water
chestnuts, drained
and chopped**

**4 Tbs. low-sodium
soy sauce**

**4 Tbs. hoisin sauce**

**1 to 2 tsp. chile
sauce, such as
sriracha**

**16 butter lettuce
or iceberg lettuce
leaves**

This fun-to-eat starter comes together quickly once all
the flavorings (onion, ginger, garlic, and lemongrass)
have been chopped. You can even pack the filling and
garnishes separately, chill overnight, then take to work
or on a picnic for a light lunch.

**1.** To make Filling: Heat oil in large skillet over medium heat.
Add onion, ginger, lemongrass, and garlic, and cook 7 to 10
minutes, or until onions are soft and beginning to brown. Add
tofu and water chestnuts, breaking tofu into small crumbles;
cook 4 minutes, or until heated through. Stir in soy sauce,
hoisin sauce, and chile sauce. Transfer to serving bowl.

**2.** Place lettuce leaves on platter, and set out remaining
Garnishes in small serving bowls. Let guests wrap tofu mixture
in lettuce leaves. Serve with grated carrots, chopped green
onions, chopped fresh mint, and chopped peanuts.

VEGAN

30 MINUTES OR LESS

MAKE IT GLUTEN-FREE Look for gluten-free tamari to replace
the soy sauce and choose a gluten-free hoisin sauce if wheat
products are an issue in your diet.

NUTRITION
INFORMATION

Calories: 88
Protein: 5 g
Total Fat: 4 g
Saturated Fat: 0.5 g
Carbohydrates: 8 g
Cholesterol: 0 mg
Sodium: 260 mg
Fiber: 2 g
Sugar: 3 g

# PEANUT-STUFFED OKRA FINGERS

YIELD: SERVES 6

Stuffed okra is a traditional Indian finger food that packs bold flavor. You can also try the filling in stuffed mushrooms instead.

**24 large fresh okra pods (1 lb.)**

**1 cup roasted unsalted peanuts**

**½ small onion, peeled and cut into chunks**

**2 cloves garlic**

**1 1-inch piece fresh ginger**

**1 jalapeño chile, seeds removed**

**½ tsp. cumin**

**½ tsp. coriander**

**½ tsp. salt**

1. Preheat oven to 425°F. Coat large baking sheet with cooking spray, or line with parchment paper.

2. Slice tops off okra. Use paring knife to split okra pods nearly in half lengthwise, leaving tip and one side intact. Pry pods open with fingers—be careful not to tear them.

3. Pulse peanuts, onion, garlic, ginger, jalapeño, cumin, coriander, and salt in food processor until very finely chopped.

4. Use fingers or small spoon to fill okra pods with peanut mixture. Place on baking sheet, and spray with cooking spray. Bake 13 to 15 minutes, or until okra has softened and filling begins to brown. Serve hot.

VEGAN

GLUTEN-FREE

30 MINUTES OR LESS

## NUTRITION INFORMATION
Calories: 177
Protein: 7 g
Total Fat: 13 g
Saturated Fat: 2 g
Carbohydrates: 12 g
Cholesterol: 0 mg
Sodium: 202 mg
Fiber: 5 g
Sugar: 3 g

**Stuffed Zucchini Rounds**
Don't love okra? Use the filling with zucchini instead. Simply cut medium zucchini into 1-inch-thick rounds, scoop out some of the seeds in the center (making sure to leave some for the bottom of the round), then fill and bake as directed.

# OVEN-CRISPED BLACK BEAN & CORN TAQUITOS

**YIELD: SERVES 6**

2 tsp. olive oil

1 medium onion, chopped (about 1 cup)

2 cloves garlic, minced (about 2 tsp.)

2 15-oz. cans black beans, rinsed and drained

2 tsp. chili powder

1 16-oz. tub prepared salsa, divided

1 cup fresh or frozen corn kernels

12 6-inch corn tortillas

¼ cup chopped cilantro

Here corn tortillas are wrapped around bean filling and baked for a healthy version of the fast-food finger food favorite. We kept these mildly spicy so kids could enjoy them, but you can always bump up the chili powder or add a little hot sauce to the filling.

**1.** Heat oil in skillet over medium heat. Cook onion 3 to 5 minutes, or until soft. Add garlic, and cook 1 minute, or until translucent and fragrant.

**2.** Stir in beans, chili powder, and 1 cup water. Reduce heat to medium-low, and simmer 10 minutes, or until most of liquid has evaporated. Remove from heat. Mash beans until mixture is thickened but still chunky and some beans remain whole. Stir in 1 cup salsa and corn, and season with salt and pepper. Cool.

**3.** Preheat oven to 425°F. Coat 2 large baking sheets with cooking spray. Spoon ¼ cup black bean mixture down center of tortilla. Roll tortilla around filling, and secure closed with toothpick. Set on prepared baking sheet. Repeat with remaining tortillas and black bean mixture. Bake 6 to 10 minutes, or until tortillas are browned and crisp.

**4.** Meanwhile, combine cilantro and remaining salsa in small bowl. Place 2 taquitos on each plate, and top with remaining salsa.

VEGAN

GLUTEN-FREE

## NUTRITION INFORMATION

Calories: 286
Protein: 11 g
Total Fat: 3 g
Saturated Fat: 0.5 g
Carbohydrates: 56 g
Cholesterol: 0 mg
Sodium: 435 mg
Fiber: 11 g
Sugar: 9 g

# DEVILED EGGS
## WITH CUMIN, YOGURT, LIME & CILANTRO

Add cilantro, a touch of lime, and cumin to deviled eggs and you've got some seriously tasty Southwest-inspired hors d'oeuvres. For a fun garnish, sprinkle with crushed tortilla chips.

SERVING:
2 DEVILED EGG
HALVES

8 eggs

16 lime slices, thinly sliced, optional

¼ cup plain low-fat Greek yogurt

2 Tbs. chopped cilantro, plus 16 small, whole leaves, for garnish

2 tsp. lime juice

1 tsp. grated lime zest

½ tsp. ground cumin

**1.** Put eggs in large saucepan or Dutch oven. Cover with cold water. Bring to boil over medium-high heat. Immediately remove from heat, cover, and let stand 12 minutes. Rinse under cold water or submerge in ice water until cool. Peel.

**2.** Halve eggs lengthwise, and scoop or squeeze yolk from each egg half into medium bowl. Arrange lime slices, if using, on plate or platter. Arrange egg halves atop lime slices or directly on platter.

**3.** In medium bowl, mash together yolks, yogurt, chopped cilantro, lime juice, lime zest, and cumin, and season with salt and pepper, if desired.

**4.** Dollop yolk mixture evenly (and generously) into egg halves with small spoon. (If any egg whites are damaged from peeling, discard these and opt for more filling in remaining egg whites.) Garnish eggs with cilantro leaves.

GLUTEN-FREE

### NUTRITION INFORMATION

Calories: 84
Protein: 8 g
Total Fat: 3 g
Saturated Fat: 1 g
Carbohydrates: 1 g
Cholesterol: 185 mg
Sodium: 66 mg
Fiber: <1 g
Sugar: <1 g

# SPICY BROCCOLI SPROUT SUSHI

YIELD: SERVES 4

**½ cup sushi rice, rinsed and drained**

**2 tsp. seasoned rice vinegar**

**2 sheets nori (roasted seaweed)**

**Hot sesame oil for sprinkling, optional**

**4 slices avocado**

**4 slices red bell pepper**

**2 slices baked seasoned Asian-style tofu, each cut into 4 thin strips**

**2 Tbs. pickled ginger, drained**

**½ cup broccoli sprouts**

Spicy sprouts, such as broccoli, arugula, or leek, give sushi rolls a delicate crunch and peppery flavor while adding protein. A sushi mat makes it easy to wrap the nori and rice tightly around fillings, but it's not necessary.

**1.** Place sushi rice and ½ cup water in small saucepan, and bring to a boil. Cover, reduce heat to low, and simmer 20 minutes, or until all liquid is absorbed. Remove from heat, and cool 20 minutes. Stir in rice vinegar.

**2.** Place 1 sheet nori on sushi mat or work surface. Spread half of warm rice over nori with back of spoon, leaving 1½-inch edges on top and bottom to seal sushi, but spreading rice all the way to both sides. Sprinkle rice with hot sesame oil, if using.

**3.** Lay 2 avocado slices, 2 bell pepper slices, and 4 tofu strips in lines down center of rice. Top with 1 Tbs. pickled ginger and ¼ cup broccoli sprouts. Brush edges of nori with water. Tightly roll nori around rice and filling, pressing bare edge at top to seal. Cut into 8 pieces with sharp knife. Repeat with remaining ingredients. Serve with soy sauce and wasabi.

VEGAN

MAKE IT GLUTEN-FREE **Substitute strips of plain extra-firm tofu for the baked tofu in the recipe.**

## NUTRITION INFORMATION

Calories: 201
Protein: 9 g
Total Fat: 6 g
Saturated Fat: 1 g
Carbohydrates: 27 g
Cholesterol: 0 mg
Sodium: 247 mg
Fiber: 3 g
Sugar: 2 g

# SALADS

If you've ever piled together a lot of tasty ingredients from the salad bar only to find that your resulting concoction was...well...only so-so, then you know that there is an art to making a good salad. The right combination of ingredients is essential to find that perfect textural balance.

What's more, salads can often veer off course and morph into fat- and calorie-laden minefields instead of the nutritional goldmines they're supposed to be. Too much dressing and too many toppings can sabotage your healthy meal choice.

With the salads in this chapter, you'll discover surprising combinations, creative topping ideas (Tempeh bacon crumbles! Candied cashews!), and lightened-up dressings that strike a perfect balance so your healthy meal (or side dish) choice *stays healthy*.

# MIX & MATCH EVERYDAY SALADS

WHEN IT COMES TO PUTTING TOGETHER TOSSED SALADS, LESS IS MORE. USING THIS MIX-AND-MATCH MENU, PICK ONE ITEM FROM EACH CATEGORY TO ASSEMBLE ANY NUMBER OF GOURMET CREATIONS TO GO WITH YOUR CHOICE OF DRESSING.

| GREENS | FRUIT | NUTS | FLAVORING | CHEESE (optional) |
|---|---|---|---|---|
| baby spinach | sliced pears | pecans | chives | Swiss |
| arugula | orange segments | almonds | red onion | feta |
| mesclun mix | dried fruit | pine nuts | garlic | mozzarella |
| romaine | diced apples | hazelnuts | green onion | goat cheese |
| Belgian endive | sliced peaches or nectarines | walnuts | shallots | Cheddar or Monterey Jack |

# GREENS GLOSSARY

**ARUGULA**

Hard to believe that not that long ago, peppery arugula were a specialty green found only in high-end restaurants and Italian eateries. These days, clamshell containers are available in most supermarkets.

**BELGIAN ENDIVE**

Belgian endive is full flavored with a hint of bitterness. The mineral-rich, compact, oval heads are grown in the dark to keep the leaves tender and creamy pale in color.

**BIBB, BOSTON, OR BUTTER LETTUCE**

These lettuces have mild flavor and tender, "buttery" leaves that are soft and require a delicate touch when handling.

**ICEBERG LETTUCE**

Iceberg has suffered from the nutrition myth that its pale, crisp, heads are low in vitamins and minerals. While they can't hold a candle to dark, leafy greens, the uniquely crisp globes offer good levels of fiber and vitamins K, C, and A.

**LOLLA ROSA**

Lolla rosa is a bronze lettuce with red edges and frilly, deeply curly leaves. It's described as having a super "lettuce" flavor.

**MÂCHE**

Mâche has the mildest flavor and the softest texture of any salad green. The leaves form pretty rosettes. It's best eaten very lightly dressed.

**MESCLUN**

Mesclun is a mixture of young lettuces that combines mild, tender leaves with heartier, more robust varieties.

**MICROGREENS**

The tiny, tender first leaves of salad greens and root vegetables are harvested and sold as microgreens.

**MIZUNA**

Mizuna is a mild mustard green with feathery leaves and a peppery flavor. The leaves are delicate and pretty and are often planted as an ornamental in gardens.

**PURSLANE**

This crunchy, lightly lemony "weed" can be found in farmers' markets. Purslane is high in omega-3 fatty acids, along with other essential nutrients.

**RADICCHIO**

The deep-red purple leaves of this Italian green add beautiful color and a distinctive, slightly bitter flavor to salads.

**ROMAINE**

Long romaine leaves are everyday salad work-horses. Be sure to choose organic whenever possible.

**SPINACH**

Popeye's favorite is a nutritional heavyweight that's an excellent source of fiber, folate, vitamin C, and vitamin A.

**SPROUTS**

Sprouts, such as mung, pea, broccoli, and sunflower are very young plant shoots that include the seed, tendril, and leaf of the green. The nutrient-dense greens add incredible texture and flavor.

**TATSOI**

Tatsoi is a small, heart-shaped leafy green related to bok choy. Rich in calcium and vitamins, it's as delicious in stir-fries as it is in salads.

**WATERCRESS**

Since Roman times, watercress has been recognized for its health-promoting properties. Modern science has proven ancient wisdom right, with the Centers for Disease Control citing watercress as its number-one powerhouse fruit or vegetable (with a perfect score of 100).

# HONEY-MUSTARD BROCCOLI SALAD

In this protein- and fiber-rich salad beluga (black) lentils are soaked overnight to shorten cooking time and enhance digestibility.

**YIELD: SERVES 4**

SALAD

**½ cup black beluga lentils, rinsed and soaked 8 hours or overnight**

**1 head broccoli, cut into florets (4 cups)**

**1 small red onion or shallot, sliced into rings (⅔ cup)**

**¼ cup chopped almonds, toasted**

HONEY-MUSTARD DRESSING

**4 Tbs. olive oil**

**1 Tbs. apple cider vinegar**

**2 tsp. raw honey or agave nectar**

**2 tsp. Dijon mustard**

**1.** To make Salad: Drain and rinse lentils, then place in medium stockpot with 1 cup water. Bring to a boil, reduce heat to medium-low, and simmer 18 minutes. Add broccoli, cover pan, and steam 2 to 3 minutes, or until broccoli and lentils are al dente.

**2.** Meanwhile, to make Honey-Mustard Dressing: Whisk together all ingredients in bowl until smooth.

**3.** Drain off any remaining liquid from broccoli and lentils, and transfer to large bowl. Add dressing, and toss to coat. Season with salt and pepper, if desired. Serve garnished with onion and almonds.

VEGAN

GLUTEN-FREE

TRY THIS SALAD **with cauliflower as well; but add the florets to the cooking water 2 to 3 minutes sooner.**

NUTRITION INFORMATION

Calories: 301
Protein: 10 g
Total Fat: 19 g
Saturated Fat: 2 g
Carbohydrates: 25 g
Cholesterol: 0 mg
Sodium: 90 mg
Fiber: 4 g
Sugar: 4 g

# CHOPPED BLACK BEAN– AVOCADO SALAD

YIELD: SERVES 4

**2 Tbs. lemon juice**

**1 Tbs. whole-grain mustard**

**2 Tbs. olive oil**

**1 cup cooked black beans**

**1 cup fresh or frozen corn, thawed**

**1 avocado, diced**

**½ cup diced sweet red pepper**

**½ cup coarsely chopped cilantro**

**¼ cup diced celery**

**2 green onions, trimmed and thinly sliced (¼ cup)**

Talk about easy! This hearty salad with southwestern flair comes together in minutes. It makes a great take-along lunch that can be made the night before.

Whisk together lemon juice and mustard in large bowl. Add oil, and whisk until smooth. Add all remaining ingredients, and gently toss to combine. Season with salt and pepper, and serve.

VEGAN

GLUTEN-FREE

30 MINUTES OR LESS

## NUTRITION INFORMATION

Calories: 238
Protein: 7 g
Total Fat: 14.5 g
Saturated Fat: 2 g
Carbohydrates: 24 g
Cholesterol: 0 mg
Sodium: 488 mg
Fiber: 9 g
Sugar: 3 g

# GRATED BEET SALAD
## WITH JICAMA & TOASTED PUMPKIN SEEDS

YIELD: SERVES 6

**2 cups grated raw beets (3 medium beets)**

**2 cups grated jicama**

**1 avocado, thinly sliced**

**1 navel orange, peeled, sectioned, each section cut into thirds**

**½ cup chopped cilantro**

**3 Tbs. thawed orange juice concentrate**

**1 Tbs. lime juice**

**½ tsp. ground cumin**

**½ tsp. ground coriander**

**1½ Tbs. olive oil**

**¼ cup toasted pumpkin seeds**

Raw beets taste similar to raw carrots in that they're sweet, juicy, and crisp. Jicama, a Mexican root vegetable that looks like a large, pale, round potato, is crunchy and mild when peeled and eaten raw. If you can't find jicama, simply substitute cubed cucumber.

**1.** Place beets in medium bowl along with jicama, avocado, orange, and cilantro.

**2.** Whisk together orange juice concentrate, lime juice, cumin, and coriander. Whisk in oil. Pour over beet mixture, and toss to mix. Season with salt and pepper, if desired. Sprinkle each serving with toasted pumpkin seeds.

GLUTEN-FREE

VEGAN

30 MINUTES OR LESS

### NUTRITION INFORMATION

Calories: 179
Protein: 5 g
Total Fat: 11 g
Saturated Fat: 2 g
Carbohydrates: 18 g
Cholesterol: 0 mg
Sodium: 136 mg
Fiber: 6 g
Sugar: 9 g

# PUMPKIN SEEDS

A single tablespoon of pumpkin seeds sprinkled on a salad can add 3 grams of protein and 1 gram of fiber along with a healthy dose of good fats.

# MATCHSTICK VEGETABLE & TOFU SALAD

YIELD: SERVES 4

**DRESSING**

**3 Tbs. low-sodium soy sauce**

**3 Tbs. rice vinegar**

**2 Tbs. light brown sugar**

**1 Tbs. toasted sesame oil**

**SALAD**

**1 8-oz. pkg. baked tofu**

**2 celery stalks**

**2 carrots, peeled**

**1 small turnip, peeled**

**½ medium cucumber, peeled**

**½ cup shiitake mushroom caps**

**¼ cup chopped cilantro**

**2 green onions, green parts only, cut into ribbons**

**½ tsp. red pepper flakes**

**2 packed cups shredded romaine lettuce or baby kale**

**¼ cup toasted cashew pieces, optional**

**1 Tbs. sesame seeds, optional**

In this Asian-style tossed salad, the vegetable matchsticks have a satisfying crunch that plays off the greens, nuts, seeds and tofu. You can also use the dressing on any tossed salad you make.

**1.** To make Dressing: Combine all ingredients in small bowl. Set aside.

**2.** To make Salad: Cut tofu, mushrooms, celery, carrots, turnip, and cucumber into matchsticks, and place in large bowl. Thinly slice shiitake mushroom caps, and add to bowl. Pour Dressing over top, and toss gently. Let stand at least 30 minutes, stirring occasionally.

**3.** Just before serving, sprinkle in red pepper flakes. Line platter or fill bowls with shredded romaine, top with tofu-vegetable mixture, and garnish with cashews and sesame seeds (if using).

VEGAN

## NUTRITION INFORMATION

Calories: 187
Protein: 10 g
Total Fat: 7 g
Saturated Fat: 1 g
Carbohydrates: 23 g
Cholesterol: 0 mg
Sodium: 617 mg
Fiber: 4 g
Sugar: 17 g

# WARM POTATO SALAD
## WITH TEMPEH BACON CRUMBLES

YIELD: SERVES 12

**TEMPEH BACON CRUMBLES**

**2 Tbs. vegetable oil**

**1 8-oz. pkg. plain tempeh, grated or finely chopped**

**1 Tbs. low-sodium soy sauce**

**1 Tbs. blackstrap molasses**

**1½ tsp. ketchup or tomato paste**

**2 drops Liquid Smoke**

SALAD

**3 lb. small red-skinned or Yukon gold potatoes, sliced ¼-inch thick**

**⅓ cup olive oil**

**1 large red onion, diced (2 cups)**

**⅓ cup apple cider vinegar**

**1 cup chopped green onions, fresh parsley, or chives, for sprinkling**

Tempeh bacon crumbles turn a carb-heavy potato salad into a more balanced side dish offering, and add great flavor. Be careful when using Liquid Smoke to flavor the tempeh as using more than the recommended amount may yield an overly smoky flavor.

**1.** To make Tempeh Bacon Crumbles: Heat oil in large skillet over medium heat. Add tempeh, and cook 3 to 5 minutes, or until browned. Stir in soy sauce, molasses, and ketchup or tomato paste, and bring to a boil. Cook 2 to 3 minutes, or until mixture is dry. Stir in Liquid Smoke 1 drop at a time. Transfer tempeh to paper-towel-lined plate to drain.

**2.** To make Salad: Place potatoes in large pot of salted water; bring to a boil. Cook 5 to 7 minutes, or until just tender.

**3.** Meanwhile, heat oil in skillet over medium-heat, add onion, and sauté 5 to 7 minutes, or until softened. Remove from heat, and whisk in vinegar and ⅓ cup water.

**4.** Drain potatoes, and transfer to large serving bowl. Stir onion mixture into potatoes. Sprinkle with Tempeh Bacon Crumbles and green onions. Serve warm.

VEGAN

## NUTRITION INFORMATION

Calories: 203
Protein: 6 g
Total Fat: 11 g
Saturated Fat: 2 g
Carbohydrates: 23 g
Cholesterol: 0 mg
Sodium: 127 mg
Fiber: 2 g
Sugar: 3 g

# CHICKPEA, ARTICHOKE HEART & TOMATO SALAD

YIELD: SERVES 2

**1½ cups cooked chickpeas or 1 15-oz. can chickpeas, rinsed and drained**

**½ 6-oz. jar water-packed artichoke hearts, rinsed, drained, and sliced**

**½ cup small pear or grape tomatoes, halved or quartered**

**⅓ cup chopped pitted Kalamata olives, optional**

**¼ cup finely chopped fresh parsley**

**¼ cup prepared balsamic vinaigrette**

**2–3 drops sriracha sauce**

**2 cups baby arugula**

**1 oz. crumbled feta cheese, optional**

The hearty ¾ cup serving of chickpeas in this salad packs about 11 grams of protein and 9 grams of fiber. Artichoke hearts, tomatoes, and baby arugula add a rainbow of antioxidants, including lycopene, beta-carotene, and vitamin C.

**1.** Toss together chickpeas, artichoke hearts, tomatoes, olives (if using), and parsley in bowl.

**2.** Season vinaigrette with sriracha. Toss chickpea mixture with vinaigrette, then stir in arugula and feta, if using. Season with salt and pepper, if desired.

GLUTEN-FREE

30 MINUTES OR LESS

## NUTRITION INFORMATION

Calories: 345
Protein: 13 g
Total Fat: 15 g
Saturated Fat: 1 g
Carbohydrates: 43 g
Cholesterol: 13 mg
Sodium: 749 mg
Fiber: 7 g
Sugar: 9 g

# GRILL-ROASTED VEGETABLE SALAD

YIELD: SERVES 4

2 large red bell peppers

2 medium-large green and/or gold zucchini, each sliced crosswise from top to bottom into 8 planks

4 Tbs. olive oil, divided

2 Tbs. coarsely chopped fresh basil leaves, plus some small whole leaves for garnish

2 tsp. white balsamic vinegar

1 Tbs. finely chopped sun-dried tomatoes

1 Tbs. chopped pitted Kalamata olives

1 clove garlic, minced (1 tsp.)

1 cup cooked red quinoa

2 cups baby or small arugula leaves, plus a few leaves for garnish

3 oz. crumbled fresh goat cheese

Make this your go-to salad for summer entertaining. Quinoa is sprinkled over top as a protein-enhancing garnish that adds textural interest. The vegetables can be roasted under the broiler if you don't have an outdoor grill.

**1.** Preheat grill on high, place bell peppers directly on grate, close lid, and cook 10 to 12 minutes, or until bell peppers are blistered and blackened in most places, turning occasionally. Transfer bell peppers to bowl, cover with foil, and let stand 20 minutes. Peel bell peppers over colander set in bowl to catch any juices; discard seeds. Cut each bell pepper into 6 long, wide strips.

**2.** Reduce grill heat to medium. Brush both sides of zucchini planks with 2 Tbs. oil, and season with salt, if desired. Grill zucchini 5 to 8 minutes, turning once. Transfer to plate, and cover loosely.

**3.** Combine remaining 2 Tbs. oil, bell pepper juices, chopped basil, vinegar, sun-dried tomatoes, olives, and garlic in small bowl to make dressing. Stir 1 Tbs. dressing into cooked quinoa. Toss arugula with 1 Tbs. dressing.

**4.** Arrange arugula on serving plates. Sprinkle ⅔ cup quinoa and 2 oz. goat cheese over servings. Top each serving with 3 pieces zucchini and 2 pieces bell pepper arranged in spoke-wheel pattern. Spoon 1 Tbs. dressing over vegetables. Top with remaining quinoa, followed by remaining zucchini and bell pepper, and remaining goat cheese. Drizzle with remaining dressing. Garnish with whole arugula and basil leaves.

GLUTEN-FREE

## NUTRITION INFORMATION

| | | |
|---|---|---|
| Calories: 305 | Saturated Fat: 5 g | Sodium: 177 mg |
| Protein: 9 g | Carbohydrates: 24 g | Fiber: 4 g |
| Total Fat: 21 g | Cholesterol: 10 mg | Sugar: 10 g |

# TATSOI, MIZUNA & EDAMAME SALAD
## WITH SESAME DRESSING

YIELD: SERVES 4

This salad calls for tatsoi and mizuna, two specialty Japanese greens that complement the flavors in the dressing. Shredded Napa cabbage and watercress will also work and are easier to find in supermarkets.

### SESAME DRESSING

**3 Tbs. roasted sesame oil**

**2 Tbs. tahini**

**2 Tbs. seasoned rice wine vinegar**

**1 Tbs. low-sodium soy sauce**

### SALAD

**1½ cups frozen shelled edamame, thawed**

**2 cups tatsoi leaves**

**2 cups mizuna**

**1 cucumber, peeled and sliced**

**1 8-oz. pkg. baked teriyaki tofu, cubed**

**1 green onion, sliced**

**1.** To make Sesame Dressing: Whisk together sesame oil, tahini, vinegar, and soy sauce in small bowl.

**2.** To make Salad: Cook edamame according to package directions. Rinse under cold water to cool. Drain well.

**3.** Divide edamame, tatsoi, mizuna, cucumber, tofu, and green onion among 4 plates. Drizzle with Sesame Dressing and serve.

VEGAN

30 MINUTES OR LESS

### NUTRITION INFORMATION

Calories: 347
Protein: 19 g
Total Fat: 21 g
Saturated Fat: 2.5 g
Carbohydrates: 21 g
Cholesterol: mg
Sodium: 729 mg
Fiber: 6 g
Sugar: 5 g

# SOUPS & STEWS

The magical melding of flavors that happens when ingredients are simmered together is what a good soup or stew is all about—and it's hard to get any better than a steaming bowl of one or the other on a chilly night—or even a cool summer evening.

Vegetarian soups and stews have one big advantage over their meat-laced counterparts, too. Because plant-based ingredients take less time to cook, hearty, satisfying recipes take less time to achieve those luscious flavor-melding results we all crave. And when a soup or stew's protein comes from plant sources, there's little fat and no cholesterol, meaning you can indulge in a second cup or bowl—or just sprinkle the first one with some cheese or a few croutons, and possibly enjoy a slice of bread alongside.

# PASILLA CHILE POSOLE

YIELD: SERVES 4

This hearty Mexican stew is flavored with mild pasilla chiles, which are sold dried in small packages. The garnishes make for a fun meal that lets everyone at the table customize their serving according to taste.

## POSOLE

**2 4- to 5-inch dried pasilla chiles**

**2 medium leeks, white and light green parts cut into 2-inch chunks**

**2 Tbs. olive oil**

**4 cloves garlic, minced (4 tsp.)**

**2 tsp. ground cumin**

**1 tsp. dried oregano**

**2 15-oz. cans white hominy, rinsed and drained**

**2 15-oz. cans, rinsed and drained, black beans**

**1 15-oz. can fire-roasted diced tomatoes**

## GARNISHES

**4 cups tortilla chips**

**2 avocados, diced**

**2 tomatoes, diced**

**¼ cup chopped green onions**

**2 limes, sliced into wedges**

**½ cup chopped cilantro**

**1.** To make Posole: Place pasilla chiles in large bowl, and cover with 3 cups boiling water. Let soak 15 minutes, or until softened. Drain chiles, and reserve liquid. Pull open chiles, and gently scrape out and discard seeds. Purée chiles in food processor with ¼ cup reserved soaking liquid. (Press purée through sieve if bits of skin remain, and discard solids.) Stir chile purée into remaining soaking liquid.

**2.** Halve leek chunks, and thinly slice into matchsticks.

**3.** Heat oil in large stockpot over medium heat. Add leeks, and sauté 5 to 7 minutes, or until softened. Add garlic, cumin, and oregano, and sauté 1 minute. Add hominy, black beans, tomatoes with juice, chile liquid, and 6 cups water; cover, and bring to a boil. Reduce heat to medium-low, and simmer 20 minutes.

**4.** Place Garnishes in bowls; pass around table when ready to serve.

VEGAN

GLUTEN-FREE

### NUTRITION INFORMATION

| | |
|---|---|
| Calories: 352 | Cholesterol: 0 mg |
| Protein: 12 g | Sodium: 588 mg |
| Total Fat: 10 g | Fiber: 16 g |
| Saturated Fat: 1 g | Sugar: 10 g |
| Carbohydrates: 64 g | |

# HOMINY

Hominy is dried and reconstituted corn kernels from which the hull and germ have been removed. Dried hominy can also be ground into white (hominy) grits. The chewy nuggets are sold canned or dried (they're cooked just like dried beans) and are wonderful in stews, casseroles, and hearty soups like posole.

# SMOKY VEGETABLE & WHEAT BERRY STEW

½ cup dried white beans

2 Tbs. olive oil

1 medium leek, white and light-green parts sliced (1 cup)

1 carrot, peeled and chopped (½ cup)

1 celery stalk, trimmed and chopped (⅓ cup)

3 cloves garlic, minced (1 Tbs.)

1 tsp. smoked paprika

5 cups low-sodium vegetable broth or water

1 14.5-oz. can diced, no-salt tomatoes with liquid

½ cup wheat berries

2 sprigs fresh sage, optional

2 cups Swiss chard greens, sliced

¼ cup chopped fresh parsley

Wheat berries and dried white beans are cooked directly within this long-simmering soup, lending body and flavor to the broth. Feel free to substitute other beans for the white beans—heirloom varieties work especially well.

**1.** Soak white beans in medium bowl of cold water overnight. Drain, and set aside.

**2.** Heat oil in large saucepan or Dutch oven over medium-high heat. Add leek, carrot, and celery, and season with salt and pepper, if desired. Cook 5 to 7 minutes, or until vegetables are brown around edges. Add garlic and smoked paprika, and sauté 1 minute. Stir in broth or water, tomatoes, wheat berries, soaked beans, and sage, if using.

**3.** Bring to a boil, cover pan almost completely, and reduce heat to medium-low. Simmer 1 hour, or until wheat berries and beans are tender, adding stock or water if soup becomes too thick. Stir in chard and parsley, and cook 5 minutes more. Season with salt and pepper, if desired.

`VEGAN`

## NUTRITION INFORMATION

Calories: 297
Protein: 11 g
Total Fat: 7 g
Saturated Fat: 1 g
Carbohydrates: 47 g
Cholesterol: 0 mg
Sodium: 254 mg
Fiber: 3 g
Sugar: 8 g

# SWISS CHARD, WHITE BEAN & POTATO SOUP

YIELD: SERVES 6

**3 cups cooked or 2 15-oz. cans cannellini or navy beans, rinsed and drained**

**2 Tbs. olive oil**

**1 large red bell pepper, chopped into ½-inch pieces (1¼ cups)**

**1 small onion, quartered and thinly sliced (1 cup)**

**4 medium new potatoes (1¼ lb.), sliced into 1-inch-thick half-moons**

**2 cloves garlic, minced (2 tsp.)**

**4 cups low-sodium vegetable broth**

**⅛ tsp. ground nutmeg**

**10 cups stemmed Swiss chard leaves, coarsely torn**

This soup may very well become your go-to winter weeknight dinner, it's so quick and so easy. Adding a few chunky pieces of potato gives it a hearty feel, and you can substitute any greens you have on hand for the chard.

**1.** Smash ¾ cup beans in bowl with back of fork to form paste; set aside.

**2.** Heat oil in large pot or Dutch oven over medium heat. Add bell pepper and onion, and season with salt and pepper, if desired. Cook 5 minutes, or until softened. Add potatoes, and cook 10 minutes, or until tender. Stir in garlic, and cook 2 minutes more.

**3.** Add broth, 1 cup water, smashed and whole beans, and nutmeg to pot; bring to a boil. Reduce heat to medium-low, and simmer 12 to 15 minutes. Add chard, and season with salt and pepper, if desired. Simmer 5 minutes, or until chard is wilted.

VEGAN

GLUTEN-FREE

30 MINUTES OR LESS

## NUTRITION INFORMATION

Calories: 288
Protein: 13 g
Total Fat: 5 g
Saturated Fat: <1 g
Carbohydrates: 48 g
Cholesterol: 0 mg
Sodium: 392 mg
Fiber: 15 g
Sugar: 5 g

# CURRIED RED LENTIL SOUP
## WITH LEMON

YIELD: SERVES 6

**2 cups red lentils, sorted, rinsed, and drained**

**1 qt. low-sodium vegetable broth**

**1 large onion, finely chopped (2 cups)**

**4 celery stalks, finely chopped (1½ cups)**

**2 large carrots, finely chopped (1½ cups)**

**2 cloves garlic, minced (2 tsp.)**

**¼ cup chopped cilantro**

**1 Tbs. curry powder**

**1 tsp. ground cumin**

**2 Tbs. lemon juice**

This deliciously easy soup is even better the second day, after the spices have had more time to mingle.

**1.** Bring lentils, vegetable broth, and 4 cups water to a simmer in large pot. Skim away foam that rises to top. Reduce heat to medium-low, cover, and simmer 5 minutes, stirring occasionally.

**2.** Add onion, celery, carrots, and garlic; simmer, uncovered, 20 minutes. Add cilantro, curry powder, and cumin, and cook 20 minutes more, or until lentils are soft. Season with salt and pepper, if desired, and stir in lemon juice.

VEGAN

GLUTEN-FREE

## NUTRITION INFORMATION

Calories: 283
Protein: 19 g
Total Fat: 2 g
Saturated Fat: <1 g
Carbohydrates: 50 g
Cholesterol: 0 mg
Sodium: 146 mg
Fiber: 13 g
Sugar: 7 g

# MOROCCAN LENTIL STEW

This exotically-flavored stew is made with easy-to-find spices and ingredients, including prepared lentil soup. It can be stretched to feed a crowd when ladled over rice, couscous, quinoa, or potatoes.

**1 Tbs. olive oil**

**1 cup chopped onion**

**3 cloves garlic, minced (1 Tbs.)**

**1 28-oz. can crushed tomatoes**

**2 18.2-oz. cartons prepared lentil soup**

**1 15-oz. can chickpeas, rinsed and drained**

**½ cup raisins or dried currants**

**2 tsp. ground cinnamon, or more to taste**

**1½ tsp. ground cumin**

**¼ tsp. red pepper flakes, or to taste**

**1.** Heat oil in medium saucepan or Dutch oven over medium heat. Add onion, and sauté 3 minutes, or until softened and translucent. Add garlic, and cook 1 minute, or until garlic is softened, but not browned, stirring constantly.

**2.** Stir in tomatoes, soup, chickpeas, raisins, cinnamon, cumin, and red pepper flakes. Season with salt and pepper, if desired. Bring stew to a simmer over medium-high heat, stirring occasionally.

**3.** Reduce heat to medium-low, and simmer, uncovered, 20 minutes, or until mixture is reduced and sauce has thickened, stirring often from bottom to prevent sticking.

VEGAN

GLUTEN-FREE

30 MINUTES OR LESS

## NUTRITION INFORMATION

Calories: 263
Protein: 11 g
Total Fat: 4 g
Saturated Fat: <1 g
Carbohydrates: 49 g
Cholesterol: 0 mg
Sodium: 642 mg
Fiber: 13 g
Sugar: 11 g

# CHICKPEA MINESTRONE

**YIELD: SERVES 6**

2 Tbs. olive oil

1 small onion, chopped (1¼ cups)

4 cloves garlic, peeled

3 large carrots, halved lengthwise and thinly sliced (2 cups)

3 stalks celery, halved lengthwise and thinly sliced (1 cup)

1 28-oz. can crushed tomatoes

2 sprigs fresh thyme

2 15-oz. cans chickpeas, rinsed and drained

4 cups low-sodium vegetable broth

1¼ cups (6 oz.) ditalini pasta

⅓ cup chopped fresh basil, plus more thinly shredded basil for garnish

Mashed and whole chickpeas give an Italian-grandma-inspired soup a hearty dose of protein and fiber. Once you get the hang of making it, you can mix things up with extra vegetables and dress the soup up with Parmesan cheese or a drizzle of good olive oil.

**1.** Heat oil in large pot or Dutch oven over medium heat. Add onion and garlic, and sauté 4 minutes, or until softened. Next add carrots and celery, and cook 5 minutes, stirring occasionally. Stir in tomatoes, add thyme sprigs, and cook 2 minutes more.

**2.** Smash ½ cup chickpeas with back of a fork to form paste. Add smashed and whole chickpeas, broth, and 2 cups water to pot. Bring to a boil, then reduce heat to medium-low, and simmer 5 minutes. Add ditalini and basil, and cook 7 to 8 minutes, stirring occasionally.

**3.** Thin soup with broth or water (if necessary), and adjust seasoning. Remove thyme sprigs, and serve garnished with shredded basil.

VEGAN

30 MINUTES OR LESS

### NUTRITION INFORMATION

Calories: 367
Protein: 14 g
Total Fat: 8 g
Saturated Fat: <1 g
Carbohydrates: 63 g
Cholesterol: 0 mg
Sodium: 588 mg
Fiber: 12 g
Sugar: 16 g

# PEANUT BUTTER

Need a quick, satisfying hit of fat, protein, and flavor? Turn to all-natural peanut butter with 5 grams of protein per tablespoon. Other nut butters have similar nutritional profiles, as well.

# SPICY PEANUT STEW

YIELD: SERVES 6

2 Tbs. olive oil

1 medium onion, diced (about 1 cup)

1 celery stalk, chopped (about ½ cup)

1 Tbs. grated fresh ginger

2 cloves garlic, minced (about 2 tsp.)

1 medium sweet potato, peeled and cut into 1-inch chunks (about 2 cups)

1 14.5-oz. can diced tomatoes with chiles

1 lb. butternut or acorn squash, cut into 1-inch chunks (3 cups)

½ lb. cauliflower florets (4 cups)

¼ cup creamy peanut butter

6 cups cooked brown rice

1 head watercress, stems removed

This West African stew gets its distinctive taste from creamy peanut butter and chile-laced chopped tomatoes. It's served over rice and garnished with watercress for a one-dish meal.

**1.** Heat oil in large pot over medium-low heat. Add onion and celery, and cook 5 minutes, or until onion is translucent, stirring occasionally. Stir in ginger and garlic, and cook 5 minutes more, or until vegetables are soft.

**2.** Add potato and tomatoes. Increase heat to medium, and cook 5 minutes, or until sauce is thickened, stirring occasionally.

**3.** Stir in 2 cups water, and season with salt and pepper. Simmer partially covered, 10 minutes. Add squash and cauliflower, and cook 15 minutes more, or until vegetables are tender.

**4.** Whisk together peanut butter and ½ cup warm water in small bowl. Add to stew, and cook 4 minutes, or until thickened, stirring constantly. Spoon over rice, and top with watercress.

VEGAN

GLUTEN-FREE

30 MINUTES OR LESS

## NUTRITION INFORMATION

Calories: 422
Protein: 11 g
Total Fat: 12 g
Saturated Fat: 2 g
Carbohydrates: 71 g

Cholesterol: 0 mg
Sodium: 770 mg
Fiber: 9 g
Sugar: 7 g

# FARMERS' MARKET CHOWDER

YIELD: SERVES 6

**4 large (or 5 small) ears corn, kernels removed and cobs reserved**

**2½ cups low-fat milk**

**2 cloves garlic, peeled and crushed, plus 3 cloves garlic, minced (1 Tbs.), divided**

**2 Tbs. unsalted butter**

**3 Tbs. olive oil, divided**

**3 cups sliced leeks (5 medium)**

**½ tsp. smoked paprika**

**⅓ cup dry sherry**

**12 oz. peeled sweet potatoes, cut into medium dice**

**½ lb. green beans, cut into ½-inch pieces**

**2 Tbs. chopped fresh cilantro**

**Lime wedges, for garnish**

While corn and leeks are essential in this summery chowder, feel free to substitute potatoes, carrots, or other root vegetables for some or all of the sweet potatoes. You could also mix in colorful yellow wax or purple beans with the green beans or use basil instead of cilantro.

**1.** Combine corn kernels, milk, and crushed garlic in saucepan. Run back of knife down cobs to release milk and pulp into saucepan, then add cobs to pan. Bring to a boil. Remove pan from heat, and let steep.

**2.** Heat butter and 1 Tbs. oil in Dutch oven over medium-low heat. Add leeks, cover, and cook 15 minutes, stirring occasionally. Add minced garlic and paprika, and cook 30 seconds. Stir in sherry, and cook 30 seconds. Add 4 cups water, and remove pot from heat.

**3.** Heat 1 Tbs. oil in skillet over medium-high heat. Add sweet potatoes, and sauté 8 minutes, or until browned; transfer to Dutch oven. Add remaining 1 Tbs. oil to same skillet, add green beans, and sauté 3 minutes. Transfer beans to plate.

**4.** Bring mixture in Dutch oven to a boil, reduce heat to medium-low, and simmer 5 minutes. Add green beans, and cook 4 minutes more.

**5.** Strain milk mixture, and discard corncobs and garlic. Stir milk mixture and 1 Tbs. cilantro into chowder. Season with salt and pepper, if desired. Sprinkle with remaining cilantro, and serve with lime wedges.

MAKE IT VEGAN **Substitute nondairy milk and olive oil for the milk and butter.**

## NUTRITION INFORMATION

| | |
|---|---|
| Calories: 280 | Cholesterol: 15 mg |
| Protein: 8 g | Sodium: 80 mg |
| Total Fat: 13 g | Fiber: 5 g |
| Saturated Fat: 4 g | Sugar: 15 g |
| Carbohydrates: 37 g | |

# VEGETARIAN PHO (VIETNAMESE NOODLE SOUP)

The national soup of Vietnam is a bowl of rice noodles, fresh herbs, and bean sprouts swimming in a fragrant broth.

## BROTH

**6 cups low-sodium vegetable broth**

**3 large shallots, sliced (1 cup)**

**½ cup dried shiitake mushrooms**

**10 cloves garlic, peeled and crushed**

**3 Tbs. low-sodium soy sauce**

**12 ¼-inch-thick coins fresh ginger**

**1 Tbs. brown sugar**

**1 Tbs. rice wine vinegar**

**1 tsp. ground black pepper**

**2 cinnamon sticks**

**2 star anise**

**5–6 fresh basil stems, leaves reserved for soup**

**5–6 cilantro stems, leaves reserved for soup**

## PHO

**1 8-oz. pkg. rice noodles**

**1 8-oz. pkg. Asian-flavor baked tofu, thinly sliced**

**2 cups soybean sprouts**

**2 cups watercress**

**4 green onions, sliced (½ cup)**

**¼ cup chopped cilantro**

**1 cup fresh basil leaves**

**1 lime, cut into wedges**

**1.** To make Broth: Place all ingredients in large pot with 8 cups water. Cover, and bring to a boil. Reduce heat to medium-low, and simmer, covered, 1 hour. Strain broth, and return to pot. Discard solids.

**2.** To make Pho: Cook rice noodles according to package directions. Drain, and rinse under cold water. Divide among 6 large soup bowls. Ladle Broth over noodles, and top with tofu, sprouts, watercress, and green onions. Serve cilantro, basil, and lime wedges on the side to be stirred into soup.

VEGAN

## NUTRITION INFORMATION

| | | |
|---|---|---|
| Calories: 290 | Saturated Fat: 1 g | Sodium: 578 mg |
| Protein: 16 g | Carbohydrates: 42 g | Fiber: 3 g |
| Total Fat: 5.5 g | Cholesterol: 0 mg | Sugar: 5 g |

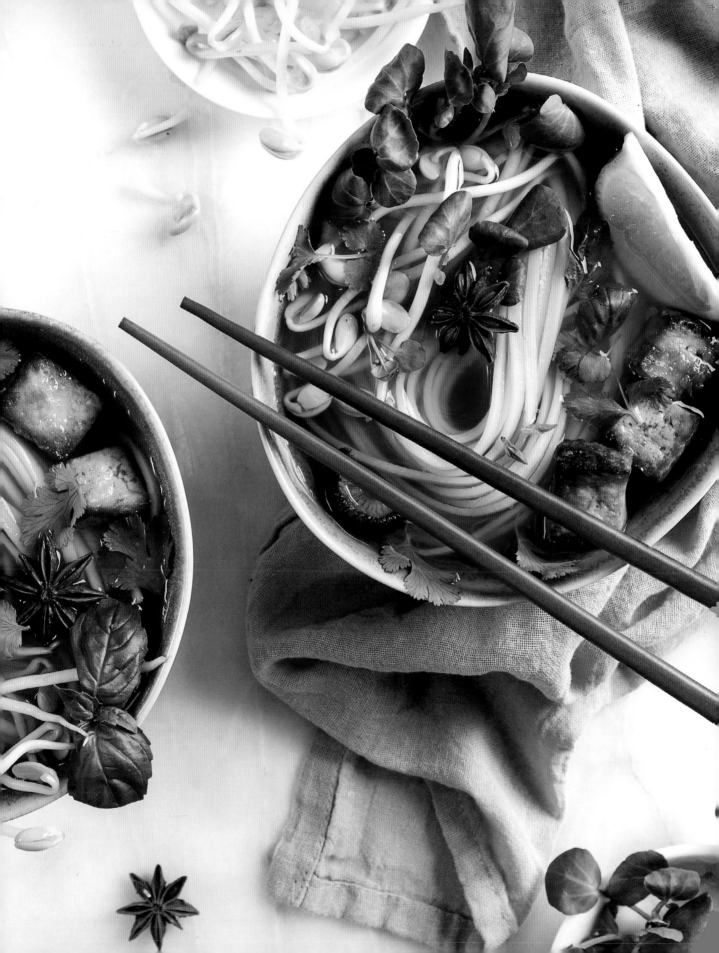

# SPLIT PEA, FENNEL & SPINACH SOUP

YIELD: SERVES 8

**2 cups chopped fresh fennel (1 bulb)**

**1 large onion, chopped (2 cups)**

**3 cloves garlic, minced (1 Tbs.)**

**1 cup dry white wine, divided**

**15 oz. dried green split peas**

**1 tsp. fennel seeds, divided**

**½ tsp. dried thyme**

**1 bay leaf**

**5 oz. baby spinach leaves**

Old-fashioned split pea soup gets a modern update with fresh and dried fennel and a last-minute addition of baby spinach that also brightens the soup's color.

**1.** Heat saucepan coated with cooking spray over medium heat. Add fennel and onion, and sauté 8 minutes. Stir in garlic, and cook 30 seconds. Add ½ cup wine, and simmer 2 minutes. Add split peas, ½ tsp. fennel seeds, thyme, bay leaf, and 7 cups water. Bring to a boil, reduce heat to medium-low, cover, and simmer 50 minutes, stirring occasionally.

**2.** Add remaining ½ cup wine, and cook, uncovered, 10 minutes, or until split peas are tender. Stir in spinach, and cook 2 minutes, or until spinach is wilted.

**3.** Remove bay leaf, and purée soup with immersion blender until smooth. Season with salt and pepper, if desired. Toast remaining ½ tsp. fennel seeds in small skillet 2 minutes, or until fragrant. Serve soup garnished with toasted fennel seeds.

## NUTRITION INFORMATION

Calories: 227
Protein: 13 g
Total Fat: 2 g
Saturated Fat: <1 g
Carbohydrates: 42 g
Cholesterol: 0 mg
Sodium: 45 mg
Fiber: 21 g
Sugar: 3 g

# NEW WORLD CHILI

**1 24-oz. jar medium tomato salsa**

**1 15.5-oz. can pinto beans, drained and rinsed**

**1 12-oz. pkg. crumbled soy "meat"**

**2 cups fresh or frozen corn kernels**

**1½ cups fresh or frozen lima beans**

**¼ cup chili powder, or to taste**

**½ tsp. hot pepper sauce, or to taste**

**¼ tsp. ground black pepper**

**1 ripe avocado, diced, for garnish**

**1 cup chopped red onions, for garnish**

This chili showcases ingredients that early explorers discovered in the New World—pinto beans, corn, tomatoes, and lima beans. Sprinkle diced avocado and chopped red onion on top for a flavorful garnish. For stovetop prep, all of the ingredients except the avocado and red onions go into the pot at once, then everything simmers for about 2 hours.

**1.** Combine all ingredients except avocado and red onions in 4-qt. slow cooker or large pot.

**2.** Cover slow cooker, and cook on low 4 to 6 hours. Or place lid on pot, and bring chili to a boil over medium-high heat; reduce heat to medium-low, and simmer, covered, stirring occasionally, 1½ to 2 hours. Season to taste with salt and pepper.

**3.** Spoon chili into bowls, and garnish each serving with diced avocados and chopped red onion.

VEGAN

GLUTEN-FREE

## NUTRITION INFORMATION

Calories: 291
Protein: 16 g
Total Fat: 7 g
Saturated Fat: 1 g
Carbohydrates: 44 g
Cholesterol: 0 mg
Sodium: 755 mg
Fiber: 13 g
Sugar: 4 g

# CHIPOTLE CHILI NON-CARNE

Spicy, smoky chipotle chile powder is added to this classic bean chili recipe for a richly flavored stew that's ready in just a half an hour. To make the chili milder, omit the chipotle powder and reduce the chili powder to 2 teaspoons.

**1 tsp. olive oil**

**1 cup finely chopped onion**

**4 cloves garlic, minced**

**1 green or yellow bell pepper, chopped**

**1 cup frozen corn**

**¼ tsp. chipotle chile powder, or to taste**

**1 Tbs. chili powder**

**1 tsp. ground cumin**

**1 tsp. dried oregano**

**4½ cups cooked black beans, or 3 15-oz. cans black beans, rinsed and drained**

**1 14½-oz. can diced tomatoes**

**1.** Heat oil in large saucepan over medium-high heat. Add onion and garlic and sauté 2 to 3 minutes. Add bell pepper and corn and sauté 2 minutes more. Stir in chipotle powder, chili powder, cumin, and oregano and cook 1 minute. Stir in beans, tomatoes, and ¾ cup water.

**2.** Reduce heat to medium-low, partially cover pan, and simmer, stirring occasionally, 20 minutes. If chili becomes too thick, add ¼ cup hot water. Season with salt and pepper, if desired.

VEGAN

GLUTEN-FREE

30 MINUTES OR LESS

## NUTRITION INFORMATION

Calories: 341
Protein: 21 g
Total Fat: 2 g
Saturated Fat: 1 g
Carbohydrates: 63 g
Cholesterol: 0 mg
Sodium: 25 mg
Fiber: 21 g
Sugar: 7 g

# SANDWICHES & WRAPS

My how the tables have turned when it comes to sandwiches! According to legend, the Earl of Sandwich invented the bread-based creations in the 17th century so he wouldn't have to leave the gambling table to eat.

These days, sandwiches are top take-along food choices—usually assembled precisely so you don't have to stay at the table. Wraps are a good example of how traditional sandwiches have evolved for added portability.

We like to stuff sandwiches and wraps with as many fresh fruits and vegetables as we can so there's really something to sink your teeth into. After all, a well-built sandwich can be a well-rounded meal.

# THE HEALTHIEST BREAD CHOICE

WHEN SHOPPING FOR BREAD, CHECK THE NUTRITION LABEL TO SEE HOW CLOSE IT COMES TO THIS IDEAL NUTRIENT RATIO:

Calories: 80

Fiber: 3 to 5 grams

Protein: 4 grams

Carbohydrates: 15 grams

Sodium: 125 milligrams

Sugar: 3 grams or less

# GREEN BEAN–ARTICHOKE WRAP
## WITH GOAT CHEESE

**YIELD: SERVES 4**

**¾ lb. green beans, trimmed**

**4 whole-grain tortillas**

**4 oz. garlic-and-herb goat cheese**

**½ cup chunky artichoke spread or artichoke tapenade**

**2 medium tomatoes, seeded and thinly sliced**

Who needs lettuce when you can stuff your wrap with crisp-tender green beans? When selecting the green beans to fill this wrap, choose the fattest, greenest ones you can find. Seeding the tomatoes before putting them in the wraps prevents sogginess if they're being made ahead.

**1.** Steam green beans 8 minutes in steamer until crisp-tender. Plunge into cold water, then drain, and pat dry.

**2.** Spread each tortilla with 2 Tbs. goat cheese and 2 Tbs. artichoke spread, leaving 1-inch edge on sides. Top with one-quarter tomato slices. Place 6 or 7 green beans in a tight bunch on top third of tortilla, then tightly roll tortilla like a burrito, folding in sides. Wrap in wax paper or foil until ready to serve.

**30 MINUTES OR LESS**

## NUTRITION INFORMATION

Calories: 299
Protein: 10 g
Total Fat: 14 g
Saturated Fat: 6 g
Carbohydrates: 33 g
Cholesterol: 19 mg
Sodium: 838 mg
Fiber: 7 g
Sugar: 4 g

# COLLARD GREEN WRAPS
## WITH MISO-GINGER SWEET POTATOES

YIELD: SERVES 4

Tofu, edamame, and mashed, seasoned sweet potatoes are wrapped in collard leaves for a flavorful lunch option with a hint of spice. The filling can also be spread on whole-grain toast or wrapped in tortillas.

**2 small sweet potatoes (1 lb.)**

**2 Tbs. white miso paste**

**1 Tbs. smooth peanut butter**

**2 Tbs. finely chopped shallot**

**1 Tbs. minced fresh ginger**

**2 cloves garlic, minced (2 tsp.)**

**1 cup frozen shelled edamame**

**¼ tsp. cayenne pepper**

**6 oz. firm silken tofu, crumbled (1 cup)**

**2 Tbs. chopped cilantro**

**8 collard green leaves, stems removed**

**1.** Preheat oven to 400°F. Cut thin slices off both ends of sweet potatoes, and poke skins with knife in several places. Bake 50 minutes, or until soft, turning once. Halve sweet potatoes, and scoop flesh into bowl. Mash in miso and peanut butter.

**2.** Meanwhile, coat skillet with cooking spray, and heat over medium heat. Sauté shallot, ginger, and garlic 3 minutes, or until soft. Add edamame, ¼ cup water, and cayenne; cook 3 minutes more. Remove from heat, and stir in tofu, cilantro, and sweet potato mixture. Cool.

**3.** Place 1 collard green leaf on work surface. Spoon ⅓ cup sweet potato mixture in center of leaf. Roll bottom edge over mixture; tuck in sides. Roll up to top edge. Place, seam-side down, and repeat with remaining ingredients.

VEGAN

---

PREP TIP **If your collard leaves are small, use two overlapping leaves to wrap the sandwich filling.**

### NUTRITION INFORMATION

| | |
|---|---|
| Calories: 179 | Cholesterol: 0 mg |
| Protein: 10 g | Sodium: 302 mg |
| Total Fat: 5 g | Fiber: 5 g |
| Saturated Fat: <1 g | Sugar: 8 g |
| Carbohydrates: 25 g | |

# BAGUETTE SANDWICHES
## WITH ROASTED RED PEPPER SPREAD

YIELD: MAKES 6
SANDWICHES

1 8-oz. container
vegan or low-fat
cream cheese,
softened

1 17-oz. jar roasted
red peppers,
drained well, finely
chopped

3 Tbs. finely minced
onion

1 clove garlic,
minced (1 tsp.)

2 18-inch whole-
grain French
baguettes

1 medium cucumber,
peeled, seeded, and
diced (¾ cup)

12 romaine lettuce
leaves

2 cups thinly sliced
radicchio

Cream cheese soaks up all the sweet, tangy flavor of roasted red peppers in an easy-to-prepare sandwich filling. Slipping cucumber between the filling and the lettuce helps keep the greens from wilting if the sandwiches are made ahead. Feel free to pile on more vegetables, like grated carrots, tomatoes, and sliced onion, too!

**1.** Combine cream cheese, roasted red peppers, onion, and garlic in bowl.

**2.** Cut each baguette into 3 6-inch pieces. Halve each piece lengthwise. Tear out some of center from bread to make space for fillings.

**3.** Spread cream cheese mixture on bottom halves of bread. Top with cucumber, lettuce, and radicchio, and cover with top half of bread.

30 MINUTES OR LESS

## NUTRITION INFORMATION

Calories: 355
Protein: 16 g
Total Fat: 6 g
Saturated Fat: <1 g
Carbohydrates: 61 g
Cholesterol: 0 mg
Sodium: 815 mg
Fiber: 3 g
Sugar: 4 g

# ROASTED VEGETABLE SANDWICHES
## WITH ZESTY WHITE BEAN SPREAD

The cumin and coriander used to season the vegetables are common spices in a number of global cuisines, so you can take the improvisation even further and add a dollop of salsa for Mexican flair, a spoonful of chutney for an Indian twist, a dab of harissa for Moroccan flavor, etc.

YIELD: SERVES 4

**VEGETABLES**

**1 tsp. ground cumin**

**1 tsp. ground coriander**

**1 tsp. salt**

**½ tsp. coarsely ground black pepper**

**2 large zucchini, sliced, ½-inch thick**

**2 medium red and/or yellow bell peppers, cut into eighths**

**3 small onions, cut into eighths**

**2 Tbs. olive oil**

**1.** To make Vegetables: Preheat oven to 375°F. Stir together cumin, coriander, salt, and pepper in small bowl. Set aside.

**2.** Toss together zucchini, bell peppers, onions, and oil in large bowl. Add cumin mixture, and toss to coat.

**3.** Divide vegetables between 2 baking sheets, and roast 30 to 45 minutes, or until tender and golden brown, turning vegetables once or twice and rotating baking sheets from top to bottom. Cool.

**4.** To make Bean Spread: Heat oil in small skillet over medium heat. Add garlic, and cook 30 seconds to 2 minutes, or until translucent and fragrant. Add beans, and coarsely mash. Stir in ¾ cup water, and cook 10 minutes, or until mixture is consistency of refried beans, stirring occasionally. Stir in lemon juice, and cool.

**5.** To assemble Sandwiches: Spread 2 Tbs. Bean Spread on each bread slice. Top 4 bread slices with 1 cup Vegetables, 2 or 3 tomato slices, and ½ cup arugula. Place remaining 4 bread slices on top. Cut in half to serve.

VEGAN

### BEAN SPREAD

**1 tsp. olive oil**

**2 cloves garlic, minced (2 tsp.)**

**1 15-oz. can cannellini beans, rinsed and drained**

**1 Tbs. lemon juice**

### SANDWICHES

**8 slices whole-grain bread**

**2 large tomatoes, sliced**

**2 cups arugula or mesclun lettuce mix**

## NUTRITION INFORMATION

Calories: 378
Protein: 15 g
Total Fat: 10 g
Saturated Fat: 1 g
Carbohydrates: 65 g
Cholesterol: 0 mg
Sodium: 830 mg
Fiber: 20 g
Sugar: 13 g

# QUICK WALNUT PÂTÉ SANDWICHES
## WITH PEARS & ARUGULA

YIELD: MAKES 8
SANDWICHES

Toasted walnuts are blended with beans and garlic to make a tasty pâté spread. Pears add a sweet, juicy crunch to sandwiches. Try them in place of tomatoes or other veggies.

### WALNUT PÂTÉ

**1 cup walnut pieces**

**1½ cups cooked cannellini beans or 1 15-oz. can cannellini beans, rinsed and drained**

**2 Tbs. lemon juice**

**2 cloves garlic, minced (2 tsp.)**

**2 tsp. olive oil**

### SANDWICHES

**16 slices whole-grain bread**

**4 large jarred roasted red bell peppers, rinsed, drained, and halved**

**2 large Anjou, Bartlett, or Concorde pears, peeled and sliced**

**2 cups baby arugula**

**1.** To make Walnut Pâté: Preheat oven to 350°F. Spread walnuts on baking sheet, and toast in oven 7 to 10 minutes, or until browned, shaking pan occasionally.

**2.** Transfer walnuts to bowl of food processor; add beans, lemon juice, garlic, oil, and ¼ cup water. Purée until smooth. Season with salt and pepper, if desired.

**3.** To make Sandwiches: Spread each of 8 bread slices with 3 Tbs. Walnut Pâté. Top each with red bell pepper half, 2 pear slices, and ¼ cup arugula. Spread remaining 8 bread slices wih 1 Tbs. Walnut Pâté. Place on top of sandwiches.

VEGAN

30 MINUTES OR LESS

### NUTRITION INFORMATION

Calories: 318
Protein: 12 g
Total Fat: 12 g
Saturated Fat: 1 g
Carbohydrates: 44 g
Cholesterol: 0 mg
Sodium: 453 mg
Fiber: 9 g
Sugar: 11 g

# SWEET & SOUR BAKED TOFU SANDWICHES

YIELD: SERVES 2

Stuff marinated, baked tofu into a crusty roll with crunchy cabbage, refrigerate it, then grab it on your way out the door the next morning for an on-the-go version of a Vietnamese bahn mi sandwich.

**1½ Tbs. low-sodium soy sauce**

**1½ Tbs. lime juice**

**1 Tbs. Thai sweet red chile sauce**

**½ Tbs. olive oil**

**½ tsp. brown sugar**

**½ 14-oz. pkg. extra-firm tofu, cut into 6 slices and patted dry**

**2 green onions, thinly sliced**

**2 Tbs. coarsely chopped roasted, unsalted peanuts**

**1 Tbs. grated fresh ginger**

**1½ cups finely shredded red cabbage**

**2 4-inch ciabatta rolls, halved lengthwise**

**1.** Preheat oven to 400°F. Lightly oil 8-inch square baking dish.

**2.** Whisk together soy sauce, lime juice, chile sauce, oil, and brown sugar in medium bowl. Add tofu slices to bowl. Marinate 10 minutes, turning twice.

**3.** Transfer marinated tofu to baking dish. Sprinkle with green onions, peanuts, and ginger. Spoon all but 1½ Tbs. marinade over top. Bake 30 minutes, or until golden. Cool.

**4.** Toss cabbage with reserved 1½ Tbs. marinade in bowl.

**5.** Hollow out excess bread from center of rolls, and discard. Place 3 tofu slices on bottom half of each roll, and top with cabbage. Close sandwiches, cut in half, and wrap tightly in plastic wrap. Store overnight in refrigerator.

VEGAN

## NUTRITION INFORMATION

Calories: 358
Protein: 18 g
Total Fat: 14 g
Saturated Fat: 2 g
Carbohydrates: 40 g
Cholesterol: 0 mg
Sodium: 748 mg
Fiber: 5 g
Sugar: 8 g

# CAROLINA-STYLE BARBECUE SANDWICHES

YIELD: SERVES 4

**1 cup apple cider vinegar**

**⅔ cup no-salt-added ketchup**

**¼ cup yellow mustard**

**3 Tbs. dark brown sugar**

**1 Tbs. molasses**

**2 tsp. Louisiana-style hot sauce**

**2 tsp. black pepper**

**1 tsp. salt**

**12 oz. seitan, drained, and cut into thin strips**

**4 hamburger-style buns**

**12 pickle chips, optional**

A tangy mustard-based sauce distinguishes Carolina-style barbecue from its sweeter Kansas City cousin. This recipe makes 2 cups of sauce, leaving plenty to serve on the side. For crunch in your sandwiches, serve with coleslaw.

Bring vinegar, ketchup, mustard, brown sugar, molasses, hot sauce, black pepper, and salt to a simmer in saucepan over medium heat. Cook 5 minutes. Transfer 1 cup sauce to bowl, and set aside. Add seitan to saucepan, and cook 10 minutes. Divide among buns. Serve with pickle chips, coleslaw, and extra sauce, if using.

NUTRITION INFORMATION

Calories: 327
Protein: 29 g
Total Fat: 2 g
Saturated Fat: 1 g
Carbohydrates: 47 g
Cholesterol: 0 mg
Sodium: 766 mg
Fiber: 2 g
Sugar: 15 g

# TEMPEH REUBENS

Thinly sliced tempeh simmered in a flavorful broth makes a great sandwich "meat" in this deli classic.

## SEASONED TEMPEH

¼ cup **Bragg Liquid Aminos**

1 small **onion,** quartered

2 cloves **garlic,** peeled

1 **bay leaf**

1 8-oz. **pkg. tempeh,** sliced

## THOUSAND ISLAND DRESSING

¼ cup **vegan mayonnaise or low-fat mayonnaise**

3 Tbs. **relish**

2 Tbs. **ketchup**

## SANDWICHES

16 slices **rye bread**

5 oz. **low-fat or vegan Monterey Jack cheese or Swiss cheese,** sliced

2 cups **sauerkraut**

**1.** To prepare Seasoned Tempeh: Combine liquid aminos, onion, garlic, bay leaf, and 2 cups water in saucepan over medium heat. Add tempeh slices, and bring to a simmer. Reduce heat to medium-low, and simmer 20 minutes. Cover, and let tempeh cool in broth.

**2.** To make Thousand Island Dressing: Stir together mayonnaise, relish, and ketchup in small bowl.

**3.** To make Sandwiches: Toast 8 slices bread. Set aside. Drain tempeh, and discard liquid, onion, garlic, and bay leaf. Place 3 slices tempeh on each slice of remaining bread. Top with cheese slices. Toast or broil 3 to 5 minutes, or until cheese has melted.

**4.** Top each sandwich with ¼ cup sauerkraut. Spread toasted bread slices with Thousand Island Dressing. Place tops on sandwiches, and slice in half.

## NUTRITION INFORMATION

Calories: 276
Protein: 14 g
Total Fat: 9 g
Saturated Fat: 1 g
Carbohydrates: 33 g
Cholesterol: 0 mg
Sodium: 971 mg
Fiber: 6 g
Sugar: 5 g

# EGGS & DAIRY

It's hard to beat eggs and dairy when it comes to a fast, easy, filling, and nourishing meal. Both are among the top sources of protein for vegetarians, with eggs clocking in at 7 grams and dairy ranging anywhere from 8 grams (1% milk) to a whopping 17 grams per serving (Greek yogurt).

Eggs and dairy play another vital role in a vegetarian diet. They are good sources of vitamin $B_{12}$, an essential vitamin the body uses to build red blood cells and the body's nervous system. $B_{12}$ cannot be found in any plant-based foods (except for trace amounts in seaweed), which means that vegans on egg- and dairy-free diets often don't get enough of the nutrient without consuming fortified foods like nutritional yeast, nondairy milk, and cereal or taking supplements. To add to the $B_{12}$ issue, as we get older, our

bodies have a harder time absorbing the vitamin, meaning we need to get more of it. One large egg provides about 18 percent of the recommended daily intake of $B_{12}$, while a cup of cottage cheese or nonfat yogurt supplies almost 58 percent.

Nutrition requirements aside, there are lots of delicious ways to work eggs and dairy into your meals without going overboard on fat or cholesterol (the two downsides to the food groups). Just be sure that when you do, you choose humane, sustainable sources that focus on animal welfare and protecting the environment.

**NOTE:** For those who don't eat eggs and/or dairy, there are substitution resources on page 147 at the end of this chapter.

# THE INCREDIBLE, EDIBLE EGG

In addition to being a good source of vitamin $B_{12}$, eggs are loaded with protein and vitamin D, plus hard-to-get choline, a nutrient that is essential for healthy cell function. Egg yolks are also rich in lutein and zeaxanthin, antioxidants that help maintain eye health.

# BUYER'S GUIDE TO EGGS
## KNOW YOUR LABELS

### FREE RANGE

This generally means that hens have access to the outdoors, but it does not guarantee they roam freely. Commercially raised hens can be as many as 10,000 to a barn, and the door is just a door. They are often uncaged within the barns, but still very crowded.

### CERTIFIED ORGANIC

Eggs with a USDA Organic seal must come from hens fed an organic vegetarian diet, free of antibiotics and pesticides. It is worth noting, however, that chickens are not naturally vegetarian—they love bugs—but it would be more difficult to qualify as organic if there were any animal parts in their feed.

### OMEGA-3 ENRICHED

Feed has higher levels of omega-3 fatty acids than usual. If hens are barn-raised, their feed probably includes flax or seaweed; if pasture-raised, omega-3s can be increased by a natural diet of bugs and grass.

### PASTURE RAISED

Hens are raised outdoors, typically at a ratio of 1,000 hens per 2.5 acres, and are fed a natural diet that can be supplemented with feed during certain times of year—like harsh winters. Look for the Humane Farm Animal Care Organization's "Certified Humane" pasture-raised label.

### HORMONE FREE

Mostly used as an advertising tool, since hormone use in egg production was banned back in the 1950s.

### FARMERS' MARKETS

Eggs at the market are extremely fresh, so they last over five weeks in the refrigerator. And, because pasture-raised hens eat a natural diet, the yolks of their eggs are a brighter orange and have a stronger flavor.

### MEDIUM, LARGE, OR EXTRA LARGE

If you mostly use eggs for omelets and the like, size doesn't really matter. But when it comes to baking, ingredient amounts are imperative to the final outcome—large eggs are the standard size used in most recipes.

*For the most up-to-date information on animal welfare and egg labeling questions, go to thehumanesociety.org.*

# HUEVOS RANCHEROS ENCHILADAS

YIELD: SERVES 6

**10 medium eggs**

**½ cup chopped onion**

**1 tsp. ground cumin**

**1½ cups cooked pinto beans**

**1 tsp. minced garlic**

**1 cup water or vegetable broth**

**1 cup cooked brown rice**

**1½ cups prepared salsa**

**½ cup reduced-fat Monterey Jack cheese**

Thin egg crêpes replace tortillas in a high-protein version of a Mexican favorite. The recipe is great for brunch because everything can be assembled the day before, then baked just before serving.

**1.** Whisk eggs with 6 Tbs. water in bowl. Season with salt and pepper, if desired. Heat 8-inch nonstick skillet coated with cooking spray over medium heat. Pour ¼ cup egg mixture into skillet, and swirl to coat bottom completely (like a crêpe). Cook 2 to 3 minutes, or until egg is firm in center. Slide onto paper-towel-lined plate. Top with paper towel. Repeat with remaining eggs to make 12 thin egg crêpes, then cool.

**2.** Wipe out skillet, coat with cooking spray, and heat over medium heat. Add onion and cumin to skillet, cover, and cook 3 minutes, or until onion is soft. Add pinto beans, garlic, and water or vegetable broth. Cover, and simmer 5 minutes. Mash some beans to thicken sauce; add cooked brown rice and ½ cup prepared salsa. Cook 5 minutes more, or until only a little liquid remains.

**3.** Roll ¼ cup filling in each egg crêpe, and place in large baking dish coated with cooking spray. Pour 1 cup prepared salsa down center of enchiladas, and sprinkle with Monterey Jack cheese. Bake 15 minutes at 350°F, or until enchiladas are heated through and cheese has melted.

GLUTEN-FREE

NUTRITION INFORMATION
Calories: 260
Protein: 17 g
Total Fat: 10 g
Saturated Fat: 4 g
Carbohydrates: 25 g
Cholesterol: 280 mg
Sodium: 748 mg
Fiber: 6 g
Sugar: 4 g

# CHEESE & MUSHROOM EGG NESTS

YIELD: SERVES 6

**6 slices whole-grain bread, crusts removed**

**4 medium cremini mushrooms, chopped (¾ cup)**

**1 green onion (white and green parts), thinly sliced (2 Tbs.)**

**1 Tbs. finely chopped fresh tarragon, plus extra leaves for garnish**

**6 large eggs**

**⅓ cup shredded Swiss cheese**

**½ tsp. smoked or regular paprika**

Omelet ingredients—eggs, cheese, mushrooms, and herbs—get a stylish makeover when baked in a "nest" of whole-grain bread. With hard-cooked yolks, the nests make wonderful take-along breakfasts that can be heated in the microwave at work.

**1.** Adjust oven rack to lowest position. Preheat oven to 325°F. Coat 6 6-oz. ramekins with cooking spray, and place on sheet pan. Flatten each bread slice with rolling pin to ⅛-inch thickness. Line prepared ramekins with bread slices, pressing against bottom and sides and overlapping where necessary (bread may extend over top).

**2.** Combine mushrooms, green onion, and tarragon in small bowl. Season with salt and pepper, and divide among ramekins. Break 1 egg carefully into each ramekin. Top with cheese and paprika; sprinkle with salt and pepper.

**3.** Bake 20 to 25 minutes, rotating pan after 10 minutes, or until whites are completely set and yolks begin to thicken but are still creamy. Bake slightly longer for hard-cooked yolks. Cool on rack 2 minutes, then unmold, and transfer to serving plates. Garnish with tarragon leaves, if desired.

## NUTRITION INFORMATION

Calories: 164
Protein: 11 g
Total Fat: 8 g
Saturated Fat: 2 g
Carbohydrates: 14 g
Cholesterol: 218 mg
Sodium: 428 mg
Fiber: 2 g
Sugar: 2 g

# SWEET POTATO & EGG STACKS

One frying pan is all you need to make these spice-laced alternatives to eggs Benedict.

**YIELD: SERVES 4**

**1 sweet potato, peeled and shredded**

**5 large eggs, divided**

**¼ tsp. ground coriander, divided**

**¼ tsp. ground cumin, divided**

**5 Tbs. vegetable oil, divided**

**1 cup crushed tomatoes with roasted onion and garlic**

**2 Tbs. lime juice**

**1 cup arugula**

**1.** Combine sweet potato, 1 egg, ⅛ tsp. coriander, and ⅛ tsp. cumin in bowl. Season with salt and pepper, if desired.

**2.** Heat 3 Tbs. oil in large skillet over medium-high heat until hot but not smoking. Scoop ⅓ cup sweet potato mixture into pan for each of 4 pancakes. Flatten gently with spatula; cook 5 minutes per side. Set aside; keep warm.

**3.** Wipe out pan, and add 1 Tbs. oil and remaining ⅛ tsp. coriander and ⅛ tsp. cumin. Stir 10 seconds over medium-high heat, add crushed tomatoes, and bring to a simmer. Reduce heat to medium-low, and simmer 5 minutes. Transfer to small bowl, and stir in lime juice.

**4.** Wipe out pan, add remaining 1 Tbs. oil, and fry remaining 4 eggs sunny side up or over easy. Season with salt and pepper, if desired.

**5.** To serve: Place 1 sweet potato pancake on each of 4 plates, top with 1 egg, ¼ cup sauce, and ¼ cup arugula.

GLUTEN-FREE

30 MINUTES OR LESS

## NUTRITION INFORMATION

Calories: 297
Protein: 10 g
Total Fat: 24 g
Saturated Fat: 3 g
Carbohydrates: 11 g
Cholesterol: 233 mg
Sodium: 111 mg
Fiber: 2 g
Sugar: 5 g

# EGGPLANT SHAKSHUKA

**YIELD: SERVES 4**

This version of shakshuka, a Middle Eastern poached-egg dish, adds eggplant and olives to the tomato sauce for a quick vegetable-stew base. Choose the freshest eggs possible for whites that will hold their shape and for more durable yolks.

**2 Tbs. olive oil**

**1 small onion, chopped (1 cup)**

**12 pitted green Greek olives, quartered**

**1½ tsp. sweet paprika**

**1½ tsp. ground cumin**

**¼ tsp. dried red pepper flakes**

**1 medium eggplant, cut into ½-inch cubes**

**1¼ cups thick crushed tomatoes**

**3 cloves garlic, minced (1 Tbs.)**

**⅓ cup chopped cilantro, divided**

**4 large eggs**

**1.** Pour oil into medium nonstick skillet. Add next 5 ingredients, and toss to combine. Mix in eggplant. Cover, and cook over medium heat 4 minutes to blend flavors, stirring occasionally. Mix in crushed tomatoes, garlic, and ¾ cup water. Bring to simmer. Cover, and cook 10 minutes, or until eggplant is tender, stirring occasionally. Stir in ¼ cup cilantro; if sauce is too thick, add 1 to 2 Tbs. water to thin it slightly. Season with salt and pepper, if desired.

**2.** Push aside eggplant mixture near top-center of skillet with wooden spoon, making deep hole. Drop in 1 egg. Repeat 3 more times, spacing eggs apart. Cover, reduce heat to medium-low, and simmer 4 minutes. Remove from heat, and let stand, covered, 1 to 2 minutes, or until egg whites are set. Sprinkle with remaining cilantro.

**GLUTEN-FREE**

## NUTRITION INFORMATION

Calories: 217
Protein: 9 g
Total Fat: 14 g
Saturated Fat: 3 g
Carbohydrates: 15 g
Cholesterol: 186 mg
Sodium: 441 mg
Fiber: 5 g
Sugar: 6 g

# GOT YOGURT?

Yogurt, cottage cheese, and ricotta cheese all deliver 15 grams or more of protein as well as being good sources of calcium and B-vitamins.

# CARROT-RICOTTA QUICHE IN A PHYLLO CRUST

YIELD: SERVES 6

**5 sheets frozen phyllo dough, thawed**

**2 large eggs**

**1½ cups low-fat ricotta cheese**

**2 Tbs. grated Parmesan cheese**

**2 cups finely grated carrots (4 large carrots)**

**¼ cup chopped shallots (2 large shallots)**

**¼ cup chopped fresh parsley**

With phyllo dough on hand, a homemade quiche crust takes only a few minutes to assemble—no rolling pin necessary! Layers of phyllo are also much lower in fat and calories than a traditional quiche crust.

**1.** Preheat oven to 350°F, and coat 9-inch pie pan with cooking spray.

**2.** Unroll phyllo, and keep under damp towel to retain moisture. Place 1 sheet phyllo on work surface, and coat with cooking spray. Top with second phyllo sheet, and coat with cooking spray. Repeat layering, coating last phyllo sheet with cooking spray. Press phyllo stack in prepared pie pan, sprayed-side down. Trim edges with scissors just to rim of pie pan.

**3.** Whisk eggs in large bowl. Whisk in ricotta and Parmesan. Fold in carrots, shallots, and parsley. Season with salt and pepper, if desired.

**4.** Bake 30 minutes, or until crust is browned, and filling is set.

## NUTRITION INFORMATION

Calories: 152
Protein: 11 g
Total Fat: 6 g
Saturated Fat: 3 g
Carbohydrates: 15 g
Cholesterol: 84 mg
Sodium: 288 mg
Fiber: 1 g
Sugar: 4 g

# GOAT CHEESE–ASPARAGUS CRUSTLESS QUICHE

**YIELD: SERVES 4**

For a pretty presentation, reserve a few asparagus tips to steam and use as a garnish for this quick supper dish. Fresh out of asparagus? Substitute broccoli florets—they're also rich in folic acid.

**1 lb. asparagus, trimmed and cut into 1-inch lengths, tips reserved for garnish, optional**

**1 tsp. olive oil**

**2 large shallots**

**2 cloves garlic, peeled**

**5 oz. fresh goat cheese**

**2 large eggs**

**5 large egg whites**

**1.** Coat 4 ramekins or a 9-inch-square baking pan with cooking spray. Toss asparagus in oil in bowl, and season with salt and pepper, if desired. Place ramekins in oven, and preheat oven to 425°F.

**2.** Meanwhile, place shallots and garlic in bowl of food processor, and process until finely minced. Add goat cheese, and process until creamy; then add eggs and egg whites, and purée until smooth. Season with salt and pepper, if desired.

**3.** Pour egg mixture over asparagus in ramekins once oven is preheated, stirring to evenly distribute vegetables. Bake 15 minutes, or until tops are light brown and tester inserted in centers comes out clean. Garnish with asparagus tips, if using.

## NUTRITION INFORMATION
Calories: 186
Protein: 16 g
Total Fat: 11 g
Saturated Fat: 6 g
Carbohydrates: 6 g
Cholesterol: 122 mg
Sodium: 244 mg
Fiber: 1 g
Sugar: 2 g

# BROCCOLI RAAB FRITTATA

YIELD: SERVES 4

**1 Tbs. olive oil**

**1 large red onion, chopped (2 cups)**

**1 small orange bell pepper, chopped, optional**

**1 Tbs. chopped oil-cured sun-dried tomatoes**

**1 Tbs. minced fresh rosemary**

**2 cups chopped broccoli raab**

**4 cloves garlic, minced (4 tsp.)**

**5 large egg whites**

**3 large whole eggs**

**¾ cup shredded Swiss or Gruyere cheese**

Any type of broccoli can be used in this recipe, but we like the play of classic Italian flavors that slightly bitter broccoli raab brings to the dish. Extra egg whites keep the frittata light and lower in cholesterol.

**1.** Preheat broiler. Coat 10-inch ovenproof skillet with cooking spray.

**2.** Heat oil in skillet over medium heat. Add onion and bell pepper (if using), sun-dried tomatoes, and rosemary; sauté 10 minutes. Add broccoli raab and garlic, and cook 10 minutes more.

**3.** Whisk together egg whites, eggs, and ⅓ cup water in bowl. Stir in cheese.

**4.** Pour egg mixture over vegetables in skillet, and cook 2 minutes, using rubber spatula to gently pull edges of frittata in toward center of skillet so uncooked egg can flow onto pan surface. When egg mixture has nearly set, place skillet under broiler 2 minutes, or until top is set and has puffed and browned slightly. Let stand 5 minutes, then run spatula around edges, and slice into wedges.

GLUTEN-FREE

## NUTRITION INFORMATION

Calories: 229
Protein: 17 g
Total Fat: 13 g
Saturated Fat: 5 g
Carbohydrates: 12 g
Cholesterol: 158 mg
Sodium: 175 mg
Fiber: 2 g
Sugar: 4 g

# BUTTERNUT SQUASH & GREENS KUKU

**YIELD: SERVES 4**

Kuku is an Iranian egg dish made with more greens than a frittata. It's traditionally served in small squares warm or at room temperature.

1 Tbs. olive oil, divided

8 oz. butternut squash, cut into ½-inch cubes (2 cups)

1 medium leek, thinly sliced

1 5-oz. pkg. baby kale (5 cups)

1 5-oz. pkg. baby spinach (5 cups)

8 large eggs

1 Tbs. grated lemon zest

3 Tbs. crumbled feta cheese

Cilantro leaves, for sprinkling

**1.** Preheat oven to 400°F.

**2.** Heat oil in large skillet over medium-high heat. Add squash, and season with salt and pepper, if desired. Cook 4 minutes, or until squash starts to soften, stirring occasionally. Reduce heat to medium, add leek, and cook 4 minutes more.

**3.** Working in batches, add kale and spinach to skillet; cook 3 to 5 minutes, or until leaves are wilted, stirring frequently.

**4.** Meanwhile, whisk eggs with lemon zest, and season with salt and pepper, if desired. Pour over wilted greens in skillet, reduce heat to medium-low, and cook 2 minutes, or until eggs begin to set on bottom, shifting vegetables around with spatula to distribute evenly.

**5.** Sprinkle kuku with feta, and transfer to oven. Bake 8 to 10 minutes, or until eggs are just cooked through and fully set, 8 to 10 minutes. Slide kuku onto platter; cool about 10 minutes. Cut into small squares, sprinkle with cilantro, and serve.

GLUTEN-FREE

## NUTRITION INFORMATION

Calories: 256
Protein: 17 g
Total Fat: 15 g
Saturated Fat: 5 g
Carbohydrates: 16 g
Cholesterol: 378 mg
Sodium: 283 mg
Fiber: 5 g
Sugar: 3 g

# SUMMER'S BOUNTY VEGETABLE TARTLETS

YIELD: MAKES
4 TARTLETS

This rustic dough is made with cream cheese and masa harina, which help boost the protein and nutrients in the individual crusts. The masa harina also gives the crusts a delectable flavor of corn tortillas, which highlights flavors of peak-season summer vegetables.

## DOUGH

**1 cup flour, plus more for rolling dough**

**¼ cup masa harina**

**¼ tsp. salt**

**4 Tbs. cold unsalted butter, cubed**

**8 oz. cold cream cheese**

## TARTLETS

**2 small zucchini, diced (1½ cups)**

**½ large onion, diced (1 cup)**

**1 medium yellow bell pepper, diced (¾ cup)**

**2 Japanese egg-plants, diced (2½ cups)**

**1 fennel bulb, diced (1 cup)**

**4½ tsp. olive oil**

**1½ tsp. minced garlic**

**1 tsp. chopped fresh thyme**

**1 tsp. chopped fresh oregano**

**1 cup drained, diced fire-roasted tomatoes,**

**16 Gaeta olives, pitted and coarsely chopped**

**1 Tbs. chopped flat-leaf parsley**

**2 oz. Fontina or Asiago cheese, grated (½ cup)**

**3 Tbs. grated Parmesan cheese**

**1 large egg**

**1.** To make Dough: Combine flour, masa harina, and salt in bowl of food processor; pulse to combine. Add butter, and pulse 10 times. Add cream cheese in small pieces, and pulse until dough comes together. Shape dough into disc; cover with plastic wrap, and chill at least 1 hour.

**2.** Cut dough into 4 equal pieces, and flatten into discs. Roll each disc into ⅛-inch-thick circle.

**3.** To make Tartlets: Preheat oven to 400°F. Toss together zucchini, onion, bell pepper, eggplants, and fennel in large bowl with oil, garlic, thyme, and oregano; season with salt and pepper, if desired.

**4.** Arrange vegetables on two baking sheets, and roast 20 minutes in oven, rotating pans from top to bottom and flipping vegetables halfway through. When tender, transfer to bowl, and cool. Reduce oven temperature to 375°F.

**5.** Add tomatoes, olives, parsley, and cheeses to roasted vegetables; toss gently; and season with salt and pepper, if desired.

**6.** Mound ¾ cup cooled filling in center of each dough round. Gently fold edges inward, forming 6 to 8 pleats as you move around the dough. Chill filled tarts 10 minutes.

**7.** Whisk egg with 2 Tbs. water. Brush dough tops lightly with egg wash, and transfer tarts to parchment-lined baking sheet. Bake 20 to 30 minutes, or until crust is golden and filling is bubbling.

> NUTRITION
> INFORMATION
>
> Calories: 348
> Protein: 10 g
> Total Fat: 24 g
> Saturated Fat: 12 g
> Carbohydrates: 26 g
> Cholesterol: 80 mg
> Sodium: 405 mg
> Fiber: 3 g
> Sugar: 5 g

# RICOTTA-BASIL STUFFED TOMATOES

Summer favorites zucchini, corn, and basil get baked in tomato shells for a light-yet-satisfying entrée.

YIELD: SERVES 4

8 large beefsteak tomatoes

2 large eggs

1 cup low-fat ricotta cheese

¼ cup finely chopped red onion

¼ cup chopped fresh basil

2 Tbs. plus 4 tsp. grated Parmesan cheese, divided

1 clove garlic, minced (1 tsp.)

1 cup corn kernels

1 cup diced zucchini plus 24 very thin zucchini slices

**1.** Preheat oven to 350°F. Slice tops off tomatoes, and scoop pulp out of centers to make stuffable tomato shells; set aside. Discard half of tomato pulp; remove seeds from and finely chop remaining half of pulp.

**2.** Whisk together eggs and ricotta in medium bowl until smooth. Stir in red onion, basil, 2 Tbs. Parmesan, and garlic. Add corn, diced zucchini, and chopped tomato pulp; stir until combined.

**3.** Fill tomatoes just to top with ½ cup ricotta mixture. Sprinkle each tomato with ½ tsp. Parmesan, and top each with 3 zucchini slices and tomato top. Place in large baking dish.

**4.** Bake 45 minutes, or until filling is puffed up and tops are browned. Let stand 10 minutes before serving. To freeze and enjoy later: Cool stuffed tomatoes completely, then place in foil-lined baking pan. Wrap tightly in foil, then in plastic wrap, and freeze. When ready to eat, thaw tomatoes completely. Preheat oven to 350°F. Bake, uncovered, 20 to 30 minutes, or until filling is hot.

GLUTEN-FREE

## NUTRITION INFORMATION

Calories: 260
Protein: 18 g
Total Fat: 10 g
Saturated Fat: 4 g
Carbohydrates: 36 g
Cholesterol: 130 mg
Sodium: 300 mg
Fiber: 6 g
Sugar: 20 g

# PROVENCAL FONDUE

YIELD: SERVES 6

A riff on the classic alpine favorite, this lightened-up fondue draws inspiration from southern France.

## FONDUE

**1 tsp. olive oil**

**1 small onion, finely diced (1 cup)**

**1 pinch salt**

**1½ cups peeled, diced tomatoes, or 1 15-oz. can diced tomatoes**

**2 cloves garlic, minced (2 tsp.)**

**2 tsp. herbes de Provence**

**1 tsp. pastis, optional**

**¼ tsp. sugar**

**2 cups shredded Gruyere cheese (8 oz.)**

**1 cup shredded Comte or Emmental cheese (4 oz.)**

**5 tsp. cornstarch**

**1 cup dry white wine**

## DIPPERS

**3 cups baguette cubes (4 oz.)**

**3 cups fresh and/or steamed vegetables**

**1.** Heat oil in fondue pot or saucepan over medium-low heat. Add onion and salt. Cover, and cook 2 to 3 minutes, or until softened. Add tomatoes, garlic, herbes de Provence, pastis (if using), and sugar; bring to a boil. Simmer 5 minutes. Transfer to bowl, and set aside.

**2.** Toss cheeses with cornstarch in bowl.

**3.** Add wine to fondue pot or saucepan, and bring to a boil over medium heat. Simmer 5 to 7 minutes, or until reduced by half. Stir in cheese mixture, and cook 3 to 4 minutes, or until cheese is melted, stirring constantly. Stir in tomato mixture, and cook 2 minutes, or until Fondue bubbles. Serve with Dippers.

### NUTRITION INFORMATION

Calories: 259
Protein: 17 g
Total Fat: 18 g
Saturated Fat: 10 g
Carbohydrates: 9 g
Cholesterol: 56 mg
Sodium: 186 mg
Fiber: 1 g
Sugar: 3 g

# MUSHROOM, CHEESE & VEGETABLE STRUDEL

YIELD: SERVES 12

## FILLING

**1 Tbs. olive oil**

**1 medium onion, chopped (1½ cups)**

**1 medium red bell pepper, diced (1 cup)**

**2 cloves garlic, minced (2 tsp.)**

**2 tsp. dried thyme**

**1 lb. white mushrooms, sliced (5 cups)**

**2 10-oz. bags baby spinach**

**¼ tsp. ground nutmeg**

**1 14-oz. pkg. firm tofu, drained**

**8 oz. Neufchatel cheese, softened**

**1 cup grated extra-sharp Cheddar cheese (4 oz.)**

## STRUDEL

**¼ cup olive oil**

**1 clove garlic, minced (1 tsp.)**

**1 tsp. dried thyme**

**1 lb. whole-wheat phyllo dough, thawed**

**½ tsp. poppy, sesame, or fennel seeds, optional**

Here's a gorgeous option for holiday meals that everyone at the table will love. Whole-wheat phyllo dough lends a wholesome, nutty taste and golden color to the finished strudel.

**1.** Preheat oven to 350°F. Coat 18- x 13-inch baking sheet with cooking spray.

**2.** To make Filling: Heat oil in pot over medium heat. Sauté onion, bell pepper, garlic, and thyme in oil 10 minutes. Add mushrooms, and cook 10 minutes, or until wilted. Stir in spinach and nutmeg, and season with salt and pepper. Cover and cook 5 to 7 minutes, or until spinach has wilted, stirring occasionally. Drain, and cool in bowl.

**3.** Purée tofu, Neufchâtel cheese, and Cheddar cheese in food processor until smooth. Stir into mushroom mixture. Season with salt and pepper.

**4.** To make Strudel: Heat oil, garlic, and thyme in small pot over medium heat 2 to 3 minutes, or until fragrant. Cool.

**5.** Cover bottom of prepared baking pan with 2 phyllo sheets, allowing sheets to overlap each other and hang off sides. Brush with garlic oil. Place 2 more phyllo sheets on top, and brush with garlic oil. Repeat 4 times, until you have a 6-layer bottom crust.

**6.** Spread Filling in crust, leaving 3-inch edge all around. Brush edges with garlic oil. Fold sides of phyllo over filling. Cover filling with 2-sheet layer of phyllo (4 sheets total), overlapping sheets in center. Brush with garlic oil. Repeat layering 2 sheets at a time until you have 4 layers (16 sheets phyllo total), brushing every second sheet with garlic oil.

Tuck under edges. Sprinkle top with seeds, if desired. Bake 45 to 50 minutes, or until golden. Let stand 15 minutes before cutting into slices.

MAKE IT VEGAN **Simply substitute vegan cream cheese and vegan Cheddar cheese.**

NUTRITION
INFORMATION

Calories: 299
Protein: 12 g
Total Fat: 15.5 g
Saturated Fat: 6 g
Carbohydrates: 31 g
Cholesterol: 24 mg
Sodium: 541 mg
Fiber: 4 g
Sugar: 2 g

# VEGANIZING RECIPES
# BY REPLACING EGGS
# & DAIRY

Veganizing Recipes just keeps getting easier and tastier. Large-chain supermarkets now carry a wide variety of dairy-free yogurt and cheese options alongside the ever-growing selection of vegetable milks, and artisanal dairy-free products like specialty cheeses are making it into the mainstream, too. Many of these products can be used to replace the dairy items in recipes throughout the book.

The eggless revolution is well underway, as well. Powdered egg replacers can be found in the baking section of supermarkets and there are even refrigerated egg-less products that look, cook and taste like scrambled eggs and can be used in baking. Then, there's aquafaba...a fancy name for chickpea (or bean) cooking liquid straight from the can that can be whipped up like egg whites and has a whole website devoted to its uses. (aquafaba.com)

For home cooks, it's also handy to have easy substitution options that can be whipped up with on-hand ingredients when needed. And, when it comes to vegan cheese, the flavor and texture of the homemade options on the following pages simply can't be beat.

## EGG REPLACERS

The market for egg replacers has exploded with new options available to home cooks. While these egg-free options won't offer the same protein count as eggs, they work well in many recipes.

You can also make your own egg replacers. Here's a quick rundown of the eggless options that can be used in baking.

> **1 Tbs. egg replacer (store-bought powder, ground chia or flaxseeds) + 2 to 3 Tbs. water = 1 egg**
>
> **¼ cup blended silken tofu = 1 egg**
>
> **3 Tbs. aquafaba (canned chickpea liquid) = 1 egg**

Replacing eggs in omelets, flans, and quiches is trickier. Firm tofu will sometimes work in scrambled dishes, and aquafaba (canned chickpea liquid) can be whipped to a beaten egg white-like consistency for meringues and soufflés.

## DAIRY REPLACERS

Prepared, plant-based yogurts, sour creams, and cream cheeses have been designed to stand in for dairy versions, which makes one-to-one substitutions a snap. The only downside to these is that they can be highly processed foods that aren't all that good for you. Always check the label before buying.

There are four whole-food dairy substitutes that are also worth mentioning.

**Canned Coconut Milk** can be used in place of heavy cream and the thick "cream" that rises to the top of the can be beaten to make whipped cream. Light Coconut Milk has about half the fat of regular, canned coconut milk. It will work in many recipes that call for full-fat coconut milk, but not all.

**Firm Tofu** can be blended with cider vinegar to replace yogurt or sour cream in recipes. Simply blend 1 cup (8 oz.) firm tofu with 1 Tbs. cider vinegar, white vinegar, or lemon juice, and use as you would yogurt or sour cream.

**Nutritional Yeast** has a nutty, cheesy flavor and can be used as a sprinkle in place of Parmesan or grated cheese. It can also be added to recipes like tofu scrambles and kale chips for cheesy flavor.

**Vegan Buttermilk** Stir 1 Tbs. vinegar into 1 cup nondairy milk and let stand until the nondairy milk is curdled and thickened.

# AQUAFABA MERINGUE

MAKES 2 CUPS

**¾ cup aquafaba (liquid from 1 15-oz. can chickpeas or white beans)**

**¼ tsp. cream of tartar**

**¾ cup granulated or cane sugar**

**½ tsp. vanilla extract**

This basic meringue recipe can be used to make cookies and pie toppings. The liquid from any cooked beans can be used as aquafaba—just make sure it's thick and has a viscosity similar to egg whites.

**1.** Beat aquafaba and cream of tartar with electric stand mixer or electric beaters 5 to 6 minutes, or until stiff peaks form.

**2.** Beat in sugar ¼ cup at a time, then beat 3 to 4 minutes, or until meringue is thick and glossy and stiff peaks form.

**3.** Beat in vanilla extract.

**4.** Use immediately to make meringues (scoop onto parchment-lined baking sheet and bake 1 to 1½ hours at 200°F) or use in other desserts.

## NUTRITION INFORMATION

Calories: 75
Protein: 0 g
Total Fat: 0 g
Saturated Fat: 0 g
Carbohydrates: 19 g
Cholesterol: 0 mg
Sodium: 1 mg
Fiber: 0 g
Sugar: 19 g

## DIY VEGAN CHEESE

### WHAT YOU'LL NEED

- large, nonreactive (stainless steel or glass) bowl for soaking
- blender or food processor
- 3 sheets cheesecloth
- large strainer

### BASIC INSTRUCTIONS

**1.** Place nuts (cashews, almonds, walnuts, macadamia nuts, brazil nuts, pine nuts, hazel nuts) or grains in bowl, and cover with at least 3 inches cold water (the nuts will swell as they soak). Soak 12 hours or overnight, away from sunlight. Drain soaking water, rinse nuts, then drain again.

**2.** Purée soaked nuts in blender or food processor 6 minutes, scraping down sides of bowl often to ensure creamy, even texture.

**3.** Drain cheese through cheese-cloth-lined strainer to eliminate excess moisture and concentrate flavors. Bake at low temperature to remove moisture and firm up final product. The longer cheese bakes, the more crumbly it becomes.

# PINE NUT CHEDDAR CHEESE

Pine nuts are so small and tender, they don't need to be soaked to make this cheese. Agar flakes lend firmness and sliceability and eliminate the need for a straining step. Try adding other ingredients, such as chopped jalapeño chiles, cumin, caraway seeds, or a dash of smoked paprika.

YIELD: MAKES 1-LB. BLOCK

| | |
|---|---|
| 1¼ cups unsweetened plain soymilk | 3 Tbs. dry white wine |
| ¼ cup agar flakes | 3 cloves garlic, peeled |
| ½ cup raw pine nuts | 2 tsp. granulated onion |
| ⅓ cup canola oil | 1¾ tsp. salt |
| ¼ cup fresh lemon juice | ¾ tsp. ground black pepper |

**1.** Line 2- to 3-cup rectangular (or whatever shape you prefer) container with 2 layers cheesecloth, allowing cheesecloth to hang over sides.

**2.** Whisk together soymilk and agar flakes in saucepan. Bring to a simmer over medium heat, and cook 8 minutes, or until agar dissolves completely and mixture is thick, stirring frequently.

**3.** Blend nuts, oil, lemon juice, wine, garlic, granulated onion, salt, and pepper in blender or food processor 5 minutes, or until smooth, scraping down sides frequently. Add soymilk mixture, and blend 2 minutes more, or until smooth. Transfer mixture to cheese-cloth-lined container; smooth top. Fold overhanging cheesecloth over cheese. Refrigerate 1 hour, or until firm. Unwrap, slice, and serve.

VEGAN

GLUTEN-FREE

TIP ON USING AGAR **The secret to success when adding agar to vegan cheeses or desserts is to simmer the flakes in plenty of liquid for about 8 minutes, or until all the bits have dissolved (once cold, undissolved agar flakes turn grainy).**

## NUTRITION INFORMATION

| | |
|---|---|
| Calories: 167 | Cholesterol: 0 mg |
| Protein: 3 g | Sodium: 522 mg |
| Total Fat: 16 g | Fiber: <1 g |
| Saturated Fat: 1 g | Sugar: 1 g |
| Carbohydrates: 5 g | |

# ALMOND FETA CHEESE

Blanched almonds give this creamy-crumbly cheese a rich texture. Unbaked, it will be smooth and spreadable. Baking will make it a bit more crumbly, like traditional feta cheese.

**YIELD: SERVES 10**

**1 cup whole blanched almonds**

**¼ cup lemon juice**

**3 Tbs. olive oil**

**1 clove garlic, peeled**

**1¼ tsp. salt**

**1.** Place almonds in medium bowl, and cover with 3 inches cold water. Let soak 24 hours. Drain soaking liquid, rinse almonds under cold running water, and drain again.

**2.** Purée almonds, lemon juice, oil, garlic, salt, and ½ cup cold water in food processor 6 minutes, or until very smooth and creamy.

**3.** Place large strainer over bowl, and line with triple layer of cheesecloth. Spoon almond mixture into cheesecloth. Bring corners and sides of cloth together and twist around cheese, forming into orange-size ball and squeezing to help extract moisture. Secure with rubber band or kitchen twine. Chill 12 hours, or overnight. Discard excess liquid.

**4.** Preheat oven to 200°F. Line baking sheet with parchment paper. Unwrap cheese (it will be soft) and transfer from cheesecloth to prepared baking sheet. Flatten to form 6-inch round about ¾-inch thick. Bake 40 minutes, or until top is slightly firm. Cool, then chill.

NUTRITION INFORMATION
Calories: 93
Protein: 2 g
Total Fat: 9 g
Saturated Fat: 1 g
Carbohydrates: 20 g
Cholesterol: 0 mg
Sodium: 292 mg
Fiber: 11 g
Sugar: <1 g

# PARMESAN-LIKE PASTA CRUMBLES

Buckwheat groats coated with garlic-infused olive oil, salt, and nutritional yeast make for a Parmesan-like topping for pasta dishes.

**YIELD: MAKES ½ CUP**

**½ cup buckwheat groats**

**2 Tbs. olive oil**

**3 cloves garlic, minced (1 Tbs.)**

**¼ cup plus 1 Tbs. nutritional yeast, divided**

**2 tsp. salt**

**1.** Place buckwheat groats in medium bowl, and cover with 3 inches cold water. Soak 12 hours. Drain.

**2.** Preheat oven to 300°F. Line baking sheet with parchment paper. Heat oil and garlic in saucepan over low heat until hot. Toss buckwheat groats with garlic oil in bowl. Stir in ¼ cup nutritional yeast and salt.

**3.** Spread buckwheat groats in even layer on prepared baking sheet. Sprinkle with remaining 1 Tbs. yeast. Bake 30 minutes, or until completely dry and crunchy. Cool, and store in airtight container.

VEGAN

NUTRITION INFORMATION
Calories: 83
Protein 4 g
Total Fat: 4 g
Saturated Fat: 1 g
Carbohydrates: 10 g
Cholesterol: 0 mg
Sodium: 584 mg
Fiber: 2 g
Sugar: <1 g

# VEGETABLES

Vegetable-forward cooking is the way of the future for all cooks, with bright, beautifully prepared produce taking center stage on the plate. It may come as a surprise to some people that vegetables do indeed contain protein (see chart, page 152). Not as much protein as beans or grains, but enough for it to add up in a veggie-rich diet.

While we could eat a pile of steamed asparagus or simple bowl of sautéed kale every night of the week (almost), the seasonings you choose are what make a vegetable dish special—and over-the-top delicious. Some ginger and soy sauce, a few sesame seeds, and...bam! You've got a dish that rivals your favorite Asian takeout. A little garlic, a scattering of olives, and a pinch of red pepper flakes and...presto! It's Italian night! You'll find these ideas—and many more—in the recipes that follow.

# TOP VEGETABLES FOR PROTEIN

SEE HOW YOUR FAVORITE VEGETABLES MEASURE UP IN TERMS OF PROTEIN.

**ARTICHOKES (1 ARTICHOKE) 2 G**

**ASPARAGUS 2 G**

**BEAN SPROUTS 1G**

**BEETS 1 G**

**BROCCOLI 1 G**

**BRUSSELS SPROUTS 2 G**

**EDAMAME 8 G**

**FENNEL (1 BULB) 1 G**

**LEAFY GREENS (KALE, COLLARDS, SPINACH, SWISS CHARD, ETC.) 2 TO 3 G**

**LIMA BEANS 6 G**

**PEAS 4 G**

**SWEET POTATO 2 G**

*Source: USDA Nutrient Data Base*

# SIZZLED SPINACH
## WITH WHITE BEANS & MOZZARELLA

YIELD: SERVES 4

This medley of Mediterranean flavors is a great make-ahead dish for company—all you have to do is sauté the spinach just before serving.

BEANS

**1 15-oz. can white beans, rinsed and drained**

**1 large red or yellow bell pepper, diced (1 cup)**

**4 oz. fresh mozzarella, drained and torn or diced**

**2 Tbs. white wine vinegar, divided**

**6 oil-packed sun-dried tomatoes, drained, finely chopped, and oil reserved**

**¼ cup chopped black olives**

**1 medium shallot, finely chopped (2 Tbs.)**

**2 Tbs. chopped fresh parsley**

**1 clove garlic, minced (1 tsp.)**

GARLICKY SPINACH

**1 Tbs. garlic oil or olive oil**

**½ cup diced red or yellow bell pepper**

**2 Tbs. minced shallot (1 medium)**

**3 cloves garlic, minced (1 Tbs.)**

**1 lb. baby spinach**

**1.** To make Beans: Toss together white beans, bell pepper, mozzarella, 1 Tbs. vinegar, and 1 Tbs. sun-dried tomato oil in medium bowl.

**2.** Stir together sun-dried tomatoes, olives, shallot, parsley, garlic, and remaining 1 Tbs. vinegar in small bowl. Stir into bean mixture. Set aside.

**3.** To make Garlicky Spinach: Heat oil in large skillet over medium heat. Add bell pepper and shallot, and sauté 3 to 5 minutes, or until vegetables begin to brown. Add garlic, and stir 30 seconds, or until fragrant. Add spinach in batches, and sauté 5 to 6 minutes, tossing with tongs, or until wilted and bright green. Season with salt and pepper, if desired. Serve Beans topped with Garlicky Spinach.

GLUTEN-FREE

30 MINUTES OR LESS

NUTRITION INFORMATION
Calories: 341
Protein: 15 g
Total Fat: 17 g
Saturated Fat: 5 g
Carbohydrates: 37 g
Cholesterol: 23 mg
Sodium: 498 mg
Fiber: 12 g
Sugar: 3 g

# ARTICHOKES STUFFED
## WITH ARUGULA PESTO

1 small lemon, sliced

1 tsp. sea salt, optional

4 large artichokes, stems trimmed to ½ inch

3 cups tightly packed chopped arugula

½ cup raw or roasted unsalted cashews

½ cup olive oil

2 Tbs. thinly sliced basil

2 Tbs. lemon juice

2 small garlic cloves, peeled

2 tsp. nutritional yeast

¾ tsp. salt

½ tsp. red pepper flakes

½ tsp. low-sodium soy sauce or wheat-free tamari

½ tsp. ground black pepper

Whole steamed artichokes have a natural elegance, but leaf-dipping can get messy. We've solved the problem by filling artichokes with a thick arugula pesto, which turns the de-choked centers into individual dipping bowls. Extra pesto can be served on the side or spooned over the artichokes as desired.

**1.** Bring 4 qt. water, lemon slices, and sea salt (if using) to a boil in large pot. Add artichokes, and return to a boil. Reduce heat to medium-low, and simmer 30 to 45 minutes, or until an outer leaf pulls off easily and base of leaf is tender.

**2.** Purée all remaining ingredients in blender until smooth.

**3.** Transfer artichokes from boiling water to bowl in sink under cold running water. Leave cooking water in pot. Place cooled artichokes on cutting board, and cut off stems. Carefully open leaves to reveal center chokes. Scoop out spiky chokes with small spoon, and discard. Return artichokes to cooking water 2 minutes to reheat.

**4.** Spoon ¼ cup pesto in center of each artichoke, and gently open outer leaves. Serve with remaining pesto for dipping.

VEGAN

NUTRITION INFORMATION

Calories: 309
Protein: 9 g
Total Fat: 22 g
Saturated Fat: 4 g
Carbohydrates: 25 g
Cholesterol: 0 mg
Sodium: 620 mg
Fiber: 10 g
Sugar: 3 g

# ARTICHOKE-POTATO MEDLEY

YIELD: SERVES 6

**1 lb. small red potatoes, quartered**

**2 10-oz. boxes frozen artichoke hearts**

**1½ Tbs. olive oil**

**½ cup pitted Kalamata olives, chopped**

**3 cloves garlic, minced (4 tsp.)**

**3 Tbs. chopped parsley**

**2 Tbs. lemon juice**

**2 tsp. grated lemon zest**

**¾ tsp. sweet or smoked paprika**

**3 hard-boiled eggs, chopped, optional**

Adding artichokes to potatoes helps boost this medley's fiber and nutrient content. For extra color, use a combination of potato varieties and serve on a bed of arugula or watercress.

**1.** Bring potatoes to a boil in large pot of salted water. Reduce heat to medium-low, and simmer 5 minutes, or until potatoes are just tender. Drain.

**2.** Return potatoes to saucepan; heat over high heat with artichokes and oil. Cook 5 minutes, or until vegetables start to brown, stirring occasionally. Add olives, garlic, parsley, lemon juice, lemon zest, and paprika. Season with salt and pepper, if desired. Cook 5 minutes more, or until fragrant and heated through. Serve garnished with chopped eggs, if using.

GLUTEN-FREE
30 MINUTES OR LESS

## NUTRITION INFORMATION

Calories: 171
Protein: 4 g
Total Fat: 7 g
Saturated Fat: 1 g
Carbohydrates: 24 g
Cholesterol: 0 mg
Sodium: 231 mg
Fiber: 7 g
Sugar: 1 g

# BRAISED LACINATO KALE

YIELD: SERVES 4

Cavolo nero, dinosaur, Tuscan, and lacinato are all names given to a long, leafy, crinkly kale variety. Serve this light vegetable dish on its own or add to grains or pasta.

**3 Tbs. olive oil**

**1 medium onion, thinly sliced (1⅓ cups)**

**3 small carrots, diced (1½ cups)**

**2 bunches lacinato kale, tough ribs removed, and leaves coarsely chopped (9 cups)**

**½ tsp. red pepper flakes**

**3 cloves garlic, peeled and thinly sliced**

**1.** Heat oil in Dutch oven over medium-high heat. Sauté onion 7 to 9 minutes, or until golden. Add carrots, and cook 2 to 3 minutes more. Add kale and ½ cup water, cover, and cook 2 to 3 minutes, or until kale has wilted. Stir in red pepper flakes and garlic, and cook 1 to 2 minutes more. Add 1¼ cups water, and bring to a simmer.

**2.** Cover, reduce heat to medium-low, and simmer 40 minutes, or until kale is tender, adding more water if necessary.

**3.** Uncover pot, increase heat to medium-high, and cook 3 minutes, or until most of liquid has evaporated. Season with salt and pepper, if desired.

GLUTEN-FREE

VEGAN

30 MINUTES OR LESS

## NUTRITION INFORMATION

Calories: 204
Protein: 6 g
Total Fat: 11 g
Saturated Fat: 2 g
Carbohydrates: 24 g
Cholesterol: 0 mg
Sodium: 100 mg
Fiber: 5 g
Sugar: 4 g

# QUICK-BRAISED BROCCOLI
## WITH SUN-DRIED TOMATOES & GOAT CHEESE

**YIELD: SERVES 6**

**2 Tbs. pine nuts**

**1½ Tbs. vegetable oil**

**2 large heads broccoli (1 lb.), cut into small florets**

**¼ cup crumbled goat cheese (2 oz.)**

**¼ cup oil-packed sun-dried tomatoes, drained and sliced**

**2 Tbs. balsamic vinegar**

This simple dish makes a satisfying weeknight supper when served over brown rice or quinoa. Sautéing the broccoli before steaming it helps caramelize its natural sugars and gives it a fuller, richer flavor.

**1.** Toast pine nuts in dry skillet over medium heat 3 to 4 minutes, stirring occasionally. Transfer to large bowl.

**2.** Heat oil in same skillet over medium-high heat. Add broccoli, and cook 2 minutes, or until florets are evenly coated with oil and beginning to soften and brown, stirring constantly. Carefully add ⅓ cup water; cover tightly with lid. Steam broccoli 4 minutes, or until water has evaporated and broccoli is tender.

**3.** Transfer broccoli to bowl with toasted pine nuts, and season with salt and pepper, if desired. Sprinkle goat cheese over broccoli, and stir in sun-dried tomatoes. Drizzle vinegar over top, and serve warm.

GLUTEN-FREE

30 MINUTES OR LESS

## NUTRITION INFORMATION

Calories: 115
Protein: 5 g
Total Fat: 8 g
Saturated Fat: 2 g
Carbohydrates: 7 g
Cholesterol: 4 mg
Sodium: 74 mg
Fiber: 3 g
Sugar: 0 g

# GINGER-GARLIC MARINATED ASPARAGUS

YIELD: SERVES 4

Here, an Asian-inspired marinade brings a balance of sweet, salty, tangy, and spicy to blanched asparagus.

**3 lb. fresh asparagus, trimmed**

**⅓ cup low-sodium soy sauce or tamari**

**⅓ cup rice vinegar**

**3 Tbs. vegetable oil**

**3 cloves garlic, minced (1 Tbs.)**

**2 Tbs. grated fresh ginger**

**1 Tbs. agave nectar or honey**

**1 Tbs. toasted sesame seeds**

**1 Thai bird chile, seeded and thinly sliced for garnish, optional**

**pinch of cayanne, or to taste**

**1.** Cook asparagus in pot of boiling salted water 5 minutes. Drain, and plunge into bowl filled with ice water.

**2.** Whisk together soy sauce, rice vinegar, oil, garlic, ginger, agave nectar, and cayenne. Pour over asparagus in large baking dish, adding water, if necessary, to submerge asparagus. Cover, and chill 4 hours, or overnight.

**3.** Drain off marinade, and arrange asparagus on plates or serving platter. Sprinkle with sesame seeds and chile slices, if using.

## NUTRITION INFORMATION

Calories: 76
Protein: 5 g
Total Fat: 3 g
Saturated Fat: 1 g
Carbohydrates: 9 g
Cholesterol: 0 mg
Sodium: 303 mg
Fiber: 3 g
Sugar: 3 g

# LEMONY ASPARAGUS
## WITH SAFFRON RICE

YIELD: SERVES 6

**1½ cups white or brown rice**

**3 cups low-sodium vegetable broth**

**1 pinch saffron threads**

**1 Tbs. vegetable oil**

**9 green onions, sliced into ¼-inch lengths (⅔ cup)**

**1–2 small fresh red chiles, thinly sliced (1 Tbs.)**

**2 cloves garlic, thinly sliced**

**1½ lb. asparagus spears, cut diagonally into 1-inch lengths (3½ cups)**

**½ cup toasted sliced almonds**

**¼ cup sliced mint leaves**

**2 lemons, cut into wedges, for garnish**

With fresh mint and lemon zest accenting asparagus spears, this stir-fry captures the brightness of spring. If you can't find toasted sliced almonds, toast your own for 3 to 5 minutes in a 300°F oven. The nutritional analysis was made for white rice (shown in the photo); brown rice would bring up the protein and fiber count.

**1.** Combine rice and broth in large saucepan, and crumble in saffron threads. Bring to a boil. Reduce heat to medium-low, cover, and simmer 20 minutes. Remove from heat, and let stand, covered, 5 minutes.

**2.** Meanwhile, heat wok over high heat, until water droplets evaporate within 1 second. Add oil, swirl to coat pan, then add green onions, chiles, and garlic; stir-fry 1 to 2 minutes, or until onions turn bright green and soften. Add asparagus, and stir-fry 2 minutes more, or until asparagus is bright green and tender. Remove from heat, stir in almonds and mint, and season with salt and pepper, if desired.

**3.** Fluff rice, and spoon onto serving plate. Top with asparagus mixture. Garnish with lemon wedges.

VEGAN

GLUTEN-FREE

30 MINUTES OR LESS

## NUTRITION INFORMATION

Calories: 276

Protein: 7 g

Total Fat: 7 g

Saturated Fat: <1 g

Carbohydrates: 47 g

Cholesterol: 0 mg

Sodium: 81 mg

Fiber: 3 g

Sugar: 3 g

# FENNEL

Crunchy and sweet when raw, tender and mildly anise-flavored when cooked, fennel adds subtle flavor and texture to soups, sauces, salads, and even quiche. Snip off the delicate tops, and sprinkle over dishes the way you would parsley, basil, or mint.

# ROASTED FENNEL QUARTERS
## WITH PARMESAN VINAIGRETTE

YIELD: SERVES 4

**2 Tbs. olive oil**

**4 cloves garlic, minced (4 tsp.)**

**1 Tbs. red wine vinegar**

**½ tsp. Dijon mustard**

**½ tsp. salt**

**⅛ tsp. freshly ground black pepper**

**3 medium fennel bulbs, quartered**

**¼ cup grated Parmesan cheese**

Roasting fennel concentrates the bulb's natural sweetness. A sprinkling of Parmesan adds crunch to the crust, but you could omit it if you wanted to keep the recipe vegan.

**1.** Preheat oven to 425°F. Coat baking sheet or roasting pan with cooking spray.

**2.** Blend oil, garlic, vinegar, mustard, salt, and pepper in mini food processor until smooth. Toss fennel with oil mixture and Parmesan in large bowl.

**3.** Place fennel on prepared baking sheet, and roast 35 to 40 minutes, or until fennel quarters are tender and outer edges are golden brown.

GLUTEN-FREE

## NUTRITION INFORMATION

Calories: 141
Protein: 4 g
Total Fat: 2 g
Saturated Fat: 2 g
Carbohydrates: 14 g
Cholesterol: 4 mg
Sodium: 474 mg
Fiber: 6 g
Sugar: <1 g

# CAULIFLOWER KITCHARI

YIELD: SERVES 4

Kitchari is an Ayurvedic dish of seasoned mung beans and rice cooked over low heat until they have a porridge-like consistency. The resulting entrée is comforting and nourishing.

**2 Tbs. plus 1½ tsp. ghee (clarified butter) divided**

**½ tsp. minced fresh ginger**

**1 tsp. cumin seeds**

**2 cups cauliflower florets**

**½ cup basmati rice, rinsed**

**⅓ cup split mung beans**

**¾ tsp. turmeric**

**½ cup frozen baby peas, defrosted**

**1 tsp. salt**

**1.** Heat 2 Tbs. ghee in saucepan over medium-high heat. When ghee is hot, stir in ginger and cumin seeds. Fry cumin seeds a few seconds, then add cauliflower, and stir-fry 4 minutes, until cauliflower is slightly browned and partially cooked. Stir in rice and beans, and fry 1 minute. Add 3½ cups water and turmeric and bring to full boil over high heat.

**2.** Reduce heat to low, partially cover, and cook, stirring occasionally, 40 minutes.

**3.** Add peas and salt, and continue cooking 5 minutes, or until rice and beans are soft. Stir in remaining 1½ tsp. ghee just before serving.

## NUTRITION INFORMATION

Calories: 256
Protein: 7 g
Total Fat: 9 g
Saturated Fat: 6 g
Carbohydrates: 38 g
Cholesterol: 25 mg
Sodium: 628 mg
Fiber: 5 g
Sugar: 3 g

# TWICE-BAKED SWEET POTATOES
## WITH DUKKA

YIELD: SERVES 8

**1 cup whole blanched almonds or hazelnuts**

**⅓ cup whole coriander seeds**

**3 Tbs. whole cumin seeds**

**1 tsp. kosher or coarse sea salt**

**2 Tbs. sumac**

**¼ cup toasted sesame seeds**

**5 medium sweet potatoes**

**1 Tbs. olive oil**

**4 oz. feta cheese, crumbled**

Sweet potatoes get mashed with olive oil and feta cheese then dusted with dukka, a nutty spice blend, for twice-baked potatoes that can be served as a main or side dish.

**1.** Preheat oven to 350°F. Spread almonds on baking sheet, and toast 5 to 7 minutes, or until light brown and fragrant. Transfer to bowl.

**2.** Meanwhile, toast coriander, cumin, and salt in skillet over medium-low heat 3 minutes, or until coriander is light brown and mixture is fragrant, swirling pan constantly. Place in bowl with almonds. Cool completely.

**3.** Coarsely grind almond-spice mixture and sumac in food processor, or grind with mortar and pestle. Transfer to bowl, and stir in sesame seeds.

**4.** Preheat oven to 350°F. Poke sweet potatoes all over with fork; bake on baking sheet 1 hour, or until soft. Cool 10 minutes.

**5.** Halve sweet potatoes, scoop out flesh into bowl, and mash with oil until smooth; fold in feta without breaking up crumbles. Place 8 potato skins on baking sheet, spoon mashed sweet potato into these skins, and sprinkle each with 1 Tbs. Dukka. Bake 10 to 15 minutes, or until piping hot.

## NUTRITION INFORMATION

Calories: 200
Protein: 6 g
Total Fat: 11 g
Saturated Fat: 3 g
Carbohydrates: 20 g
Cholesterol: 13 mg
Sodium: 316 mg
Fiber: 4 g
Sugar: 6 g

# THAI GREEN BEAN CURRY
## WITH PINEAPPLE & SWEET POTATOES

This stew owes its velvety consistency to blended sweet potatoes, which thicken the curry base along with light coconut milk. When buying red curry paste, check the label to make sure it doesn't contain any fish or meat-based ingredients.

**YIELD: SERVES 4**

1 Tbs. vegetable oil

3 large shallots (½ cup)

1½ Tbs. red curry paste

3 cloves garlic, minced (1 Tbs.)

2 tsp. minced fresh ginger

1 8-oz. can pineapple chunks, juice reserved

2 medium sweet potatoes, peeled and cut into 1-inch chunks (2½ cups)

¾ lb. green beans

¾ cup light coconut milk

Basil or cilantro leaves, for garnish

**1.** Heat oil in medium saucepan over medium heat. Add shallots, and sauté 5 minutes. Add curry paste, garlic, and ginger, and sauté 30 seconds, or until fragrant. Add 2½ cups water and reserved pineapple juice. Cover, and simmer 10 minutes. Add 1 cup sweet potato chunks, and cook 10 to 15 minutes, or until sweet potatoes are tender.

**2.** Blend mixture in saucepan with immersion blender or in blender or food processor until smooth. Return to saucepan, add remaining 1½ cups sweet potatoes, and bring to a boil. Cover, and simmer 5 minutes. Stir in pineapple chunks, green beans, and coconut milk; cover; and simmer 7 to 10 minutes, or until green beans are crisp-tender. Garnish with basil, and serve.

VEGAN

GLUTEN-FREE

### NUTRITION INFORMATION

Calories: 341
Protein: 15 g
Total Fat: 17 g
Saturated Fat: 5 g
Carbohydrates: 37 g
Cholesterol: 23 mg
Sodium: 498 mg
Fiber: 12 g
Sugar: 3 g

# ROASTED BEET QUARTERS
## WITH MUSTARDY CRUMBLES

YIELD: SERVES 4

**2½ Tbs. olive oil, divided**

**½ cup panko breadcrumbs**

**1½ Tbs. Dijon mustard**

**6 small golden beets, peeled, quartered, leafy tops reserved (1 lb.)**

**6 small red beets, peeled, quartered, leafy tops reserved and chopped**

NUTRITION
INFORMATION
Calories: 191
Protein: 5 g
Total Fat: 9 g
Saturated Fat: 1 g
Carbohydrates: 26 g
Cholesterol: 0 mg
Sodium: 353 mg
Fiber: 4 g
Sugar: 12 g

Once you've made the topping for these roasted beets, you'll want to find other ways to use the simple, surprising "crumbles." Be sure to roast the golden beets separately from the red beets so that the colors remain distinct.

**1.** Preheat oven to 375°F. Coat baking sheet with cooking spray.

**2.** Heat 1 Tbs. oil in large skillet over medium heat. Add breadcrumbs and mustard, and cook 7 to 8 minutes, or until crumbs are deep golden, mixing, pressing, and separating with flexible spatula or back of fork. Transfer to plate. Wipe out skillet, and set aside.

**3.** Toss golden beets with ½ Tbs. oil in bowl, and spread on half of prepared baking sheet. Repeat with ½ Tbs. oil and red beets. Roast beets 35 minutes, or until tender, turning after 25 minutes if flat sides become too dark.

**4.** Meanwhile, heat remaining ½ Tbs. oil in reserved skillet over medium heat. Add beet greens, and sauté 2 minutes, or until wilted. Season with salt and pepper, if desired.

**5.** Arrange roasted beets on platter, slightly mounded in center. Sprinkle with sautéed greens and breadcrumb crumbles.

VEGAN

# BRAISED LEBANESE EGGPLANT
## WITH CHICKPEAS

Slow-cooking eggplant in tomato sauce makes it incredibly silky and tender. Choose a marinara sauce that has as few ingredients as possible so the flavors don't overwhelm the eggplant.

**YIELD: SERVES 6**

2 Tbs. olive oil

1 large onion, diced (1½ cups)

6 medium Japanese eggplants, halved lengthwise and cut into 2-inch pieces

1 clove garlic, minced (1 tsp.)

½ tsp. ground allspice

¼ tsp. ground cumin

1 cup marinara sauce

1 Tbs. red wine vinegar

1 15-oz. can chickpeas, rinsed and drained

2 large mint sprigs, plus 2 Tbs. chopped mint

**1.** Preheat oven to 325°F. Heat oil in Dutch oven over medium-high heat. Add onion, and sauté 7 minutes, or until soft. Stir in eggplant, and cook 5 minutes, or until beginning to brown. Add garlic, allspice, and cumin, and cook 1 minute more.

**2.** Stir in marinara sauce, vinegar, and ⅔ cup water, and bring to a simmer. Reduce heat to medium, and simmer 5 minutes. Remove from heat, and stir in chickpeas. Season with salt and pepper. Lay mint sprigs on top of eggplant mixture, cover, and transfer pot to oven. Cook 45 to 50 minutes, or until eggplant is tender. Remove mint sprigs, and stir in chopped mint. Serve hot or at room temperature.

GLUTEN FREE

VEGAN

## NUTRITION INFORMATION

Calories: 188
Protein: 7 g
Total Fat: 6 g
Saturated Fat: 1 g
Carbohydrates: 29 g
Cholesterol: 0 mg
Sodium: 427 mg
Fiber: 8 g
Sugar: 11 g

# EGGPLANT PARMESAN
## WITH CREAMED SPINACH

Colorful creamed spinach replaces some of the ooey-gooey factor of the excess cheese that usually goes on top of this Italian classic.

**YIELD: SERVES 4**

½ **cup all-purpose flour**

½ **cup panko breadcrumbs, divided**

½ **cup grated Parmesan cheese**

**1 large egg**

**4 ¾-inch-thick center-cut eggplant slices**

**1 9-oz. bag frozen spinach**

**1 oz. reduced-fat cream cheese**

**¾ cup prepared refrigerated thick marinara sauce**

½ **cup packed coarsely grated mozzarella or fontina cheese**

### NUTRITION INFORMATION
Calories: 295
Protein: 16 g
Total Fat: 12 g
Saturated Fat: 5 g
Carbohydrates: 34 g
Cholesterol: 72 mg
Sodium: 558 mg
Fiber: 6 g
Sugar: 7 g

**1.** Position rack in center of oven, and preheat to 375°F. Coat baking sheet with cooking spray.

**2.** Place flour in pie dish or soup plate. Add panko and Parmesan to second pie dish or soup plate; whisk to blend. Reserve 2 Tbs. panko mixture. Add egg to third pie dish or soup plate; whisk to blend. Season eggplant with salt and pepper, if desired. Coat slices with flour, then egg, then panko mixture; press to adhere. Coat slices on both sides with cooking spray, and arrange on baking sheet.

**3.** Bake eggplant 12 minutes, or until bottoms are brown and crisp. Loosen slices from sheet, and flip over. Bake 12 to 13 minutes longer, or until both sides are brown and crisp, and eggplant is tender.

**4.** Meanwhile, coat large skillet with cooking spray; add spinach. Toss over medium-high heat 2 to 3 minutes, or until wilted. Scrape into towel-lined sieve, and firmly press out excess liquid. Transfer spinach to work surface, and finely chop.

**5.** Recoat skillet with cooking spray. Add spinach, cream cheese, and 1 Tbs. reserved panko mixture. Cook over medium-high heat 3 to 4 minutes, or until mixture is very thick, adding remaining 1 Tbs. reserved panko (if necessary) to thicken.

**6.** Spread marinara sauce atop eggplant on baking sheet. Spoon or spread spinach over top, leaving border of sauce visible. Sprinkle with mozzarella, and bake 4 to 5 minutes, or until topping is heated through.

# LATE SUMMER SUCCOTASH

What better way to make the most of end-of-summer produce than with a sunny succotash that can also be served cold as a salad? If you can't find white balsamic vinegar, try white wine vinegar or apple cider vinegar.

**2 cups shelled lima beans or 1 10-oz. pkg. frozen baby lima beans, thawed**

**1 Tbs. butter**

**1 tsp. olive oil**

**1 small red onion, diced (1 cup)**

**1 clove garlic, minced (1 tsp.)**

**1 cup fresh or frozen corn**

**1 cup cherry tomatoes, halved**

**2 Tbs. chopped fresh parsley**

**2 Tbs. chopped fresh basil**

**1 Tbs. white balsamic vinegar**

**1.** If using fresh lima beans, bring large pot of salted water to a boil. Add beans, and blanch 2 to 3 minutes, or until tender but not soft.

**2.** Heat butter and oil in large skillet over medium-high heat. Add onion, and sauté 5 to 7 minutes, or until it begins to brown. Add garlic, and cook 1 minute more.

**3.** Stir in lima beans, and sauté 5 minutes. Add corn and tomatoes, and sauté 1 minute more, or until heated through, but tomatoes have not released their juices. Remove from heat, and stir in parsley, basil, and vinegar. Serve warm or chilled.

GLUTEN-FREE

30 MINUTES OR LESS

## NUTRITION INFORMATION

Calories: 179
Protein: 7 g
Total Fat: 4.5 g
Saturated Fat: 2 g
Carbohydrates: 28 g
Cholesterol: 8 mg
Sodium: 240 mg
Fiber: 6 g
Sugar: 5 g

# PASTA & NOODLES

Kids love it. Adults crave it. And...diet gurus usually tell you to avoid it. But does pasta have to be such a divisive food subject? Not when you make it right.

Half and half is the rule of thumb when it comes to healthy pasta and noodle choices. Half of what goes into your bowl, casserole, or plate should be pasta, while the other half (or even more) of the recipe should be vegetables and low-fat protein sources. This "better half" helps balance out the carbohydrate content of pasta by adding nutrients and keeping calories down in the finished dish. And generous amounts of good-for-you extras make it tastier, too!

# ROSEMARY-PARMESAN SPAGHETTI & SQUASH

Using both spaghetti pasta and spaghetti squash in this lets you get all the noodle-y satisfaction of real pasta with the extra nutrient boost and reduced calorie count of spaghetti squash.

**YIELD: SERVES 4**

1 small spaghetti squash (1½ to 2 lbs.)

4 oz. multigrain thin spaghetti or angel hair pasta

⅓ cup chopped walnuts

2 Tbs. olive oil

¼ cup plain dry breadcrumbs

3 cloves garlic, minced (1 Tbs.)

1 Tbs. chopped fresh rosemary

¼ cup grated Parmesan cheese

**1.** Preheat oven to 375°F.

**2.** Pierce squash in several places with knife. Microwave 3 minutes on high power to soften. Slice off stem and blossom ends, and stand squash upright. Cut straight down length of squash. Remove seeds with spoon. Place squash halves cut-side down on rimmed baking sheet, and add 1½ cups water to cover baking sheet surface. Bake 30 minutes, or until squash yields when pressed.

**3.** Cool squash 10 minutes cut side up. Scrape with fork to release strands. Transfer strands to bowl.

**4.** Cook pasta according to package directions. Drain, and add to squash strands, mixing with two forks.

**5.** Toast walnuts in small skillet over medium-high heat 5 minutes, or until browned and fragrant. Transfer to plate, and set aside.

**6.** Wipe out skillet, then heat oil in skillet over medium heat. Add breadcrumbs, and cook 1 minute. Add garlic and rosemary, and sauté 2 minutes, or until fragrant, and breadcrumbs are toasted. Add breadcrumbs to squash mixture, and toss to combine. Serve sprinkled with walnuts and cheese.

MAKE IT VEGAN **Omit the Parmesan and use nutritional yeast or Parmesan Crumbles from p. 149.**

## NUTRITION INFORMATION

Calories: 309
Protein: 10 g
Total Fat: 16 g
Saturated Fat: 3 g
Carbohydrates: 37 g
Cholesterol: 4 mg
Sodium: 151 mg
Fiber: 6 g
Sugar: 6 g

# WHOLE-GRAIN & HIGH-PROTEIN PASTAS

Cooks now have more choices than ever to make their pasta dishes wholesome, starting with whole-grain and high-protein options. Whole-grain pastas and noodles have about the same protein content as pasta made with white flour, but they contain more fiber and nutrients, making them healthier, slower-digesting complex carbohydrates. High-protein pastas are usually made with bean and nut flours (in addition to wheat flour) to boost their protein content.

# SHELLS
## WITH ASPARAGUS, PEAS, FETA & MINT

YIELD: SERVES 6

1 lb. asparagus, cut into 1-inch pieces

12 oz. whole-wheat pasta shells

1½ cups fresh or frozen baby peas

2 Tbs. garlic oil, such as Garlic Gold

3 green onions, thinly sliced (⅓ cup)

1 cup sliced fresh basil

½ cup coarsely chopped fresh mint

1 Tbs. grated lemon zest

3 oz. feta cheese, crumbled (¾ cup), optional

One large pot of boiling water is all it takes to make a pasta medley full of fresh spring vegetables. Blanching the vegetables in the boiling water also adds flavor to the pasta.

**1.** Bring large pot of water to a boil. Add asparagus, and cook 4 minutes, or until crisp-tender. Remove asparagus with slotted spoon; transfer to serving bowl.

**2.** Add pasta to boiling water; cook 5 minutes. Add peas, return water to a boil, and cook 2 minutes. Drain pasta and peas, reserving ¼ cup cooking water, and return pasta and peas to pot. Stir in reserved cooking water, asparagus, garlic oil, green onions, basil, mint, and lemon zest. Season with salt and pepper, if desired; transfer back to serving bowl; and sprinkle with feta cheese, if using.

30 MINUTES OR LESS

NUTRITION INFORMATION

Calories: 315
Protein: 13 g
Total Fat: 9 g
Saturated Fat: 3 g
Carbohydrates: 51 g
Cholesterol: 13 mg
Sodium: 403 mg
Fiber: 8 g
Sugar: 4 g

**Seasonal Substitutions**

Asparagus gives this recipe a springtime flair; here's how to make the dish the rest of the year by substituting the following for the asparagus:

**Summer:** diced zucchini

**Fall:** finely diced butternut squash

**Winter:** broccoli

# SPAGHETTI
## WITH SAUTÉED LEEKS, WHITE BEANS & WALNUTS

YIELD: SERVES 6

1 Tbs. olive oil

3 medium leeks, white and light green parts chopped (6 cups)

1 medium yellow bell pepper, seeded and thinly sliced (1 cup)

¼ tsp. red pepper flakes

1½ cups cooked white or cannellini beans, or 1 15-oz. can cannellini beans, rinsed and drained

1 cup low-sodium vegetable broth

3 cloves garlic, minced (1 Tbs.)

12 oz. whole-wheat spaghetti

3 oz. crumbled feta cheese (¾ cup), optional

⅓ cup chopped toasted walnuts

Although few Italian cooks would ever serve this much sauce over a plate of pasta, avid vegetable lovers will appreciate the generous serving of chunky leek-and–white bean sauce.

**1.** Heat oil in large saucepan over medium-high heat. Add leeks, bell pepper, and red pepper flakes; sauté 10 minutes, or until vegetables begin to brown. Stir in beans, vegetable broth, and garlic. Reduce heat to low, and simmer 5 minutes. Season with salt and pepper, if desired.

**2.** Meanwhile, cook spaghetti according to package directions until al dente, about 7 minutes. Drain. Divide spaghetti among 6 bowls or plates. Spoon sauce over each serving of pasta, and sprinkle with feta cheese, if desired, and walnuts.

30 MINUTES OR LESS

### NUTRITION INFORMATION

Calories: 379
Protein: 13 g
Total Fat: 8 g
Saturated Fat: <1 g
Carbohydrates: 67 g
Cholesterol: 0 mg
Sodium: 350 mg
Fiber: 13 g
Sugar: 7 g

# LEEKS

Why haven't sweet, subtle leeks become a mainstay in American cooking? While their culinary cousins (onions, shallots, and garlic) tend to take a supporting role in recipes, leeks have enough color, texture, and flavor to be given star treatment in a wide variety of dishes, from sauces, soups, and stews, to omelets and grilled dishes.

# BEET LINGUINE
## WITH CASHEW RICOTTA

YIELD: SERVES 4

A creamy-garlicky cashew ricotta complements the sweet flavors of beets and caramelized onions in this colorful dish. The recipe makes 1 cup of cashew ricotta; save the remaining ½ cup for another use.

### CASHEW RICOTTA

1 large head garlic

4 tsp. olive oil, divided

2 cups raw cashews, soaked 2–4 hours

4 tsp. nutritional yeast

2 Tbs. fresh lemon juice

1 tsp. sea salt

5 tsp. apple cider vinegar

### LINGUINE

½ lb. beets, greens removed

1½ Tbs. olive oil, divided

1 medium red onion, chopped (1½ cups)

1½ tsp. balsamic vinegar

1½ tsp. mirin (rice wine)

8 oz. whole-wheat linguine

**1.** To make Cashew Ricotta, Preheat oven to 400°F. Slice off garlic top, drizzle with 1 tsp. oil, and wrap garlic head in foil. Roast 1 hour, or until soft. Cool, then squeeze roasted garlic from cloves into food processor.

**2.** Rinse and drain cashews, and add to food processor with remaining 1 Tbs. oil, yeast, lemon juice, vinegar, and salt. Blend until smooth.

**3.** To make Linguine: Boil beets in large saucepan of water 35 to 40 minutes, or until tender. Drain, peel, and coarsely chop.

**4.** Heat 1 Tbs. oil in large skillet over medium heat. Add onion, and cook 15 to 20 minutes, or until beginning to caramelize. Stir in vinegar, and mirin, and cook 2 minutes. Blend onion mixture and beets in food processor until smooth. Season with salt and pepper, and keep warm.

**5.** Cook pasta according to package directions. Drain, and reserve 3 Tbs. cooking water. Toss pasta with beet sauce, remaining 1½ tsp. oil, and reserved pasta water. Top with Cashew Ricotta.

VEGAN

### NUTRITION INFORMATION

| | |
|---|---|
| Calories: 400 | Cholesterol: 0 mg |
| Protein: 13 g | Sodium: 181 mg |
| Total Fat: 15 g | Fiber: 10 g |
| Saturated Fat: 3 g | Sugar: 8 g |
| Carbohydrates: 58 g | |

# LINGUINE
## WITH GRILL-ROASTED TOMATOES & ZUCCHINI PESTO

**YIELD: SERVES 4**

**6 large cloves garlic, peeled**

**3½ Tbs. plus ⅛ tsp. olive oil, divided**

**8 oz. uncooked whole-wheat linguine**

**¼ cup raw sunflower seeds, divided**

**2 cups cherry tomatoes**

**4 small zucchini, halved, then cut into thin slices lengthwise**

**3 cups fresh basil leaves**

**1 oz. grated Parmesan cheese**

Grilled zucchini and garlic get puréed with toasted sunflower seeds, fresh basil, and Parmesan to make a rich, mellow pesto. If storing pesto in the fridge, top the sauce with a thin layer of olive oil to preserve its bright-green color.

**1.** Preheat grill or grill pan to medium-high heat. Place garlic cloves on square of foil, drizzle with ⅛ tsp. oil, and wrap into flat package. Grill 20 minutes. Open packet to cool slightly.

**2.** Meanwhile, cook pasta according to package directions.

**3.** Toast sunflower seeds in skillet 5 to 6 minutes over medium heat. Transfer to plate, and set aside.

**4.** Thread tomatoes onto skewers. Brush tomatoes and zucchini with 2 Tbs. oil, and grill 6 minutes, or until tomatoes begin to shrink and zucchini is tender.

**5.** Transfer garlic, basil, and 2 Tbs. toasted sunflower seeds to food processor, and blend until finely ground. Add 1 cup grilled zucchini, remaining 1½ Tbs. oil, and Parmesan; blend until smooth.

**6.** Drain pasta, and toss with pesto, remaining zucchini, and tomatoes. Sprinkle with remaining sunflower seeds.

### NUTRITION INFORMATION
Calories: 452
Protein: 16 g
Total Fat: 20 g
Saturated Fat: 4 g
Carbohydrates: 55 g
Cholesterol: 6 mg
Sodium: 132 mg
Fiber: 6 g
Sugar: 9 g

**Veg Pestos**
Build your pasta sauce repertoire around an assortment of vegetable pestos. Here are few combinations to try in place of the zucchini and sunflower seeds:

**green beans and almonds**
**broccoli and hazelnuts**
**fava beans and cashews**
**kale and walnuts**

# MUSHROOM RAVIOLI
## WITH GREEN PEA PURÉE

YIELD: SERVES 4

Homemade ravioli is a great make-ahead dish when you use wonton wrappers for the pasta. Place filled ravioli on a parchment-lined baking sheet and freeze until hard. Store in a resealable plastic bag in the freezer.

MUSHROOM
RAVIOLI

**2 Tbs. olive oil**

**½ small onion, chopped (½ cup)**

**1 clove garlic, minced (1 tsp.)**

**½ tsp. chopped fresh thyme**

**8 oz. wild mushroom mix or assorted mushrooms, chopped (3 cups)**

**2 Tbs. sherry**

**24 wonton wrappers**

GREEN PEA PURÉE

**2 cups frozen peas, thawed**

**¾ cup low-sodium vegetable broth**

**2 Tbs. grated Parmesan cheese, plus more for garnish, if desired**

**1.** To make Mushroom Ravioli: Heat oil in skillet over medium-high heat. Add onion, and cook 5 to 7 minutes, or until translucent and starting to brown. Stir in garlic and thyme, and cook 1 minute more. Add mushrooms, and increase heat to high. Sauté mushrooms 7 minutes, or until all liquid has evaporated. Add sherry to pan and cook 1 minute, or until sherry has evaporated. Transfer to bowl, and cool 20 minutes.

**2.** Place 1 wonton wrapper on work surface. Brush edges with water. Spoon 1 tsp. mushroom mixture in center of wrapper and fold into triangle, pressing edges to seal. Repeat with remaining wrappers and mushroom mixture.

**3.** To make Green Pea Purée: Blend peas, broth, and cheese in blender until smooth. Transfer to saucepan, and warm over medium heat. Season with salt and pepper, and set aside.

**4.** Bring large pot of salted water to a boil over high heat. Add ravioli and cook 2 minutes, or until cooked through. Drain. Spoon Pea Purée onto plates, and top with ravioli. Sprinkle with Parmesan cheese, if desired.

## NUTRITION INFORMATION

| | |
|---|---|
| Calories: 292 | Cholesterol: 7 mg |
| Protein: 11 g | Sodium: 637 mg |
| Total Fat: 8.5 g | Fiber: 5 g |
| Saturated Fat: 1.5 g | Sugar: 6 g |
| Carbohydrates: 42 g | |

# ZUCCHINI-CORN CANNELLONI

YIELD: SERVES 4

Baked cannelloni is a lighter alternative to lasagna and has the same big, bold flavors.

## SAUCE

1½ tsp. olive oil

½ small onion, finely chopped (½ cup)

1 clove garlic, minced (1 tsp.)

½ tsp. rubbed sage

½ tsp. dried oregano

1 14.5-oz. can diced fire-roasted tomatoes

1 tsp. balsamic vinegar

## CANNELLONI

1 Tbs. olive oil

1 medium onion, chopped (1½ cups)

1 medium zucchini, finely diced (1½ cups)

½ cup fresh or frozen corn kernels

2 cloves garlic, minced (2 tsp.)

½ tsp. rubbed sage

1 cup low-fat ricotta cheese

4 Tbs. Parmesan cheese, divided

1 large pinch ground nutmeg

16 no-cook lasagna noodles

½ cup low-fat shredded mozzarella cheese, optional

**1.** To make Sauce: Heat oil in saucepan over medium heat. Add onion, and sauté 7 minutes, or until soft. Add garlic, sage, and oregano; stir until combined. Add tomatoes and vinegar, and season with salt and pepper, if desired. Cover, reduce heat to medium-low, and simmer 10 minutes. Purée with immersion blender.

**2.** To make Cannelloni: Heat oil in skillet over medium heat. Add onion; sauté 10 minutes. Add zucchini and corn; increase heat to medium-high. Sauté 3 to 5 minutes, or until beginning to brown. Stir in garlic and sage; remove from heat. Stir in ricotta, 2 Tbs. Parmesan, and nutmeg.

**3.** Bring large pot of salted water to a boil. Add noodles, and cook 3 minutes, or until noodles bend without breaking. Drain, and cool in large bowl of cold water. Drain again, pat dry, and stack on cutting board. Halve noodles width-wise.

**4.** Preheat oven to 350°F. Spoon ½ cup Sauce into 9-inch square baking dish.

**5.** Spoon 3 Tbs. zucchini mixture down center of 1 halved noodle. Roll into a tube, and place seam-side down in dish. Repeat with remaining noodles and filling. Pour remaining Sauce over Cannelloni in dish. Sprinkle with remaining 2 Tbs. Parmesan and mozzarella, if using. Bake 25 minutes, or until cheese melts and Sauce is bubbly.

## NUTRITION INFORMATION

Calories: 314

Protein: 15 g

Total Fat: 10 g

Saturated Fat: 4 g

Carbohydrates: 42 g

Cholesterol: 24 mg

Sodium: 536 mg

Fiber: 4 g

Sugar: 12 g

MAKE-AHEAD TIP Cool cannelloni, and cover tightly with foil. Refrigerate 3 days, or freeze up to 1 month. Thaw, and reheat, covered, in 350°F oven 20 to 25 minutes, or until hot in center.

# TOFU & SPINACH STUFFED SHELLS

YIELD: SERVES 6

Olive oil–poached garlic gives tofu a deep, mellow flavor, while miso and vinegar provide a cheese-like tang.

**6 oz. jumbo pasta shells**

**12 cloves garlic, peeled and thinly sliced**

**¼ cup olive oil**

**1 16-oz. block firm tofu, drained, rinsed, and patted dry**

**2 Tbs. unpasteurized apple cider vinegar**

**2 tsp. lemon juice**

**2 tsp. white miso**

**5 oz. baby spinach leaves (6 cups)**

**1 24-oz. jar prepared pasta sauce**

**2 Tbs. chopped Kalamata olives, optional**

**2 Tbs. chopped green olives, optional**

**1.** Preheat oven to 375°F.

**2.** Cook pasta shells according to package directions. Drain, rinse, and drain again, then place on clean kitchen towel to cool and dry.

**3.** Bring garlic and olive oil to a simmer in small skillet over medium heat. Reduce heat to low, and simmer 15 minutes, or until garlic is soft and golden. Remove from heat, and set aside.

**4.** Crumble tofu into bowl of food processor, and blend with vinegar, lemon juice, miso, garlic, and oil until smooth. Transfer to medium bowl.

**5.** Heat large saucepan over medium heat. Add spinach and 2 Tbs. water, and cook 3 to 4 minutes, or until leaves are wilted. Transfer to strainer, and squeeze out excess liquid. Roughly chop, and stir into tofu mixture.

**6.** Spoon 2 Tbs. filling into each pasta shell, and place in single layer in large baking dish. Cover with pasta sauce, sprinkle with olives (if using), and bake 45 minutes, or until sauce is bubbling. Let stand 10 minutes before serving.

VEGAN

## NUTRITION INFORMATION

| | |
|---|---|
| Calories: 343 | Cholesterol: 0 mg |
| Protein: 13 g | Sodium: 562 mg |
| Total Fat: 14 g | Fiber: 5 g |
| Saturated Fat: 2 g | Sugar: 11 g |
| Carbohydrates: 42 g | |

# SPINACH-ARTICHOKE MINI LASAGNAS

YIELD: MAKES 24
MINI LASAGNAS

1 16-oz. pkg. frozen
chopped spinach,
thawed and drained

1 15-oz. can water-
packed artichoke
hearts, drained and
chopped

1 16-oz. container
reduced-fat ricotta
cheese

12 oz. shredded
mozzarella cheese,
divided (3 cups)

½ cup grated
Parmesan cheese

1 large egg, lightly
beaten

3 Tbs. prepared
pesto

¼ cup red wine

1 25-oz. jar spaghetti
sauce

72 refrigerated
or thawed frozen
dumpling or wonton
wrappers

Muffin cups make perfect single-serving lasagnas when you use dumpling or wonton wrappers as the lasagna noodles.

**1.** Stir together spinach, artichoke hearts, ricotta, 2 cups mozzarella, Parmesan, egg, and 2 Tbs. pesto in large bowl. Set aside.

**2.** Bring wine to a boil in small saucepan over medium-high heat. Boil until reduced by half. Stir in remaining 1 Tbs. pesto, then spaghetti sauce, and bring to just a simmer. Remove from heat.

**3.** Preheat oven to 375°F, and coat two 12-cup muffin pans with cooking spray. Press 1 dumpling wrapper into bottom of each muffin cup. Spoon 2 Tbs. cheese mixture into dumpling wrapper. Top with 1½ tsp. sauce. Repeat layering dumpling wrapper, cheese mixture, and sauce. Top with dumpling wrapper, and crimp or turn down edges as you would a pie. Spread 1 Tbs. sauce over top. Sprinkle lasagnas with remaining 1 cup mozzarella.

**4.** Bake 10 to 12 minutes, or until cheese on top is melted and bubbling. Cool 5 minutes before unmolding and serving.

## NUTRITION INFORMATION

| | |
|---|---|
| Calories: 361 | Cholesterol: 63 mg |
| Protein: 20 g | Sodium: 764 mg |
| Total Fat: 17 g | Fiber: 4 g |
| Saturated Fat: 8 g | Sugar: 3 g |
| Carbohydrates: 30 g | |

# HERBED TOFU LASAGNA
## WITH ZUCCHINI

Simple, fresh flavors and an innovative way with tofu—it's blended with herbs and seasonings until creamy and ricotta-like—make this lasagna one you'll want to make year-round.

**YIELD: SERVES 10**

**2 14-oz. pkg. firm tofu, well drained**

**½ cup chopped fresh basil**

**⅓ cup chopped fresh Italian parsley**

**⅓ cup pine nuts, toasted**

**2 cloves garlic, peeled**

**2 Tbs. lemon juice**

**1 tsp. salt**

**½ tsp. red pepper flakes**

**¼ tsp. sugar**

**1 Tbs. olive oil**

**4 medium zucchini, cut into ½-inch slices (about 3 cups)**

**5 cups marinara sauce**

**16 no-cook lasagna noodles (9 oz.)**

**1.** Preheat oven to 350°F. Coat 13- x 9-inch baking dish with cooking spray. Combine tofu, basil, parsley, pine nuts, garlic, lemon juice, salt, red pepper flakes, and sugar in food processor; blend until smooth and similar to ricotta in texture.

**2.** Put oil and zucchini in large nonstick skillet. Sauté 3 to 5 minutes over medium-high heat, or until just tender.

**3.** Spread 3 Tbs. marinara sauce over bottom of prepared baking dish. Cover with layer of noodles, overlapping slightly, half of tofu mixture, and half of zucchini mixture. Top with another layer of noodles, remaining tofu and zucchini, and ½ cup sauce. Finish with another layer of noodles and remaining sauce.

**4.** Cover with foil, and bake 1 hour. Let rest 10 minutes before serving.

VEGAN

## NUTRITION INFORMATION

| | |
|---|---|
| Calories: 314 | Cholesterol: mg |
| Protein: 18 g | Sodium: 617 mg |
| Total Fat: 12 g | Fiber: 6 g |
| Saturated Fat: 1 g | Sugar: 10 g |
| Carbohydrates: 36 g | |

# TORTILLA LASAGNA
## WITH SWISS CHARD

YIELD: SERVES 6

Italy meets Mexico in this easy casserole made where corn tortillas are used as the lasagna noodles.

**2 tsp. olive oil**

**1 lb. Swiss chard, stems and leaves separated, chopped**

**1 large onion, chopped (about 1½ cups)**

**4 cloves garlic, minced (about 4 tsp.)**

**4½ cups tomato sauce, divided**

**1½ cups fresh basil leaves, chopped**

**9 6-inch corn tortillas, divided**

**2 cups part-skim ricotta cheese**

**3 oz. part-skim mozzarella cheese, grated (about 1 cup)**

**3 Tbs. grated Romano cheese**

**1.** Preheat oven to 375°F. Heat oil in large pot over high heat. Add chard stems and onion, and cook 8 minutes, or until soft, stirring often. Add chard leaves and garlic. Cover, and cook over medium-low heat 5 minutes, or until chard leaves are tender. Season with salt and pepper.

**2.** Combine 2½ cups tomato sauce and basil. Spread ½ cup tomato-basil sauce over bottom of 10-inch springform pan. Arrange 3 tortillas in single layer (overlapping slightly) over sauce.

**3.** Season ricotta with salt and pepper. Spread 1 cup ricotta over tortillas in pan. Top with ½ cup tomato-basil sauce, half of chard mixture, ⅓ cup mozzarella and 1 Tbs. Romano cheese. Repeat layering with 3 more tortillas, 1 cup ricotta, ½ cup tomato-basil sauce, remaining chard mixture, ⅓ cup mozzarella, and 1 Tbs. Romano cheese; place remaining tortillas on top. Spread remaining 1 cup tomato-basil sauce over tortillas; cover with foil, and bake 45 minutes.

**4.** Remove foil, sprinkle with remaining ⅓ cup mozzarella, and 1 Tbs. Romano cheese, and bake, uncovered, 10 minutes more. Let stand 5 minutes, then unmold, and cut into wedges. Serve with warmed remaining tomato sauce on the side.

## NUTRITION INFORMATION

| | |
|---|---|
| Calories: 419 | Cholesterol: 24 mg |
| Protein: 19 g | Sodium: 715 mg |
| Total Fat: 13 g | Fiber: 7 g |
| Saturated Fat: 4.5 g | Sugar: 8 g |
| Carbohydrates: 56 g | |

# SMOKED TOFU FARFALLE CASSEROLE

YIELD: SERVES 6

Here's a new twist on Mom's beloved tuna noodle casserole. We lightened the cream sauce, added lots of veggies, and replaced the tuna with smoked tofu, which adds richness and depth to the flavor.

4 tsp. olive oil

1 small yellow bell pepper, chopped (about 1 cup)

1½ cups frozen baby peas

3 cloves garlic, minced (about 1 Tbs.)

2½ tsp. minced fresh thyme

8 oz. farfalle pasta (bows)

1¾ cups low-fat milk

3 Tbs. all-purpose flour

3 oz. sharp Cheddar cheese, grated (about ¾ cup)

6 oz. smoked tofu, diced

3 Tbs. Italian-seasoned breadcrumbs

**1.** Preheat oven to 425°F. Heat 1 tsp. oil in 6-qt. Dutch oven over medium heat. Add bell pepper, and cook, stirring often, 3 minutes. Stir in frozen peas, garlic, and thyme, and cook, stirring often, 2 minutes more. Transfer to bowl and set aside.

**2.** Wipe out Dutch oven; fill with water, and bring to a boil. Add pasta, and cook about 4 minutes, or until just al dente. Drain and transfer to clean bowl. Drizzle with 2 tsp. olive oil, and toss to coat. Return Dutch oven to stove.

**3.** Heat 1½ cups milk in Dutch oven over medium heat until almost simmering. Whisk together remaining ¼ cup milk with flour in small bowl, then whisk into hot milk. Cook over medium-low heat, whisking constantly, 2 minutes, or until sauce thickens and bubbles. Remove from heat, and stir in cheese. Season to taste with salt and pepper. Add pasta, bell pepper mixture, and tofu, and stir to combine.

**4.** Mix breadcrumbs with remaining 1 tsp. oil in small bowl; sprinkle over casserole. Bake uncovered, 20 minutes, or until golden. Serve hot.

### NUTRITION INFORMATION

| | |
|---|---|
| Calories: 348 | Cholesterol: 20 mg |
| Protein: 16 g | Sodium: 537 mg |
| Total Fat: 9 g | Fiber: 4 g |
| Saturated Fat: 4 g | Sugar: 8 g |
| Carbohydrates: 49 g | |

# SPICY ASIAN STIR-FRY
## WITH WHOLE-WHEAT LINGUINE

Whole-wheat linguine works well in Asian noodle stir-fry dishes like this one.

**YIELD: SERVES 4**

8 oz. whole-wheat linguine noodles

1 Tbs. peanut oil

1 small onion, thinly sliced (1 cup)

2 cloves garlic, minced (2 tsp.)

1 small head bok choy, chopped into 2-inch pieces (1½ cups)

1½ cups broccoli florets

⅓ cup snow peas, halved

½ red bell pepper, thinly sliced (½ cup)

2 Tbs. hoisin sauce

1 Tbs. chili garlic sauce

¼ cup chopped peanuts

**1.** Cook pasta according to package directions. Drain, reserving 1 cup cooking water, and set pasta aside.

**2.** Meanwhile, heat oil in large skillet or wok over medium heat. Add onion and garlic, and sauté 5 to 7 minutes, or until onion is golden.

**3.** Add bok choy, broccoli, snow peas, and bell pepper. Stir-fry 5 minutes. Add ½ cup water, cover, and simmer 5 minutes. Stir in hoisin and chili garlic sauces. Stir in noodles, adding ½ cup reserved cooking water. Add more water if mixture seems too dry. Garnish each serving with 1 Tbs. chopped peanuts.

VEGAN

30 MINUTES OR LESS

### NUTRITION INFORMATION

Calories: 330
Protein: 13 g
Total Fat: 9 g
Saturated Fat: 1 g
Carbohydrates: 55 g
Cholesterol: 0 mg
Sodium: 205 mg
Fiber: 10 g
Sugar: 7 g

# SINGAPORE HAWKER NOODLES
## WITH GOLDEN TOFU & COCONUT

Street food vendors all over Southeast Asia offer versions of this delicious rice noodle dish.

**YIELD: SERVES 4**

**6 oz. dried brown rice vermicelli**

**2 cups thinly sliced napa cabbage**

**1 cup chopped cilantro**

**1 stalk celery, quartered lengthwise and thinly sliced**

**2 small shallots, peeled**

**1½ tsp. vegetable oil**

**8 oz. firm tofu, drained and cubed**

**½ cup lemon juice**

**4 tsp. sugar**

**2 tsp. sriracha sauce or other Asian hot sauce**

**¾ tsp. coarse salt**

**2 cloves garlic, minced (2 tsp.)**

**½ cup toasted unsweetened coconut flakes**

**1.** Cook noodles according to package directions. Drain, and rinse noodles under cold water, then drain again. Transfer noodles to large bowl, and add cabbage, cilantro, celery, and shallots. Gently toss to mix.

**2.** Heat oil in medium nonstick skillet over medium-high heat. Add tofu, and cook 12 to 15 minutes, or until golden brown on two or three sides, turning occasionally. Remove from heat, and set aside.

**3.** Whisk together lemon juice, sugar, sriracha, salt, and garlic in small bowl. Pour sauce over noodle mixture, and toss to coat. Divide noodle mixture among serving bowls. Top with tofu cubes, and garnish with coconut flakes.

VEGAN

GLUTEN-FREE

30 MINUTES OR LESS

## NUTRITION INFORMATION

Calories: 342
Protein: 10 g
Total Fat: 12 g
Saturated Fat: 7 g
Carbohydrates: 46 g
Cholesterol: 0 mg
Sodium: 447 mg
Fiber: 4 g
Sugar: 7 g

# PEANUT NOODLES
## WITH CRUNCHY CELERY

**¼ cup toasted sesame oil**

**¼ cup low-sodium soy sauce**

**¼ cup smooth peanut butter**

**2 Tbs. lemon juice**

**2 Tbs. brown sugar**

**1 Tbs. plus 1 tsp. minced fresh ginger**

**2 cloves garlic, minced (2 tsp.)**

**1 tsp. chili garlic sauce**

**½ lb. whole-grain linguine**

**1½ cups thinly sliced celery stalks**

**½ cup chopped celery leaves, plus 1 cup whole or torn celery leaves**

**⅓ cup finely chopped roasted peanuts, optional**

The classic combo of celery and peanut butter gets a tasty update in this noodle salad. Choose very fresh celery with plenty of dark leaves that are the color of parsley.

**1.** Process sesame oil, soy sauce, peanut butter, lemon juice, brown sugar, ginger, garlic, and chili garlic sauce in blender or food processor until smooth. Transfer to glass measuring cup.

**2.** Cook pasta in boiling, salted water according to package directions. Drain, and cool in strainer 20 minutes, tossing occasionally to prevent sticking.

**3.** Transfer pasta to large bowl, and season with salt, if desired. Add sliced celery, chopped celery leaves, half of peanuts (if using), and ½ cup sauce; toss to combine. Garnish with remaining peanuts (if using) and whole or torn celery leaves. Drizzle with remaining sauce, if desired. Serve at room temperature.

VEGAN

## NUTRITION INFORMATION

Calories: 314
Protein: 12 g
Total Fat: 12 g
Saturated Fat: 2 g
Carbohydrates: 49 g
Cholesterol: 0 mg
Sodium: 425 mg
Fiber: 6 g
Sugar: 6 g

# COCONUT SOBA NOODLES
## WITH GINGER KALE

YIELD: SERVES 4

**1 cup cilantro leaves**

**6 cloves garlic, coarsely chopped**

**1 jalapeño chile, chopped**

**1 Tbs. grated fresh ginger plus ¼ cup thinly sliced fresh ginger, divided**

**1 tsp. ground turmeric**

**3 tsp. vegetable or peanut oil, divided**

**1 15-oz. can light coconut milk**

**2 Tbs. lime juice**

**1 6-oz. pkg. soba noodles**

**1 Tbs. low-sodium soy sauce**

**3 cloves garlic, peeled and smashed**

**8 oz. curly kale, roughly chopped (4 cups)**

**¼ cup chopped roasted peanuts, optional**

Japanese soba noodles are made with buckwheat, which gives them a rich, nutty flavor. Some brands of soba noodles are 100 percent buckwheat. Their flavor is intense, but they are suitable for gluten-free diets.

**1.** Purée cilantro, garlic, chile, grated ginger, turmeric, and 1 tsp. oil in food processor until green paste forms.

**2.** Heat saucepan over medium heat. Add paste, and sauté 30 seconds. Whisk in coconut milk and ½ cup water. Reduce heat to low, and simmer 15 minutes without boiling. Stir in lime juice, and season with salt and pepper, if desired.

**3.** Cook noodles according to package directions. Whisk together soy sauce and 2 Tbs. water in small bowl.

**4.** Heat remaining 2 tsp. oil in wok over high heat. Add sliced ginger and garlic, and stir-fry 15 seconds. Add kale, and cook 1 minute. Pour in soy sauce mixture, cover, and steam 30 seconds. Uncover, and stir-fry 1 minute, or until kale is wilted.

**5.** Serve noodles topped with kale, coconut sauce, and peanuts, if using.

VEGAN

## NUTRITION INFORMATION

Calories: 307
Protein: 10 g
Total Fat: 12 g
Saturated Fat: 7 g
Carbohydrates: 41 g
Cholesterol: 0 mg
Sodium: 472 mg
Fiber: 4 g
Sugar: 1 g

# BEANS & LENTILS

Beans and lentils make their way into many, many dishes throughout this book. So why give them a separate chapter? Because the inexpensive and incredibly versatile little legumes are the superstars of the plant-based protein world.

With 7 to 9 grams of protein, 6 to 9 grams of fiber, plenty of complex carbohydrates, and no cholesterol per half-cup (cooked), beans and lentils are some of the most nutritious foods you can eat, period. In fact, the World Health Organization (WHO) gives them top billing (along with fruits and vegetables) for their role in a healthy diet.

Beans and lentils make their way into traditional cuisines around the globe, from spicy Mexican chilaquiles (p. 234) and tangy, tomato-ey Middle Eastern cabbage rolls, to homey Italian soups, like ribollita (p. 227) and good ol' Southern black-eyed peas with greens, meaning you don't have to look hard to find a legume dish you'll love.

# A PERFECT POT
# OF DRIED BEANS

Use this basic recipe to prepare beans. Adding aromatics (such as onion, garlic, and herbs) will flavor the beans and their broth, but leave a neutral flavor for any type of recipe. Kombu (dried kelp) helps reduce beans' gas-producing properties.

**2 cups dried beans, presoaked, if desired**

**½ onion, peeled, optional**

**2 cloves garlic, crushed, optional**

**1 bay leaf, optional**

**1 strip kombu, optional**

**Sprigs of fresh or dried herbs, optional**

Place beans, optional aromatics, and 8 to 10 cups water in large pot or saucepan, and bring to a boil over medium-high heat. Boil 15 minutes. Reduce heat to medium-low, and simmer presoaked beans for 30 minutes; dried beans for 2 hours, or until beans are tender and creamy, adding more water if necessary. Remove aromatics before serving or using beans.

## NUTRITION INFORMATION

Per ½ cup
Calories: 124
Protein: 7 g
Total Fat: <1 g
Saturated Fat: 0 g
Carbohydrates: 23 g
Cholesterol: 0 mg
Sodium: 2 mg
Fiber: 12 g
Sugar: 1 g

# BEAN SOAKING TIME

### NO SOAK

Believe it or not, you don't have to soak dried beans before you cook them. Simply simmer in plenty of water 1 to 2 hours or until beans are done.

### QUICK SOAK

Bring 1 cup beans and 4 cups water to a boil in large saucepan. Reduce heat to medium-low, and simmer 2 minutes. Remove from heat, cover, and let stand 1 hour. Drain, then cook beans in large pot of water 40 minutes to 1 hour, or until done.

### LONG SOAK

Place 1 cup beans in large bowl, and cover with 6 cups water. Let soak 4 to 24 hours. Drain, then cook beans in large pot of water 40 minutes to 1 hour, or until done.

# NEW YEAR'S BLACK-EYED PEAS & GREENS

YIELD: SERVES 6

**½ lb. dried black-eyed peas (1¼ cups)**

**1 bay leaf**

**2 Tbs. red wine vinegar**

**1¾ tsp. salt, divided**

**1 12-oz. bunch kale, stems removed, leaves torn into pieces**

**2 Tbs. lemon juice, divided**

**2 large tomatoes, seeded and diced (1½ cups)**

**2 Tbs. olive oil**

**4 green onions, sliced (½ cup)**

**¼ cup finely chopped fresh parsley**

**1 Tbs. finely chopped fresh oregano**

"Eat poor on New Year's, and eat fat the rest of the year," goes the saying in the American South, where black-eyed peas are eaten at New Year's for luck. The peas are said to represent coins and are served alongside greens, which represent paper money. The dish tastes wonderful the rest of the year as well.

**1.** Set peas in saucepan, and cover with boiling water; let sit 1 hour. Drain, return peas to saucepan, cover with fresh water, and add bay leaf. Bring to a boil, and cook 20 minutes. Add vinegar and 1 tsp. salt, and cook 10 to 25 minutes longer, or until peas are tender but keep their shape.

**2.** Bring large pot of salted water to a boil. Add kale, and boil 3 to 5 minutes, or until tender. Drain, and toss with 1 tsp. lemon juice.

**3.** Toss tomatoes with ¼ tsp. salt in colander. Let sit, shaking occasionally, to drain juices.

**4.** Combine remaining ½ tsp. salt, remaining 5 tsp. lemon juice, oil, green onions, parsley, and oregano in large bowl.

**5.** Drain peas, and remove bay leaf. Add to bowl with lemon juice and herbs, and mix well. Add tomatoes, and mix again. Serve warm, with kale on side.

**VEGAN**

**GLUTEN-FREE**

## NUTRITION INFORMATION

| | |
|---|---|
| Calories: 195 | Cholesterol: 0 mg |
| Protein: 10 g | Sodium: 701 mg |
| Total Fat: 6 g | Fiber: 8 g |
| Saturated Fat: <1 g | Sugar: 6 g |
| Carbohydrates: 28 g | |

# CANNELLINI AL GRATIN

YIELD: SERVES 12

**1½ lb. dried cannellini beans**

**6 sprigs plus 1½ Tbs. chopped fresh thyme, divided**

**3 sprigs plus 3 Tbs. chopped fresh parsley, divided**

**½ medium onion, unpeeled, plus 1 large onion, diced (2 cups)**

**3 whole cloves**

**1 medium fennel bulb, quartered and diced (2 cups)**

**12 cloves garlic (6 peeled and halved; 6 minced), divided**

**3 Tbs. olive oil, divided**

**2 cups diced carrots**

**1 tsp. white wine vinegar**

**¾ cup grated Parmesan cheese, divided**

**1½ cups fresh breadcrumbs**

This hearty, crumb-topped main dish is ideal for parties. It will serve six to eight people generously and still leave plenty to freeze in small portions for easy weeknight suppers. Using dried beans gives the dish superior texture and the beans a chance to soak up all the flavors of the garlic and herbs.

**1.** Soak beans in large bowl of cold water overnight. Drain.

**2.** Put beans in 6-qt. Dutch oven, and add enough water to cover by 2 inches. Tie together thyme and parsley sprigs, and add to pot. Pierce onion half with cloves, and add to pot. Add fennel fronds and stalks to pot with 6 halved garlic cloves. Partially cover, and bring to a boil. Uncover, reduce heat to medium-low, and simmer 35 to 40 minutes, or until beans are just tender. Drain beans, and reserve cooking liquid. Discard herb bundles, onion, and fennel. Wipe out Dutch oven for next step.

**3.** Preheat oven to 400°F. Heat 2 Tbs. oil in Dutch oven over medium-high heat. Add carrots and diced fennel, and season with salt, if desired. Cover, and cook 10 minutes, or until beginning to brown, stirring frequently. Add diced onion, season with salt (if desired), and cook, covered, 6 to 8 minutes, or until onion is soft and bottom of pan is browning, stirring occasionally. Add minced garlic, and cook 1 minute, or until fragrant. Remove pot from heat, and stir in vinegar, using spatula to scrape up any browned bits of onion stuck to bottom of pot. Add beans, chopped thyme, 2 Tbs. chopped parsley, ½ cup Parmesan, and 1½ to 2 cups bean cooking liquid. (Liquid should come to about 1½ to 2 inches below top of beans; add more if necessary.) Stir well to combine.

**4.** Combine breadcrumbs, remaining 1 Tbs. chopped parsley, and remaining ¼ cup Parmesan in small bowl. Drizzle remaining 1 Tbs. oil into crumb mixture, and combine to moisten breadcrumbs. Spread breadcrumb mixture over bean mixture. Bake gratin, uncovered, 40 to 45 minutes, or until top is browned and juices have bubbled down below surface, leaving brown rim around edge of crust. Cool at least 20 to 25 minutes to allow beans to finish absorbing juices. Serve warm.

## NUTRITION INFORMATION

Calories: 285
Protein: 17 g
Total Fat: 5 g
Saturated Fat: 1 g
Carbohydrates: 43 g
Cholesterol: 4 mg
Sodium: 150 mg
Fiber: 11 g
Sugar: 4 g

# TRUFFLED WILD MUSHROOMS OVER WHIPPED WHITE BEANS

**YIELD: SERVES 4**

Truffle oil and earthy wild mushrooms turn a simple combination into a sublime main dish. Try making the whipped beans with cooked red lentils for a change.

**2 tsp. olive oil, divided**

**1 medium leek, white and pale green parts chopped (about ½ cup)**

**3 cups cooked cannellini beans, or 2 15-oz. cans cannellini beans, rinsed and drained**

**½ cup low-sodium vegetable broth**

**2 cloves garlic, minced (2 tsp.)**

**2 tsp. chopped fresh thyme**

**1 lb. wild mushrooms, halved**

**¼ cup chopped fresh parsley**

**2 tsp. truffle oil**

**1.** Heat 1 tsp. oil in large skillet over medium heat. Add leek and sauté 2 minutes. Stir in beans, broth, garlic, and thyme. Cover, reduce heat to low, and simmer 8 minutes. Season with salt and pepper. Transfer bean mixture to food processor, and blend until creamy and smooth. Return to skillet, cover, and keep warm.

**2.** Heat remaining 1 tsp. oil in medium skillet over high heat. Add mushrooms and sauté 8 minutes, or until soft and brown. Season with salt and pepper, and stir in parsley.

**3.** Spoon whipped bean mixture into shallow bowls. Top with equal portions of mushrooms. Drizzle each serving with ½ tsp. truffle oil, and serve.

GLUTEN-FREE

VEGAN

30 MINUTES OR LESS

## NUTRITION INFORMATION

Calories: 299
Protein: 15 g
Total Fat: 7 g
Saturated Fat: 1 g
Carbohydrates: 46 g
Cholesterol: 0 mg
Sodium: 691 mg
Fiber: 17 g
Sugar: 2 g

# RIBOLLITA
## WITH ORCA BEANS

YIELD: SERVES 8

**2½ tsp. olive oil**

**1 medium onion, chopped (1½ cups)**

**1 large carrot, chopped (¾ cup)**

**1 celery stalk, chopped (½ cup)**

**2½ tsp. dried Italian seasoning**

**3 cups chopped savoy cabbage or kale (7 oz.)**

**3 cups chopped Swiss chard (12 oz.)**

**2 cups chopped plum tomatoes**

**4 cups low-sodium vegetable broth**

**2 cups cooked Orca beans, 2 cups cooking liquid reserved**

**5 cloves garlic, minced (5 tsp.)**

**1 chipotle chile in adobo sauce, minced**

**2 cups rustic Italian bread cubes**

**½ cup grated Parmesan or Romano cheese, optional**

Heirloom Orca beans have clearly been an inspiration to cooks and gardeners. In addition to the whale-reference name, the legumes are also called vaquero (which means cowboy in Spanish) and calypso beans. Creamy and starchy, Orca beans work well in hearty soups and stews. If you can't find Orcas, you can use cranberry beans as a substitute.

**1.** Heat oil in large pot or Dutch oven over medium heat. Add onion; sauté 8 minutes, or until soft and translucent. Add carrot, celery, and Italian seasoning; sauté 5 minutes, or until celery is softened. Stir in cabbage, Swiss chard, and tomatoes; cook 15 minutes, or until cabbage and chard have wilted. Stir in broth, beans with reserved cooking liquid, garlic, and chipotle chile. Bring mixture to a boil, reduce heat to medium-low, and simmer 20 minutes, or until vegetables are tender.

**2.** Add bread cubes to soup, gently stir, and cook 5 minutes more, or until bread is soaked. Season with salt and pepper, if desired. Serve sprinkled with cheese (if using). If making the soup ahead, reserve bread to add at the time of reheating, just before serving.

HEIRLOOM JEWELS **Shapely, speckled, and colorful heirloom beans can add interest and extra flavor to everyday bean dishes. To use them, simply substitute a similar-sized heirloom bean for the type called for in a recipe.**

### NUTRITION INFORMATION

Calories: 156
Protein: 7 g
Total Fat: 2 g
Saturated Fat: <1 g
Carbohydrates: 29 g

Cholesterol: 0 mg
Sodium: 276 mg
Fiber: 10 g
Sugar: 6 g

## FREEZING BEANS

Cooked beans freeze well for future use in recipes. For recipe prep ease, freeze 1½ cups cooked beans (the amount found in a 15-oz. can) in 1-quart resealable plastic bags.

# CORNBREAD SHEPHERD'S PIE

YIELD: SERVES 4

**2 15-oz. cans pinto beans, rinsed and drained, liquid reserved**

**3 Tbs. tomato paste**

**1 Tbs. olive oil**

**1 large red onion, cut into ¼-inch dice (2½ cups), divided**

**2½ Tbs. chili powder**

**3 medium plum tomatoes, seeded and chopped (1½ cups), divided**

**6 Tbs. whole-grain cornbread and muffin mix**

**1⅓ cups plain nonfat Greek yogurt, divided**

**1 large egg**

**1½ Tbs. sugar**

Serve this easy, make-ahead dish with bell peppers, radishes, and shredded lettuce that can be sprinkled over each serving. To reheat, warm the shepherd's pie in a 350-degree oven for 20 minutes.

**1.** Place oven rack in top position, and preheat oven to 425°F. Coat 9-inch pie dish with cooking spray. Whisk reserved bean liquid with tomato paste in bowl.

**2.** Heat oil in large skillet over medium-high heat. Add 2 cups onion. Cover, and cook 4 minutes, or until onion begins to soften, stirring occasionally. Add chili powder, and stir 10 seconds to coat onions. Stir in tomato paste mixture, 1 cup tomatoes, beans, and 1½ cups water. Bring to simmer, stirring occasionally. Reduce heat to low, and simmer uncovered, 6 minutes, or until flavors blend and chili liquids thicken. Season with salt and pepper, if desired.

**3.** Meanwhile, combine cornbread mix, ⅓ cup yogurt, egg, sugar, and 1 Tbs. water in medium bowl.

**4.** Spread chili beans in prepared pie dish. Pour cornbread batter over beans, spreading with back of spoon. Bake 10 minutes, or until cornbread is set and golden.

**5.** Meanwhile, finely chop remaining ½ cup onion. Place in small bowl; mix in remaining ½ cup tomatoes, and season with salt and pepper, if desired.

**6.** Divide shepherd's pie among shallow bowls. Serve with tomato salsa and remaining 1 cup yogurt.

## NUTRITION INFORMATION

| | |
|---|---|
| Calories: 380 | Cholesterol: 47 mg |
| Protein: 22 g | Sodium: 556 mg |
| Total Fat: 6 g | Fiber: 16 g |
| Saturated Fat: 1 g | Sugar: 20 g |
| Carbohydrates: 63 g | |

# CHORIZO & PINTO BEAN TACOS

**YIELD: SERVES 6**

We love soy chorizo sausage because it adds spice and texture to recipes without a processed fake meat flavor. Here, it fills out a simple bean filling for homemade tacos that can be on the table in under 30 minutes.

**12 6-inch corn tortillas**

**1 Tbs. canola oil**

**1 small red onion, divided: half of onion diced, half sliced**

**1 clove garlic, minced (1 tsp.)**

**4 oz. soy chorizo sausage**

**1 10-oz. can diced tomatoes with chiles**

**2 15-oz. cans pinto beans, rinsed and drained**

**1 small avocado, sliced**

**⅓ cup crumbled queso fresco or grated Cheddar cheese**

**¼ cup chopped cilantro**

**1.** Preheat oven to 350°F. Wrap tortillas in foil, and place in oven to warm.

**2.** Heat oil in nonstick skillet over medium-high heat. Add diced onion, and sauté 3 minutes. Add garlic, and cook 1 minute more. Crumble soy sausage into pan, and sauté 1 minute. Stir in diced tomatoes, and bring mixture to a simmer. Reduce heat to medium-low, and cook 4 to 5 minutes, or until slightly thickened. Stir in beans, and cook 2 minutes more, or until beans are warmed through.

**3.** To assemble tacos: Fill tortillas with 3 Tbs. bean mixture. Top with sliced onions, avocado, cheese, and cilantro. Serve with salsa and hot sauce, if desired.

GLUTEN FREE

30 MINUTES OR LESS

## NUTRITION INFORMATION

Calories: 366
Protein: 10 g
Total Fat: 13.5 g
Saturated Fat: 2 g
Carbohydrates: 48 g
Cholesterol: 7 mg
Sodium: 807 mg
Fiber: 9 g
Sugar: 4 g

# BLACK BEAN TOSTADAS
## WITH KIWI SALSA

YIELD: SERVES 4

½ **cup chopped white onion, plus ⅓ cup minced white onion, divided**

**1 Tbs. lime juice**

**¼ tsp. salt**

**3 medium kiwifruit, peeled and diced**

**½ cup coarsely chopped cilantro**

**1 Tbs. finely chopped jalapeño chile**

**3 dried New Mexico chiles, seeded and cut into small pieces**

**2 tsp. olive oil**

**1 15-oz. can black beans, drained, liquid reserved**

**4 tostada shells**

**1 cup plain nonfat Greek yogurt**

Marinating onions in lime juice for just 15 minutes develops the flavors of a quick-stir fruit salsa. Taste the jalapeño before you add it to the salsa; fresh chiles can vary in heat and intensity.

**1.** Toss together chopped onion, lime juice, and salt in bowl. Let stand 15 minutes, stirring occasionally. Stir in kiwifruit, cilantro, and jalapeño.

**2.** Grind dried chiles to fine particles (like sugar) in spice mill or coffee grinder; set aside.

**3.** Heat oil in nonstick skillet over medium heat. Add minced onion, cover, and cook 5 minutes, or until softened, stirring occasionally. Add beans, ½ cup reserved bean liquid, and 2½ tsp. ground chiles. Mash beans, leaving some whole for texture. Cook 5 minutes, or until mixture is thickened but moist, stirring often.

**4.** Place 1 tostada shell on each plate. Divide bean mixture among tostadas, leaving ½-inch border. Top each with ¼ cup yogurt and ¼ cup salsa; dust with ground chiles. Serve with remaining salsa.

GLUTEN-FREE

## NUTRITION INFORMATION

Calories: 241
Protein: 12 g
Total Fat: 6 g
Saturated Fat: 1 g
Carbohydrates: 37 g
Cholesterol: 0 mg
Sodium: 325 mg
Fiber: 7 g
Sugar: 13 g

# CHILAQUILES

YIELD: SERVES 6

This festive Mexican dish can be customized to suit your flavor preferences or what's on hand in your fridge. Use a mild salsa for younger palates, or experiment with a different cheese, such as mozzarella.

2 15.5-oz. cans black beans, rinsed and drained

1 cup prepared chipotle salsa

2 cloves garlic, peeled

1 tsp. dried oregano

1 Tbs. plus 1 tsp. olive oil, divided

1 cup low-sodium vegetable broth

2 cups arugula

3 Roma tomatoes, diced (1 cup)

¼ cup chopped cilantro

2 green onions, sliced (about ¼ cup)

1 Tbs. fresh lime juice

1 9-oz. bag tortilla chips

4 oz. shredded Cheddar or Monterey Jack cheese (about 2 cups)

1 avocado, diced, optional

**1.** Blend beans in food processor 1 minute, until mostly smooth. Add salsa, garlic, and oregano, and blend 1 minute.

**2.** Heat 1 tsp. oil in pot over medium-high heat. Add bean mixture and broth, and whisk until combined. Bring to a boil and simmer 5 minutes, stirring occasionally.

**3.** Combine arugula, tomatoes, cilantro, green onions, lime juice, and remaining 1 Tbs. oil in medium bowl.

**4.** Fold chips into simmering black bean mixture. Cook 3 to 5 minutes, or until chips are soft and slightly chewy.

**5.** Transfer to 2-quart casserole or deep serving dish. Sprinkle cheese on top and let stand 5 minutes. Top with arugula salad and avocado, if desired, and serve.

## NUTRITION INFORMATION

Calories: 355
Protein: 14 g
Total Fat: 12.5 g
Saturated Fat: 2.5 g
Carbohydrates: 52 g
Cholesterol: 4 mg
Sodium: 632 mg
Fiber: 10 g
Sugar: 4 g

# SWEET POTATO & BLACK BEAN ENCHILADAS

Need a dish for a potluck or holiday party? These spicy enchiladas fit the bill.

YIELD: SERVES 8 (MAKES 16 ENCHILADAS)

SAUCE

1 15-oz. can tomato sauce

1 tsp. ancho chile powder

1 tsp. chili powder

1 tsp. garlic powder

1 tsp. onion powder

1 tsp. dried oregano

½ tsp. chipotle chile powder

FILLING

1 Tbs. olive oil

1 small onion, diced (1 cup)

1½ lb. sweet potatoes, peeled and diced (3 cups)

1 15-oz. can diced tomatoes, drained

1 16-oz. jar prepared medium salsa

2 cloves garlic, minced (2 tsp.)

1 chipotle chile in adobo sauce, drained and minced

1 15-oz. can black beans, rinsed and drained

1 12-oz. round queso fresco, divided

ENCHILADAS

16 6-inch corn tortillas, warmed

2 limes, cut into wedges

1 avocado, sliced

½ cup sour cream, for garnish

Cilantro sprigs, for garnish

**1.** To make Sauce: Bring all ingredients to a simmer in saucepan over medium heat. Whisk to combine, then remove from heat. Season with salt and pepper, if desired.

**2.** To make Filling: Heat oil in separate saucepan over medium heat. Add onion, and sauté 3 to 5 minutes, or until soft. Add sweet potatoes, tomatoes, salsa, garlic, chipotle chile, and ½ cup water; bring to a boil. Reduce heat to medium-low, and simmer 30 to 40 minutes, or until sweet potatoes are soft. Mash mixture with potato masher until combined. Add black beans, and cook 5 minutes. Stir in half of queso fresco, and remove from heat.

**3.** To assemble Enchiladas: Preheat oven to 350°F. Brush 13- x 9-inch baking dish with oil. Spread ½ cup Sauce in bottom of dish. Fill tortillas with Filling. Roll, and pack close together seam-side down in baking dish. Top with remaining Sauce and queso fresco. Bake 15 minutes.

**4.** Adjust oven to broil. Broil Enchiladas 5 minutes, or until cheese is browned and bubbly. Let rest 10 minutes before serving. Garnish with lime wedges, avocado slices, sour cream, and cilantro sprigs, if using.

GLUTEN-FREE

### NUTRITION INFORMATION

Calories: 435
Protein: 13 g
Total Fat: 15 g
Saturated Fat: 5 g
Carbohydrates: 65 g
Cholesterol: 20 mg
Sodium: 963 mg
Fiber: 11 g
Sugar: 11 g

# MIXED DAL
## WITH TOMATO TARKA

Red lentils, yellow split peas, and mung beans give this traditional Indian dish a lovely golden color. To simplify the recipe, you could just make it with 1 cup of a single dried lentil or split pea. Split peas are also members of the high-protein legume family, along with beans and lentils.

⅓ cup dried red lentils

⅓ cup dried split yellow or green peas

⅓ cup dried split mung beans

3 Tbs. melted butter, ghee, or vegetable oil, divided

2 Tbs. grated fresh ginger, divided

1 tsp. ground turmeric

4 cups baby spinach leaves (4 oz.)

1 tsp. salt

2 tsp. whole cumin seeds

1 medium onion, chopped (1½ cups)

1 tsp. garam masala

⅛ tsp. cayenne pepper

3 cloves garlic, minced (1 Tbs.)

1 large tomato, diced

Cilantro leaves for garnish, optional

**1.** Rinse and drain lentils, split peas, and mung beans; place in large bowl, and cover with hot water. Soak 30 minutes. Drain.

**2.** Combine drained lentil mixture, 1 Tbs. butter, 1 Tbs. ginger, turmeric, and 6 cups water in saucepan; bring to a boil. Cover, and simmer 1 hour, or until legumes are very soft. Whisk with wire whisk to break up lentils. Add spinach and salt, cover, and simmer 10 minutes more.

**3.** Meanwhile, heat remaining 2 Tbs. butter in small skillet over medium heat. Add cumin seeds; cook 30 seconds to 1 minute, or until seeds darken. Add onion, garam masala, and cayenne, and cook 3 to 5 minutes, or until onions soften and begin to brown. Stir in garlic and remaining 1 Tbs. ginger; cook 1 minute. Add tomato, and cook 2 to 3 minutes more, or until tomato releases juices and most of liquid has evaporated.

**4.** Stir tomato mixture into lentil mixture. Season with salt and pepper, if desired; garnish with cilantro, if using.

GLUTEN-FREE

---

MAKE IT VEGAN **Use vegetable or coconut oil in place of the ghee.**

### NUTRITION INFORMATION

Calories: 306
Protein: 14 g
Total Fat: 10 g
Saturated Fat: 6 g
Carbohydrates: 42 g

Cholesterol: 14 mg
Sodium: 716 mg
Fiber: 14 g
Sugar: 6 g

# WARM SPICED LENTIL BOWL
## WITH YOGURT AND SMOKED ALMONDS

YIELD: SERVES 4

This hearty one-bowl meal comes together in under 30 minutes.

**2½ tsp. toasted sesame oil**

**2½ tsp. whole cumin seeds**

**1 medium carrot, chopped (⅓ cup)**

**1 rib celery, chopped (¼ cup)**

**1 medium leek, trimmed and chopped (white and light green parts)**

**3 cups low-sodium vegetable broth**

**1 cup brown lentils, rinsed and drained**

**3 cloves garlic, minced (1 Tbs.)**

**⅓ cup smoked almonds, coarsely chopped**

**½ cup plain nonfat Greek yogurt**

**1.** Heat oil in large saucepan over low heat. Add cumin seeds, and cook 1 minute, or until fragrant. Stir in carrot, celery, and leek. Increase heat to medium-high, and sauté 3 minutes. Stir in broth and lentils. Bring mixture to a simmer, reduce heat to low, and cook 20 minutes, or until lentils are tender. Stir in garlic, and cook 5 minutes more. Season with salt and pepper, if desired.

**2.** Ladle lentil mixture into 4 bowls, and garnish with almonds and yogurt.

GLUTEN-FREE

30 MINUTES OR LESS

### NUTRITION INFORMATION

Calories: 309
Protein: 18 g
Total Fat: 10 g
Saturated Fat: 0 g
Carbohydrates: 39 g
Cholesterol: 0 mg
Sodium: 187 mg
Fiber: 14 g
Sugar: 7 g

# MIDDLE EASTERN STUFFED CABBAGE ROLLS

YIELD: SERVES 4

Crinkly savoy cabbage leaves (which pull apart more easily than white cabbage) are stuffed with a combination of lentils, currants, and olives, then blanketed in a spicy tomato sauce. Serve over rice.

1 Tbs. olive oil

1 small onion, finely chopped (1 cup)

2 cloves garlic, minced (2 tsp.)

¾ cup dried French or green lentils

8 large savoy cabbage leaves, ribs removed

⅓ cup dried currants

½ cup pitted Kalamata olives, quartered

3 Tbs. lemon juice, divided

1 15-oz. can low-sodium tomato sauce

2 tsp. ground cumin

1½ tsp. dried marjoram

¼ tsp. ground allspice

**1.** Heat oil in saucepan over medium heat. Add onion, and cook 3 minutes. Add garlic, and cook 30 seconds. Add lentils and 4 cups water. Bring to a boil, reduce heat to medium-low, and simmer 15 minutes, or until tender. Drain.

**2.** Bring pot of water to a boil. Blanch cabbage leaves 6 minutes, or until tender. Rinse under cold water, and drain.

**3.** Mash half of lentil mixture in bowl. Stir in remaining lentils, currants, olives, and 1 Tbs. lemon juice.

**4.** Combine tomato sauce, ½ cup water, remaining 2 Tbs. lemon juice, cumin, marjoram, and allspice in bowl. Spray 8-inch square baking dish with cooking spray, then coat bottom with ½ cup sauce.

**5.** Preheat oven to 375°F. Lay 1 cabbage leaf on work surface. Spoon ⅓ cup lentil mixture in center of leaf, fold sides inward, and roll tightly. Place seam-side down in dish. Repeat with remaining leaves and filling. Pour remaining sauce over rolls; cover with foil.

**6.** Bake cabbage rolls, covered, 1 hour. Uncover, baste with sauce, bake 10 minutes more, and serve.

GLUTEN-FREE

VEGAN

## NUTRITION INFORMATION

| | |
|---|---|
| Calories: 303 | Cholesterol: 0 mg |
| Protein: 12 g | Sodium: 632 mg |
| Total Fat: 9 g | Fiber: 11 g |
| Saturated Fat: 1 g | Sugar: 18 g |
| Carbohydrates: 49 g | |

MAKE-AHEAD TIP **Refrigerate foil-covered cabbage rolls 3 days, or freeze 1 month. If frozen, thaw overnight in refrigerator before baking.**

# MORE TIKKA MASALAS

YIELD: SERVES 4

This mild veg version of an Indian restaurant favorite shows that Indian food doesn't have to be ultra-spicy to be good.

1 Tbs. vegetable oil

½ medium onion, diced

1 Tbs. garam masala

1 Tbs. tomato paste

2 tsp. grated fresh ginger

1 serrano chile, minced

2 15-oz. cans chickpeas, rinsed and drained

1 28-oz. can crushed tomatoes

½ cup low-fat Greek yogurt

¼ cup chopped cilantro

**1.** Heat oil in skillet over medium heat. Add onion, and sauté 5 minutes, or until softened.  Add garam masala, tomato paste, ginger, and  serrano chile, and season with salt, if desired.  Sauté 1 minute more.

**2.** Stir in chickpeas and tomatoes. Bring to a boil, reduce heat to medium-low, and simmer 15 minutes. Remove from heat, and stir in yogurt and cilantro.

VEGAN

GLUTEN-FREE

30 MINUTES OR LESS

## NUTRITION INFORMATION

Calories: 328
Protein: 16 g
Total Fat: 9 g
Saturated Fat: 1 g
Carbohydrates: 52 g
Cholesterol: 2 mg
Sodium: 582 mg
Fiber: 5 g
Sugar: 11 g

**More Masalas**
Once you have the basic sauce for this dish down, the possibilities are endless for easy weeknight meals. Here are a few combinations to try:

**Tofu and Spinach:** Substitute 1 lb. cubed extra-firm tofu for the chickpeas and add 2 cups baby spinach leaves.

**Red Lentils and Green Beans:** Replace the chickpeas with 1½ cups cooked red lentils and 2 cups fresh green beans.

**Okra and Paneer:** Replace the chickpeas with 1 cup frozen, thawed okra and 2 cups paneer (cheese cubes).

# CHICKPEA CROQUETTES

YIELD: SERVES 4

Whole chickpeas give these sautéed croquettes (held together with chickpea flour!) a hearty texture. Garnish with crumbled vegan feta cheese, if desired.

## TOPPING

**1 cucumber, sliced (1 cup)**

**1 cup cherry tomatoes, quartered**

**2 green onions, chopped**

**2 Tbs. lemon juice**

**1 Tbs. olive oil**

## CROQUETTES

**1 cup chickpea flour**

**2 tsp. ground cumin**

**1 tsp. chili powder**

**½ tsp. salt**

**1 15-oz. can chickpeas, rinsed and drained**

**4 green onions, chopped (½ cup)**

**½ cup diced red bell pepper**

**¼ cup chopped fresh parsley**

**2 Tbs. lemon juice**

**1 Tbs. olive oil**

**2 cloves garlic, minced (2 tsp.)**

**1.** To make Topping: Toss together cucumber, tomatoes, green onions, lemon juice, and oil in bowl. Season with salt and pepper, if desired, and set aside.

**2.** To make Croquettes: Whisk together chickpea flour, cumin, chili powder, and salt in bowl. Whisk in ¾ cup hot water. Stir in remaining ingredients, and season with salt and pepper, if desired.

**3.** Coat nonstick skillet with cooking spray; heat over medium heat. Scoop 4 ¼-cup dollops of chickpea mixture into skillet, and reduce heat to medium-low. Cook 3 to 4 minutes, or until golden. Flip with spatula, and cook 3 to 4 minutes more. Repeat with remaining chickpea mixture. Serve each Croquette topped with ¼ cup Topping.

VEGAN
GLUTEN-FREE

## NUTRITION INFORMATION

Calories: 314
Protein: 12 g
Total Fat: 11 g
Saturated Fat: 1 g
Carbohydrates: 45 g
Cholesterol: 0 mg
Sodium: 534 mg
Fiber: 9 g
Sugar: 6 g

# CHICKPEA-STUFFED ZUCCHINI

A cheesy-crunchy topping makes this easy summer dish a kid favorite. Try it with other beans or lentils as well.

**4 large zucchini, halved lengthwise**

**1 Tbs. olive oil**

**1 medium onion, chopped (1½ cups)**

**1 red bell pepper, chopped (1 cup)**

**1 cup cooked chickpeas**

**3 tomatoes, chopped (1 cup)**

**2 tsp. dried thyme**

**1 cup shredded reduced-fat Cheddar cheese**

**4 oz. low-fat plain yogurt**

**½ tsp. paprika**

**½ cup crushed potato chips**

**1.** Preheat oven to 400°F. Scoop out seeds and flesh from zucchini to create ¼-inch-thick shell. Chop flesh, and set aside. Place zucchini shells in baking dish coated with cooking spray.

**2.** Heat oil in large skillet over medium heat. Add onion, bell pepper, chickpeas, tomatoes, thyme, and chopped zucchini, and sauté 5 minutes, or until tender.

**3.** Fill each zucchini shell with ½ cup chickpea mixture. Stir together cheese, yogurt, and paprika in small bowl. Spoon 2 Tbs. cheese mixture atop stuffing in each zucchini, then sprinkle each with 1 Tbs. crushed potato chips. Bake 20 minutes, or until stuffed zucchini are heated through and crispy on top.

GLUTEN-FREE

30 MINUTES OR LESS

## NUTRITION INFORMATION

Calories: 341
Protein: 19 g
Total Fat: 15 g
Saturated Fat: 5 g
Carbohydrates: 39 g
Cholesterol: 17 mg
Sodium: 370 mg
Fiber: 9 g
Sugar: 16 g

# WHOLE GRAINS

When the Harvard School of Public Health specifies whole grains on its Healthy Eating Plate and gives them the same space and attention as protein, then you know the tasty seeds and kernels are more than just another type of carbohydrate. Regularly consuming grains that are minimally processed and left intact (without the bran or germ removed) has been linked to reduced risk of heart disease, type 2 diabetes, obesity, strokes, and certain cancers.

Another major advantage to opting for whole grains is their higher protein levels. Take quinoa, which has twice as much protein (4 grams per ½-cup serving) as white rice. That extra protein, along with the increased amounts of fiber and nutrients in whole grains, helps balance out blood sugar levels and keeps you feeling fuller longer. That extra protein can also contribute to increased energy levels throughout the day.

The only downside to whole grains is how, well, wholesome their name sounds. Like eating them is some sort of obligation. Yes, they're really good for you, but tender quinoa, chewy barley, creamy millet, and nutty brown rice, even when they're just steamed and served as a side dish, can be some of the purest meal pleasures.

## WHOLE GRAINS GUIDE

**ANCIENT WHEAT GRAINS** The whole-grain wheat products on the market today can trace their origins back thousands of years. In the kitchen, the tender-chewy-nutty kernels have one major advantage: It's hard to mess them up or ruin their texture by overcooking. Here's a quick rundown of the most common varieties you can find. They are also interchangeable in recipes (though cooking times may vary), which means you can easily substitute what you have on hand in a recipe.

**HULLED BARLEY** The homey cereal grain best known for soups and stews can be found whole, cracked, or ground into barley grits. Pearled barley is a faster, less nutritious option than hulled barley because its bran coating has been removed. Protein: 3 g/½ cup cooked barley

**WHEAT BERRIES** These are exactly what they sound like—whole wheat kernels that can be cooked and eaten like barley or other grains. Protein: 5 g/½ cup cooked wheat berries

**FARRO** The warrior whole grain! Farro reputedly was the chief sustenance of the Roman legions and may be an original strain of every subsequent wheat variety ever grown. Protein: 4 g/½ cup cooked farro

**SPELT** The European wheat variety has been cultivated for over 7,000 years. Some gluten-sensitive people find they can eat spelt and breads made with spelt flour. Protein: 5 g/½ cup cooked spelt

**FREEKEH** Freekeh (pronounced *free-kuh*) is the name for green wheat grains that have been roasted to give them a chewy texture and rich, nutty flavor. Protein: 3 g/½ cup cooked freekeh

**KAMUT** Kamut is the trademarked name for Khorasan wheat, an ancient variety that hails from Persia. Protein: 5 g/½ cup cooked Kamut

# HOW TO COOK WHOLE GRAINS

IN ADDITION TO THE PACKAGE DIRECTIONS, HERE ARE THREE MORE WAYS TO COOK WHOLE GRAINS.

### PILAF-STYLE

This method offers several ways of adding flavor to whole grains. First, by sautéing the grains in fat to toast them. Second, by adding aromatics (onion, garlic, herbs, spices) to the sautéing process. And finally, by cooking the grains in just enough of a flavorful liquid like broth, fruit or vegetable juice, etc., for the grains to absorb as they plump and get tender.

### PASTA-STYLE

For fluffy grains that work well in cold dishes and salads, cook them, uncovered, in a large pot of boiling salted water. Drain, then return to pot so that any excess moisture evaporates.

### PRESSURE COOKER

This method can be used with hearty, longer-cooking grains. Add 4 cups water and 1 to 2 Tbs. oil (2 Tbs. when cooking barley and oats) to the pressure cooker for every 1 cup uncooked grains. Lock pressure cooker lid, turn heat to high, and bring pressure cooker up to high pressure. Reduce heat just enough to maintain pressure at high, and cook 15 minutes for brown rice, 18 minutes for barley, 25 minutes for wild rice, and 35 minutes for kamut, triticale, oats, sorghum, or wheat berries.

## GLUTEN-FREE WHOLE GRAINS

Lucky us! Thanks to growing interest in gluten-free whole grains, there are more varieties available to home cooks than ever. And you don't need to be watching your gluten consumption to enjoy them.

**OATS**  This versatile comfort food is packed with protein, B vitamins, calcium, iron, and beta-glucan, an especially heart-healthful form of fiber that has been shown to lower LDL ("bad") cholesterol. Protein: 4 g/½-cup serving

**BUCKWHEAT**  Related to rhubarb, buckwheat is a complete protein grain that is available raw or roasted (kasha). Protein: 3 g/½-cup serving

**QUINOA**  Quinoa is one of two whole grains (along with buckwheat) that contain all eight amino acids that make up a "complete" protein. Protein: 4 g/½-cup cooked quinoa

**SORGHUM**  The bead-like grains are sold unhulled, making them a nutrient-packed whole grain to add to recipes. Protein: 4 g/½-cup cooked sorghum

**MILLET**  A staple cereal in Africa, Asia, and India, millet can be cooked 15 minutes (for chewy, al dente grains) or 30 minutes (for a creamy mush). Protein: 3 g/½-cup cooked millet

**AMARANTH**  Cultivated in Asia, Africa, and South America for centuries, amaranth is high in iron, fiber, and calcium, as well as many other nutrients. Protein: 5 g/½-cup cooked amaranth

**TEFF**  The minuscule grain is a nutritional giant that's high in protein, fiber, and minerals (especially iron) and boasts 17 times more calcium than barley or wheat. Protein: 5 g/½-cup cooked teff

# PERUVIAN BAKED QUINOA & CHEESE

Think of this recipe as a protein-packed, gluten-free alternative to mac 'n' cheese.

2 tsp. olive oil

1 medium leek, white and pale green parts halved and sliced (1 cup)

½ cup diced red bell pepper

½ cup diced green bell pepper

1½ cups quinoa, rinsed and drained

2 cloves garlic, minced (2 tsp.)

2 large eggs

1 cup nonfat milk

1½ cups grated Cheddar cheese (4 oz.), plus more for sprinkling, optional

**1.** Heat oil in medium saucepan over medium heat. Add leek and bell peppers; cover, and cook 5 minutes, or until tender. Stir in quinoa and garlic, and cook, uncovered, 3 to 4 minutes, or until quinoa grains turn opaque.

**2.** Add 3 cups water, and season with salt. Cover, reduce heat to medium-low, and simmer 3 to 4 minutes more, or until most liquid has been absorbed. Remove from heat, and let stand 5 minutes.

**3.** Preheat oven to 350°F. Coat 13- x 9-inch baking dish with cooking spray. Whisk together eggs and milk in large bowl. Fold in quinoa mixture and cheese. Transfer to prepared baking dish, and bake 30 to 35 minutes, or until browned around the edges and on top.

GLUTEN-FREE

## NUTRITION INFORMATION

Calories: 241
Protein: 12 g
Total Fat: 10 g
Saturated Fat: 4.5 g
Carbohydrates: 27 g
Cholesterol: 72 mg
Sodium: 295 mg
Fiber: 2 g
Sugar: 3 g

# OAT-LOVERS' GLOSSARY

### OAT GROATS
Whole oats that have been toasted, hulled, and cleaned. In addition to being cooked as a hot cereal, groats can be used to make a chewy grain dish similar in texture to spelt or farro.

### STEEL CUT/PINHEAD/
### SCOTTISH OATS
Toasted oat groats that have been broken into three to four pieces.

### ROLLED/OLD-FASHIONED
Oat groats that are steamed and rolled flat for quicker cooking. Rolled oats or quick-cooking oats workbest in baked goods. For oatmeal that's both creamy and chewy, look for thick-cut rolled oats.

### QUICK-COOKING OATS
Oat groats that have been broken into pieces then rolled flat so that they will cook in 4 to 5 minutes. The tender choice for baked goods.

### INSTANT OATS
Thin, precooked rolled oats that need only be rehydrated with a hot liquid.

# SAVORY OATS WITH BRIE
## & CHERRY TOMATOES

YIELD: SERVES 4

**2 tsp. olive oil or butter**

**1 shallot, chopped**

**2 cups cherry tomatoes, halved**

**½ tsp. salt, optional**

**2 cups old-fashioned rolled oats**

**1 clove garlic, minced (1 tsp.)**

**1½ oz. Brie, cut into small cubes**

**¼ cup fresh basil leaves, torn**

**1 Tbs. toasted pine nuts**

Oats aren't just for breakfast! Give them the savory treatment and they make a luscious, creamy grain bowl. Sub any cheese for the Brie, any chopped nuts for the pine nuts, and any fresh herb for the basil in this one-bowl dinner.

**1.** Heat oil in skillet over medium-high heat. Add shallot, tomatoes, and salt (if using). Cook 5 minutes, or until shallot has softened and tomatoes start releasing their juices. Add oats; cook 1 minute more.

**2.** Stir in garlic and 4 cups water, and bring to a boil. Reduce heat to medium-low, and simmer, uncovered, 10 minutes. Remove from heat, and dot with Brie. Sprinkle with basil and pine nuts.

GLUTEN-FREE

30 MINUTES OR LESS

MAKE IT VEGAN **Substitute diced avocado or cubed, baked tofu for the cheese.**

## NUTRITION INFORMATION

Calories: 252
Protein: 11 g
Total Fat: 9 g
Saturated Fat: 2 g
Carbohydrates: 32 g
Cholesterol: 11 mg
Sodium: 363 mg
Fiber: 5 g
Sugar: 4 g

# MILLET AND CARAMELIZED BRUSSELS SPROUTS
## WITH WALNUTS AND CRANBERRIES

In this recipe, the millet and the Brussels sprouts cook in about the same amount of time. Then all you need is a quick toss with the nuts, dried fruit, and dressing to finish the dish. The medley is just as good cold the next day, too!

**YIELD: SERVES 4**

**1¼ lb. Brussels sprouts, trimmed and quartered lengthwise**

**5 Tbs. canola or grapeseed oil, divided**

**¾ cup millet**

**⅔ cup toasted chopped walnuts**

**⅔ cup chopped dried cranberries**

**3 Tbs. chopped fresh parsley**

**2 Tbs. balsamic vinegar**

**1 Tbs. pure maple syrup**

**1 tsp. lemon juice**

**½ tsp. grated lemon zest**

**1.** Preheat oven to 475°F. Toss Brussels sprouts with 2 Tbs. oil in large bowl, and season with salt, if desired. Arrange sprouts in single layer in 13- x 9-inch baking dish. Roast 20 to 24 minutes, or until brown and tender, stirring once. Cool 5 minutes.

**2.** Meanwhile, heat large saucepan over medium heat. Add millet, and cook 6 to 8 minutes, or until golden. Add 2 cups water, and bring to a boil. Reduce heat to medium-low, cover, and simmer 20 minutes, or until liquid is absorbed. Transfer millet to large bowl. Cool 5 minutes. Fold Brussels sprouts, walnuts, cranberries, and parsley into millet.

**3.** Whisk together remaining 3 Tbs. oil, vinegar, syrup, lemon juice, and lemon zest in bowl. Stir into millet mixture, and season with salt, if desired.

VEGAN

GLUTEN-FREE

30 MINUTES OR LESS

## NUTRITION INFORMATION

Calories: 375
Protein: 8 g
Total Fat: 22 g
Saturated Fat: 2 g
Carbohydrates: 42 g

Cholesterol: 0 mg
Sodium: 26 mg
Fiber: 7 g
Sugar: 14 g

# MILLET

Of all the so-called pseudograins (gluten-free items like quinoa, buckwheat, amaranth, and teff are actually seeds), millet might just be the most versatile. A staple cereal in Africa, Asia, and India, nutty-tasting hulled millet can be cooked into pilafs, simmered longer for a smooth breakfast cereal, stirred raw into baked goods for extra crunch, sprouted for salads, ground into flour, and even popped like popcorn.

# MIXED-GRAIN TABBOULEH
## WITH ROASTED EGGPLANT, CHICKPEAS & MINT

Combining quinoa with bulgur improves the texture and nutritional profile of this cold grain salad. Roasted eggplant and chickpeas round out the dish, making it ideal for a take-along lunch or a light summer supper.

**3 medium eggplants, cut into ½-inch cubes (8 cups)**

**¾ tsp. salt, divided**

**¾ tsp. ground black pepper, divided**

**3½ Tbs. olive oil, divided**

**¼ cup quick-cooking bulgur**

**⅔ cup quinoa, rinsed and drained**

**⅔ cup chopped fresh mint, plus sprigs for garnish**

**⅓ cup chopped cilantro**

**1 cup small grape tomatoes, halved**

**2 Tbs. lemon juice**

**1 cup cooked chickpeas**

**½ cup finely chopped red onion**

**1.** Preheat oven to 450°F. Coat large rimmed baking sheet with cooking spray. Spread eggplant cubes in single layer on baking sheet, spray lightly with cooking spray, and sprinkle with ¼ tsp. each salt and pepper. Drizzle with 1½ Tbs. oil; toss to coat. Roast eggplant 20 minutes. Turn; stir, then roast 10 minutes more, or until tender and browned. Cool on baking sheet.

**2.** Bring large pot of salted water to a boil. Add bulgur, and boil 4 minutes. Mix in quinoa, and boil 12 minutes, or until both grains are tender but still have some texture. Drain. Transfer to large bowl, and cool, fluffing with fork. Mix chopped mint and cilantro into grains, then mix in cooled eggplant and tomatoes.

**3.** Whisk together lemon juice, remaining 2 Tbs. oil, ½ tsp. salt, and ½ tsp. pepper in medium bowl. Add chickpeas and red onion; marinate 15 minutes, then fold chickpea mixture into grains. Garnish with mint sprigs.

VEGAN

---

**MAKE IT GLUTEN-FREE** Substitute cooked millet for the bulgur.

## NUTRITION INFORMATION

Calories: 395
Protein: 12 g
Total Fat: 16 g
Saturated Fat: 2 g
Carbohydrates: 56 g

Cholesterol: 0 mg
Sodium: 694 mg
Fiber: 12 g
Sugar: 10 g

# SORGHUM & SUN-DRIED TOMATO PESTO TABBOULEH

YIELD: SERVES 6

Tender-chewy, round sorghum grains can stand in for small pasta shapes and Israeli couscous. Here, it's used in a simple Middle Eastern grain salad.

½ cup sorghum, rinsed and drained

½ cup prepared sun-dried tomato pesto

1 English cucumber, peeled and diced (2 cups)

2 cups halved grape or cherry tomatoes

1 cup chopped fresh basil, parsley, or cilantro

8 green onions, thinly sliced (1 cup)

2 Tbs. lemon juice

1. Combine sorghum and 1 cup water in medium saucepan; bring water to a boil. Cover pan, reduce heat to medium-low, and simmer 1 hour, or until grains are tender. Drain, and transfer to bowl.

2. Stir pesto into hot sorghum, then allow mixture to cool. Once sorghum is cool, stir in remaining ingredients, and season with salt and pepper, if desired. Let stand 1 hour or refrigerate overnight for best flavor.

GLUTEN-FREE

MAKE IT VEGAN  **Choose a vegan sun-dried tomato pesto for the dressing.**

## NUTRITION INFORMATION

Calories: 175
Protein: 4 g
Total Fat: 10 g
Saturated Fat: 1 g
Carbohydrates: 20 g
Cholesterol: 0 mg
Sodium: 23 mg
Fiber: 3 g
Sugar: 6 g

# SORGHUM

Would you believe the United States is the number-one producer of sorghum in the world—and yet few people have ever tasted it? The gluten-free movement has brought this tasty grain into the spotlight and onto supermarket shelves. Elsewhere in the world, sorghum is used to make everything from couscous and bread to alcoholic beverages.

# QUINOA

At this point, quinoa needs almost no introduction. Gluten-free and high in protein and fiber, the South American staple is now used in prepared pastas, snack foods, and breakfast cereals; there's even quinoa shampoo. Quinoa has had its own United Nations–designated International Year (2013). But the real appeal of quinoa remains its taste and its versatility. Red, white, and black varieties of quinoa are interchangeable in recipes—most chefs choose the color that goes best with other ingredients.

# QUINOA–SWEET POTATO BOWL
## WITH CHIMICHURRI

SWEET POTATOES
AND QUINOA

**2 large sweet
potatoes, skin-on,
finely diced
(1½–2 lb.)**

**1 tsp. olive oil**

**1 cup red quinoa,
rinsed and drained**

**2 small, ripe yet firm
avocados, peeled
and sliced, optional**

CHIMICHURRI

**¼ cup olive oil**

**3 cups loosely
packed Italian
parsley leaves,
roughly chopped**

**3 Tbs. lemon juice**

**2 cloves garlic,
minced (2 tsp.)**

**½ tsp. sweet paprika**

**¼ tsp. red pepper
flakes**

Chimichurri has its roots in Argentina, where it is usually slathered over grilled meat. Here, it lends spicy, garlicky goodness to a hearty bowl of sweet potatoes and quinoa. For extra protein and fiber, you could also add ¼ cup cooked beans.

**1.** To make Sweet Potatoes and Quinoa: Preheat oven to 425°F. Toss sweet potatoes with oil on large baking sheet, and spread in single layer. Season with salt and pepper, if desired, and roast 15 to 20 minutes, or until soft, stirring halfway through.

**2.** Meanwhile, bring quinoa and 2 cups water to a boil in small saucepan. Reduce heat to medium-low, cover, and cook 15 minutes, or until tender. Season with salt, if desired.

**3.** To make Chimichurri: Warm oil in small saucepan over medium heat. Blend parsley, lemon juice, garlic, paprika, and red pepper flakes in food processor until coarsely chopped. Pour in warm oil, and pulse quickly until blended.

**4.** Divide sweet potatoes and quinoa among 4 bowls. Top each serving with 3 Tbs. Chimichurri, and garnish with sliced avocado, if using. Drizzle with extra Chimichurri, if desired.

VEGAN

GLUTEN-FREE

## NUTRITION INFORMATION

| | |
|---|---|
| Calories: 443 | Cholesterol: 0 mg |
| Protein: 10 g | Sodium: 131 mg |
| Total Fat: 14 g | Fiber: 10 g |
| Saturated Fat: 2 g | Sugar: 9 g |
| Carbohydrates: 71 g | |

# ROASTED OYSTER MUSHROOM BOWLS
## WITH MILLET & LENTILS

YIELD: SERVES 4

Soft millet, chewy lentils, and crispy-edged roasted oyster mushrooms are tossed with a thyme-laced vinaigrette for a one-bowl meal that's elegant enough for company. If you can't find tamari-flavored roasted pumpkin seeds, use roasted and salted pumpkin seeds.

### MILLET AND MUSHROOMS

**1 cup uncooked millet**

**1¼ lb. oyster mushrooms, torn into bite-size pieces (5½ cups)**

**1 medium red onion, sliced (1½ cups)**

**4 tsp. olive oil**

**2 Tbs. fresh thyme**

**1 15-oz. can lentils, rinsed and drained**

**½ cup tamari-flavored roasted pumpkin seeds, optional**

### DRESSING

**2 Tbs. olive oil**

**1 Tbs. apple cider vinegar**

**1 Tbs. pure maple syrup**

**1 Tbs. low-sodium soy sauce**

**1 Tbs. fresh thyme, or 1 tsp. dried thyme**

**1 clove garlic, minced (1 tsp.)**

**½ tsp. Dijon mustard**

**1.** Preheat oven to 425°F. Coat large baking sheet with cooking spray.

**2.** To make Millet and Mushrooms salad: Bring 2½ cups water to a boil in medium saucepan. Add millet; reduce heat to medium-low. Cover, and simmer 15 to 20 minutes, or until millet has softened and absorbed all liquid. Lightly fluff with fork.

**3.** Meanwhile, spread mushrooms and onion on prepared baking sheet. Drizzle with oil, and sprinkle with thyme. Season with salt and pepper, if desired, and toss to coat. Roast 20 minutes, or until mushrooms are browned.

**4.** To make Dressing: Whisk together all ingredients in small bowl.

**5.** Stir lentils and half of Dressing into millet. Divide among bowls, top with roasted mushrooms and onion, and drizzle with remaining Dressing. Sprinkle with pumpkin seeds, if using.

VEGAN

30 MINUTES OR LESS

### NUTRITION INFORMATION

Calories: 456
Protein: 18 g
Total Fat: 14 g
Saturated Fat: 2 g
Carbohydrates: 67 g

Cholesterol: 0 mg
Sodium: 264 mg
Fiber: 16 g
Sugar: 8 g

# AMARANTH, ROASTED TOMATO & EGGPLANT STACKS
## WITH PESTO

Pesto-laced amaranth soaks up all the juices of roasted eggplant and tomato slices. The directions here are for individual servings, but you could also make the recipe in a baking dish for a family-style entrée.

**YIELD: SERVES 4**

3½ Tbs. olive oil, divided

6 large plum tomatoes

¾ tsp. sugar

¾ tsp. salt

½ tsp. balsamic vinegar

½ large globe eggplant (10 oz.)

½ cup amaranth

¼ cup plus 2 tsp. prepared basil pesto, divided

2 mozzarella balls, each cut into 6 slices

**1.** Preheat oven to 450°F. Line baking sheet with parchment paper. Halve tomatoes lengthwise and remove seeds and ribs but not stems. Season cavity of each tomato half with pinch of sugar, pinch of salt, and 3 drops balsamic vinegar. Drizzle ½ tsp. olive oil over each tomato half.

**2.** Slice eggplant into 12 slices. Brush each slice on both sides with oil, place on baking sheet with tomato halves, and season with salt, if desired. Roast 15 minutes. Flip eggplant slices, and roast 15 minutes more, or until eggplant is browned and tender and tomatoes are wrinkled and lightly browned. Cool veggies on pan 10 minutes. Reduce oven temperature to 350°F.

**3.** Bring 1 cup water to a boil in saucepan; stir in amaranth. Reduce heat to medium-low, cover, and cook 20 minutes, or until water is absorbed. Cool 5 minutes, stirring once or twice. Transfer to bowl, and stir in ¼ cup pesto.

**4.** Line baking sheet with parchment, and brush with oil. Arrange tomato halves on parchment. Spoon 1 Tbs. amaranth mixture into each tomato, top with 1 slice eggplant, 1 slice mozzarella, and dab of remaining pesto. (You may have extra amaranth mixture.) Bake 6 to 8 minutes, or until warmed through.

`GLUTEN-FREE`

---

MAKE IT VEGAN **Substitute vegan cheese or cashew cheese (p. 343) for the mozzarella.**

### NUTRITION INFORMATION
Calories: 357
Protein: 12 g
Total Fat: 24 g
Saturated Fat: 7 g
Carbohydrates: 25 g
Cholesterol: 28 mg
Sodium: 577 mg
Fiber: 7 g
Sugar: 7 g

# AMARANTH

"Pigweed" may not seem all that appetizing, but call the grain-like herb by its other name—amaranth—and you've got a protein-packed winner. Amaranth has been cultivated in Asia, Africa, and South America for centuries, but the leaves, seeds, and flour have only recently made their way into North American recipes. Amaranth is high in iron, fiber, and calcium, as well as many other nutrients.

# GREENS & QUINOA PIE

Spring greens are wilted then mixed with quinoa and cheese for a golden, crustless, gluten-free pie.

YIELD: SERVES 6

½ cup quinoa, rinsed and drained

1 large bunch chicory (1 to 1¼ lb.), cut into bite-sized pieces (bottom 1½ inches of hard stems removed)

1 head romaine lettuce, shredded

3 Tbs. olive oil, divided

2 medium onions, thinly sliced (2 cups)

2 green onions, thinly sliced (¼ cup)

¼ cup chopped fresh dill

¼ cup crumbled feta cheese, preferably Greek (1 oz.)

¼ cup grated aged goat cheese or Swiss cheese (1 oz.)

3 eggs, lightly beaten

**1.** Place quinoa in small saucepan, and toast over medium heat 2 to 3 minutes, or until almost dry. Add 1 cup water, and season with salt, if desired. Cover, and bring to a boil. Reduce heat to medium-low, and simmer, covered, 15 minutes. Remove from heat, and transfer to large bowl.

**2.** Heat large pot over medium heat. Add chicory, and cook 3 to 5 minutes, or until wilted, stirring frequently or tossing with tongs. Add romaine, and wilt 1 to 2 minutes more. Transfer greens to strainer, and squeeze out excess moisture. Transfer to cutting board, and chop into small pieces. Stir greens into quinoa.

**3.** Preheat oven to 350°F. Heat 1 Tbs. oil in skillet over medium-high heat. Add onions, and sauté 10 minutes, or until browned. Add cooked onions, green onions, dill, feta cheese, and goat cheese to quinoa mixture. Stir in eggs; season with salt and pepper, if desired.

**4.** Pour 1 Tbs. oil into 9-inch pie pan, and place in oven. Heat 5 minutes, or until oil is hot. Swirl oil to coat bottom of pan, then spread quinoa mixture in pan with spatula. Bake 20 minutes. Drizzle pie with remaining 1 Tbs. oil, and bake 20 to 30 minutes more, or until golden brown.

GLUTEN FREE

## NUTRITION INFORMATION

Calories: 233
Protein: 10 g
Total Fat: 13 g
Saturated Fat: 4 g
Carbohydrates: 20 g
Cholesterol: 115 mg
Sodium: 149 mg
Fiber: 7 g
Sugar: 4 g

# MILLET FRITTERS
## WITH FETA, SPINACH & GOLDEN RAISINS

These skillet-browned cakes have a Greek feel to them with the sage, spinach, and golden raisins. Serve with a spicy prepared tomato sauce or dollops of olive tapenade. The recipe will work with other cooked whole grains as well.

YIELD: SERVES 6

**2 cups cooked millet**

**1 medium onion, chopped (1½ cups)**

**3 large eggs, lightly beaten**

**2 cloves garlic, minced (2 tsp.)**

**1 tsp. finely chopped fresh sage, or ½ tsp. dried sage**

**½ tsp. kosher salt**

**2 cups finely chopped fresh spinach**

**½ cup breadcrumbs, plus more if needed**

**⅓ cup feta cheese**

**½ cup golden raisins**

**2 Tbs. olive oil**

**1.** Stir together millet, onion, eggs, garlic, sage, and salt in medium bowl. Stir in spinach, breadcrumbs, feta, and raisins; let stand 5 minutes. If fritters still feel wet, add more breadcrumbs. You should be able to pinch together mixture and have it stick together without oozing. Shape into 12 ½-cup fritters.

**2.** Heat oil in large skillet over medium heat. Add 6 fritters, making sure not to overcrowd pan; cover; and cook 5 to 10 minutes, or until bottoms of fritters are browned. Flip, and cook 5 minutes more, or until browned on second side. Repeat with remaining fritters.

30 MINUTES OR LESS

MAKE IT GLUTEN-FREE **Use gluten-free breadcrumbs.**

NUTRITION
INFORMATION

Calories: 253
Protein: 8 g
Total Fat: 10 g
Saturated Fat: 3 g
Carbohydrates: 33 g
Cholesterol: 106 mg
Sodium: 317 mg
Fiber: 3 g
Sugar: 10 g

# STUFFED EGGPLANT
## WITH LENTILS & MILLET

**YIELD: SERVES 4**

Whole grains make great fillings for vegetables like these hearty stuffed eggplant halves. Millet freezes well, too, so you might want to double or triple the recipe and freeze the extras for fast, filling weeknight meals.

### EGGPLANT

**2 eggplants, halved lengthwise**

**2 Tbs. plus 1 tsp. olive oil, divided, plus more to coat pan**

**1 small onion, chopped (1 cup)**

**1½ cups chopped button mushrooms**

**½ cup millet**

**⅓ cup green lentils**

**3 Tbs. toasted pine nuts**

**½ tsp. ground allspice**

**pinch of cayenne pepper**

**2½ Tbs. chopped fresh mint**

### TOMATO SAUCE

**1 Tbs. olive oil**

**2 cloves garlic, minced (2 tsp.)**

**2 tsp. tomato paste**

**3 medium tomatoes, peeled, seeded, and chopped (1½ cups)**

**1.** To make Eggplant: Preheat oven to 450°F. Lightly score cut sides of each eggplant half all around to within ¼ inch of edges. Sprinkle with salt, if desired.

**2.** Lightly oil roasting pan, and heat in oven 2 minutes. Place eggplant halves cut-side down in hot roasting pan, and bake 10 minutes. Flip. Spread 1 tsp. oil on each eggplant half. Bake 15 minutes, or until flesh is just tender. Cool 10 minutes.

**3.** Heat remaining 1 Tbs. oil in saucepan over medium heat. Add onion, and sauté 7 minutes, or until beginning to brown. Remove ¼ cup onion, and set aside. Add mushrooms to pan, increase heat to medium-high, and sauté 3 minutes, or until tender. Transfer mushrooms to bowl.

**4.** Reduce heat to medium, return ¼ cup onion to pan; add millet, and sauté 2 minutes. Add lentils and 2 cups water, cover, and bring to a boil. Reduce heat to medium-low, and simmer, covered, 20 minutes, or until lentils are tender. Remove from heat; let stand, covered, 10 minutes. Transfer to bowl with mushroom mixture.

**5.** To make Tomato Sauce: Heat oil in saucepan over medium-low heat. Add garlic, and cook 30 seconds. Stir in tomato paste. Add tomatoes, increase heat to medium-high, and cook 2 minutes. Add ½ cup water, and bring to a boil. Reduce heat to medium, and simmer, partially covered, 10 minutes, or until sauce is slightly thickened.

**6.** Reduce oven temperature to 400°F. Scoop out eggplant flesh, leaving ¼-inch-thick edges for shells. Chop eggplant flesh, and add to mushroom-millet mixture. Add pine nuts, and stir in allspice and Aleppo pepper. Spoon 1 cup filling into each eggplant shell, top each with 2 Tbs. Tomato Sauce, and bake 15 minutes. Serve with remaining Tomato Sauce, and garnish with mint.

VEGAN

> ### NUTRITION INFORMATION
> Calories: 371
> Protein: 11 g
> Total Fat: 18 g
> Saturated Fat: 2 g
> Carbohydrates: 47 g
> Cholesterol: 0 mg
> Sodium: 36 mg
> Fiber: 13 g
> Sugar: 9 g

# WHITE BEAN, BULGUR & NECTARINE SALAD

YIELD: SERVES 4

½ cup bulgur wheat

5 nectarines, pitted, cut into wedges, and thinly sliced

2 cups torn fresh basil leaves

1 cup cooked cannellini or navy beans

¾ cup finely diced red onion

3 Tbs. lemon juice

2 Tbs. olive oil

1 clove garlic, minced (1 tsp.), optional

Tiny whole grains such as bulgur, quinoa, and millet pair well with fresh fruit in salads because they soak up all the sweet juices. Cannellini beans add a creamy texture and make the salad filling enough to be served as a main course.

**1.** Cook bulgur according to package directions. Drain, cool, and transfer to large bowl.

**2.** Stir nectarines, basil, beans, onion, lemon juice, oil, and garlic (if using) into bulgur. Season with salt and pepper, if desired. Chill 1 to 4 hours before serving.

## NUTRITION INFORMATION

Calories: 276
Protein: 9 g
Total Fat: 8 g
Saturated Fat: 1 g
Carbohydrates: 47 g
Cholesterol: 0 mg
Sodium: 114 mg
Fiber: 9 g
Sugar: 16 g

# BULGUR

Most often used to make tabbouleh, bulgur is a form of whole wheat that has been precooked, dried, and ground.

# WARM FARRO PILAF
## WITH DRIED CRANBERRIES

This recipe calls for pearled farro, which cooks much faster than whole regular farro, and it doesn't require soaking before it is prepared.

**FARRO**

**1 Tbs. olive oil**

**1 medium carrot, cut in half**

**1 celery rib, cut in half**

**½ small onion**

**1¼ cups pearled farro**

**4 cups no-chicken broth or water**

**PILAF**

**2 Tbs. olive oil**

**½ medium onion, diced (⅔ cup)**

**½ lb. kale, center stem removed, chopped (4 packed cups)**

**2 cloves garlic, minced (2 tsp.)**

**½ tsp. Aleppo pepper or ¼ tsp. red pepper flakes**

**½ cup dried cranberries**

**⅓ cup toasted pine nuts**

**1.** To make Farro: Heat oil in saucepan over medium-high heat. Add carrot, celery, and onion. Cook 3 to 5 minutes, or until vegetables start to brown. Add farro, and stir to coat grains with oil. Pour in broth, and bring mixture to a simmer. Reduce heat to low, and cover. Cook 20 minutes, or until just tender; drain. Discard carrot, celery, and onion. Cool Farro.

**2.** To make Pilaf: Heat oil in large skillet over medium-high heat. Sauté diced onion 5 to 7 minutes. Add kale, and cook 5 to 7 minutes, or until just wilted. Reduce heat to medium, and stir in garlic and Aleppo pepper. Cook 1 minute, then add Farro, and sauté 3 to 5 minutes, or until warmed through. Remove from heat, and stir in dried cranberries and pine nuts. Season with salt and pepper, if desired. Serve warm.

VEGAN

## NUTRITION INFORMATION

Calories: 329
Protein: 10 g
Total Fat: 13 g
Saturated Fat: 1 g
Carbohydrates: 49 g
Cholesterol: 0 mg
Sodium: 370 mg
Fiber: 6 g
Sugar: 10 g

# RICE & BARLEY
## WITH GINGERED ADZUKI BEANS

**YIELD: SERVES 4**

⅓ **cup short-grain brown rice, rinsed**

⅓ **cup hulled barley, rinsed**

¾ **tsp. salt**

**2 Tbs. minced fresh ginger**

**1 Tbs. dark sesame oil**

**1 15-oz. can adzuki beans, drained and rinsed**

**2 Tbs. mirin (sweet rice wine)**

**1 tsp. umeboshi vinegar**

¼ **cup thinly sliced green onions (white and light green parts)**

The Japanese have long enjoyed rice with barley. The combination is a common accompaniment in bento boxes (shown, right) and makes a delicious side dish or base for a one-bowl meal.

**1.** Combine rice, barley, and 3 cups water in medium saucepan. Bring to a boil, and add ¼ tsp. salt. Reduce heat, and simmer, uncovered, about 30 minutes, or until water reaches level of grains. Reduce heat to low, cover, and cook 5 minutes more, or until grains are dry. (Do not disturb steam holes that have formed.) Remove from heat, and let stand 5 minutes.

**2.** Meanwhile, heat ginger and sesame oil in medium skillet over medium heat until ginger begins to sizzle, about 3 minutes. Add beans, mirin, vinegar, and remaining ½ tsp. salt. Cook over medium-high heat, stirring often, about 3 minutes, or until liquid evaporates.

**3.** Stir beans into cooked rice and barley. Taste, and add more salt if desired. Sprinkle with chopped green onions.

### NUTRITION INFORMATION

Calories: 296
Protein: 11 g
Total Fat: 4 g
Saturated Fat: 0 g
Carbohydrates: 52 g
Cholesterol: 0 mg
Sodium: 686 mg
Fiber: 11 g
Sugar: 3 g

# RICE GUIDE

RICE COMES IN THREE DIFFERENT SIZES OR "GRAINS."

### LONG-GRAIN
Cooks up light and fluffy with distinct grains. Best In: Pilafs, fried rice, Indian recipes, steamed side dishes

### MEDIUM-GRAIN
Shorter and softer than long-grain; sticky when cool. Best In: Rice and beans, casseroles, and Mediterranean dishes

### SHORT-GRAIN
Soft, creamy, and sticky when cooked (chopstick friendly!). Best In: Rice pudding, risotto, sushi, and stir-fry sides

# TOFU, VEGGIE BURGERS & MEAT SUBSTITUTES

Think of tofu, tempeh, seitan, and other meat substitutes as neutral-tasting blank canvasses on which you can splash your favorite flavors. Mexican, Asian, Indian, Italian—you name it, the plant-based protein powerhouses take to it—even burgers can be given added flair when they're made with non-meat options.

This chapter contains recipes that will convert even the most reluctant meat substitute cook into a fan. They range in difficulty from super-simple to elegantly sophisticated so you have something to try—or turn to—for every occasion.

# THAI LEMONGRASS TOFU SKEWERS

YIELD: SERVES 4

Pressing and draining tofu before marinating it gives it a chewy texture that goes well with barbecue flavors.

**16 oz. extra-firm tofu**

**1 stick lemongrass, tender white part peeled and chopped**

**1 shallot, finely chopped**

**2 tsp. minced fresh ginger**

**⅓ cup low-sodium soy sauce**

**⅓ cup fresh lime juice**

**¼ cup light brown sugar**

**1 Tbs. toasted sesame oil**

**5 green onions, trimmed, each cut into 4 batons**

**20 snap peas**

**16 Boston lettuce leaf cups**

**½ cup loosely packed mint leaves**

**¼ cup dry-roasted peanuts, chopped**

**1.** Drain tofu between 2 cutting boards set on angle over sink, 1 hour. Cut into 16 cubes.

**2.** Purée lemongrass, shallot, and ginger to paste in food processor. Whisk together soy sauce, lime juice, brown sugar, sesame oil, and 2 Tbs. water in bowl. Transfer half of soy sauce mixture to bowl for dipping sauce. Add lemongrass mixture to remaining soy sauce mixture.

**3.** Toss together tofu, green onions, snap peas, and lemongrass–soy sauce mixture, and marinate 30 minutes.

**4.** Oil grill grates, and preheat grill to medium. Thread 4 tofu cubes, 5 green onions, and 5 snap peas onto each of 4 skewers. Place on grill, close hood, and cook 4 minutes. Turn, close hood, and cook 4 minutes more. Transfer to platter. Slide skewer ingredients off with lettuce; garnish with mint, peanuts, and sauce.

**VEGAN**

## NUTRITION INFORMATION

Calories: 281
Protein: 16 g
Total Fat: 14 g
Saturated Fat: 2 g
Carbohydrates: 26 g
Cholesterol: 0 mg
Sodium: 603 mg
Fiber: 4 g
Sugar: 16 g

# COOK'S GUIDE TO TOFU TYPES

### SILKEN

Ultra-smooth and jiggly soft, silken tofu is ideal for puréeing as a base for soups, dressings, dips, and sauces. It also makes excellent dessert puddings and pie fillings.

### SOFT

Whenever you want curds or crumbles for scrambles or egg-like salads, reach for soft tofu. Similarly, it can replace ricotta in lasagna or stuffed shells. Soft tofu can also be puréed, but the results will be thicker and heavier than what you'd get with silken tofu.

### FIRM/EXTRA-FIRM

The most versatile choice, firm tofu can go both ways. It crumbles well for scrambles or eggless salad, but blotted or pressed, it holds its shape as slabs or cubes.

### SUPER-FIRM

Dense and dry, super-firm tofu is an especially good stand-in for feta cheese. Crumbled into stews, it absorbs flavors and adds texture.

### SPROUTED

You won't find chewy bits of sprouted soybeans in blocks of sprouted tofu, but you will get more nutrients (and more fat and calories). It comes in an array of textures—silken, soft, firm, extra firm.

### BAKED

Chewy, dense baked tofu is the most straightforward substitute for meat in stir-fries, casseroles, fajitas, sandwiches, and salads. It comes pre-seasoned in an array of flavors, such Italian, teriyaki, and Mexican.

# BROILED TOFU & STEAMED MUSTARD GREENS
## WITH SPICY MANGO SAUCE

Mustard greens serve as a bed for broiled tofu with a hot mango sauce. Other greens to try in this recipe: Asian mustard greens, broccoli raab, Chinese broccoli, or collard greens.

**YIELD: SERVES 8**

**2 Tbs. canola oil**

**1 small onion, quartered and thinly sliced (½ cup)**

**1 small red bell pepper, coarsely chopped (½ cup)**

**¾ cup hot mango chutney**

**1 medium tomato, coarsely chopped (¾ cup)**

**2 16-oz. pkg. extra-firm tofu, drained and patted dry**

**2 12-oz. bunches mustard greens, thick stems removed**

**1.** Heat oil in medium-size saucepan over medium heat. Add onion and bell pepper, cover, and cook 10 to 15 minutes, or until vegetables are soft, stirring occasionally. Stir in mango chutney and tomato. Cover, and simmer 5 minutes more. Keep warm.

**2.** Preheat oven to broil, and place oven rack in highest position. Coat baking sheet with nonstick cooking spray. Halve each tofu block crosswise to make pieces the size and thickness of sandwich bread. Cut each tofu piece into 4 triangles. Brush each tofu triangle on both sides with mango mixture (it's OK if some bell pepper and onion bits stick to tofu); season with salt and pepper, if desired; and place on prepared baking sheet. Broil 4 to 5 minutes. Flip triangles, and brush with more mango mixture. Broil 4 to 5 minutes more, or until browned and crispy.

**3.** Meanwhile, bring 1 cup water to a boil in large pot. Add mustard greens, cover, and steam 5 to 7 minutes or until greens are crisp-tender, turning occasionally with tongs to make sure greens cook evenly.

**4.** Divide mustard greens among serving plates. Top each serving with 2 tofu triangles, and drizzle with ¼ cup mango sauce.

VEGAN

GLUTEN-FREE

30 MINUTES OR LESS

## NUTRITION INFORMATION
Calories: 246
Protein: 14 g
Total Fat: 10 g
Saturated Fat: 1 g
Carbohydrates: 29 g
Cholesterol: 0 mg
Sodium: 490 mg
Fiber: 5 g
Sugar: 22 g

# VEGETABLE POT PIE

A lot of good things are tucked beneath the crust of this crowd-pleasing recipe.

## FILLING

**2 cups diced potatoes**

**1 cup sliced carrots**

**3 Tbs. olive oil, divided**

**16 oz. firm tofu, drained and cubed**

**¼ cup plus 2 Tbs. tamari, divided**

**½ tsp. granulated garlic, divided**

**2 cups sliced mushrooms**

**2 cups diced onions**

**1 cup chopped broccoli**

**2 cloves garlic, minced (2 tsp.)**

**¼ cup flour**

**2 cups low-sodium vegetable broth**

**½ cup plain vegetable milk**

**3 Tbs. red wine**

**1 Tbs. chopped fresh thyme**

**1 Tbs. chopped fresh sage**

**1 tsp. hoisin sauce**

**½ tsp. vegan Worcestershire sauce**

## CRUST

**1 ¼ cups flour**

**½ cup vegetable shortening, cut into small pieces**

**1 tsp. chopped fresh rosemary**

**1 tsp. chopped fresh sage**

**1.** To make Filling: Cook potatoes and carrots in boiling salted water 10 minutes. Drain and set aside.

**2.** Heat 1 Tbs. oil in skillet over medium-high heat. Brown tofu in oil 5 minutes. Stir in 2 Tbs. tamiari, ¼ tsp. granulated garlic and ⅛ tsp. cayenne, and cook until liquid has evaporated.

**3.** Heat 1 Tbs. oil in Dutch oven over medium heat. Add mushrooms, and cook 2 minutes. Add onion, broccoli, and garlic, and sauté 6 to 7 minutes.

**4.** Add remaining 1 Tbs. oil to pot, and sprinkle vegetables with flour. Stir until all vegetables are coated. Stir broth into vegetables, and cook 3 to 4 minutes, or until sauce thickens. Stir in all remaining ingredients, then spread Filling in casserole dish.

**5.** Preheat oven to 375°F. To make Crust: Combine all ingredients in bowl, and mix with fork until mixture is crumbly. Stir in 4 Tbs. water until dough forms. Roll dough out to size of casserole dish on floured work surface. Drape dough over Filling in casserole dish, and prick all over with fork. Bake 45 minutes, or until crust is golden.

VEGAN

## NUTRITION INFORMATION

| | |
|---|---|
| Calories: 394 | Cholesterol: <1 mg |
| Protein: 12 g | Sodium: 978 mg |
| Total Fat: 22 g | Fiber: 4 g |
| Saturated Fat: 6 g | Sugar: 5 g |
| Carbohydrates: 36 g | |

# GREEK MEATBALLS
## WITH FETA CHEESE

YIELD: SERVES
12 (MAKES 48
MEATBALLS)

Seitan and cottage cheese get blended together for veg meatballs that will fool even diehard omnivores. This recipe makes a lot—leftovers are great in sandwiches or can be reheated.

**3 8-oz. pkg. plain seitan, rinsed and drained**

**1 8-oz. pkg. low-fat cottage cheese or ricotta**

**1 cup unseasoned breadcrumbs**

**1 small onion, finely chopped (1 cup)**

**1 large egg, lightly beaten**

**3 Tbs. lemon juice**

**2 Tbs. finely chopped fresh dill**

**2 Tbs. finely chopped fresh mint and/or parsley, plus more for garnish**

**2 tsp. ground cumin**

**1 tsp. baking soda**

**½ tsp. allspice**

**¼ tsp. ground cinnamon**

**2 Tbs. olive oil**

**1 25-oz. jar tomato sauce**

**1 cup crumbled feta cheese, optional**

**1.** Pulse seitan in food processor until finely ground. Transfer to bowl, and add all ingredients except oil, tomato sauce, and feta. Mash mixture with hands or potato masher until mixture comes together. Season with salt and pepper, if desired. Chill 30 minutes.

**2.** Preheat oven to 350°F. Coat baking dish with oil. Scoop seitan mixture into golf ball–size meatballs, and place in prepared baking dish. Bake 20 minutes.

**3.** Pour tomato sauce over meatballs, and sprinkle with feta (if using). Bake 30 minutes, or until sauce is bubbly.

MAKE IT VEGAN **Substitute crumbled firm tofu for the cottage cheese or ricotta and a flax- or chia seed egg (p. 147) for the egg, and omit the feta cheese.**

## NUTRITION INFORMATION

Calories: 168
Protein: 21 g
Total Fat: 4 g
Saturated Fat: <1 g
Carbohydrates: 14 g
Cholesterol: 16 mg
Sodium: 684 mg
Fiber: 2 g
Sugar: 4 g

# SEITAN 101

Because of its chewy texture, seitan is a natural choice for recipes where you want a "meaty" mouthfeel. Nicknamed "wheat meat," seitan hails originally from China, where it is often used in Buddhist vegetarian cooking. Seitan is made by kneading a dough of flour, water, and seasonings (such as soy sauce, tomato paste, or fresh herbs) to release the gluten, or wheat protein. The dough is cut into smaller pieces, simmered in liquid, and sautéed for a firm, chewy texture. Seitan can also be baked, stir-fried, or ground into patties.

Give packaged seitan a quick rinse to remove the high-sodium broth, and pat dry with paper towels. Tear it into bite-sized pieces with your hands, or pull it apart with a fork. Because packaged seitan is ready to eat, cook just long enough to heat through. Overcooking can make it tough and rubbery.

# HOMEMADE SEITAN

We've added light seasonings to this recipe so that this recipe for seitan will work in any dish, but feel free to play around with flavors and shapes. This tried-and-true favorite can be used in any recipe calling for seitan.

**2 cups vital wheat gluten**

**½ cup nutritional yeast**

**2 tsp. garlic powder**

**5 cups low-sodium vegetable broth, divided**

**2 Tbs. low-sodium soy sauce**

**½ small onion, diced**

**1 clove garlic, crushed**

**1.** Combine wheat gluten, yeast, and garlic powder in large bowl. Stir in 1 cup broth and soy sauce until dough forms, adding more broth if necessary. Knead dough in bowl with spoon 3 minutes, or until elastic. Shape into 2 loaves.

**2.** Place loaves in large saucepan, and add remaining 4 cups broth, onion, garlic, and enough water to cover seitan. Cover, and bring to a boil over medium heat. Reduce heat to medium-low, and simmer 30 to 45 minutes, or until seitan is firm. Remove from heat, and cool in broth.

# BRAISED SEITAN CUTLETS IN MUSHROOM & RED WINE SAUCE

**YIELD: SERVES 2**

1 8-oz. pkg. seitan, drained and halved into 2 thin cutlets

1 Tbs. unbleached flour

1 Tbs. olive oil

¼ lb. mushrooms, sliced

¼ cup chopped onion

2 cloves garlic, minced (2 tsp.)

½ cup red wine

1 tsp. Dijon mustard

½ tsp. thyme

1 tsp. cornstarch

½ cup low-sodium vegetable broth

¼ cup chopped parsley

If you can't find large seitan slabs for cutlets, simply use smaller pieces: dust them in flour, sauté, then add to sauce before serving.

**1.** Coat seitan pieces in flour. Heat oil in large skillet or Dutch oven over medium-high heat. Add seitan, and cook 1 to 2 minutes on each side, pressing pieces down to brown evenly. Remove seitan from skillet, and keep warm.

**2.** Add mushrooms, onion, and garlic to skillet. Sauté 7 to 10 minutes, or until softened and lightly browned. Whisk together red wine, mustard, and thyme in measuring cup. Add to mushroom mixture; season with salt and pepper, if desired; and cook 2 to 3 minutes, or until slightly thickened. Whisk together cornstarch and vegetable broth in same measuring cup, then add to mushroom mixture. Simmer 2 to 3 minutes, or until thickened, stirring constantly. Place seitan cutlets on plates, top with mushroom sauce, and sprinkle with parsley.

VEGAN

30 MINUTES OR LESS

## NUTRITION INFORMATION

Calories: 260
Protein: 34 g
Total Fat: 7 g
Saturated Fat: 1 g
Carbohydrates: 16 g

Cholesterol: 0 mg
Sodium: 399 mg
Fiber: 3 g
Sugar: 3 g

# WEEKNIGHT POT PIE

YIELD: SERVES 6

**4 cups broccoli florets (halved if large)**

**1¼ cups prepared creamy portobello mushroom soup, such as Imagine**

**¾ cup light mayonnaise or soy mayonnaise**

**1 tsp. dry sherry or cooking sherry**

**¼ tsp. poultry seasoning (or ⅛ tsp. each ground thyme and ground sage)**

**1 lb. seitan, cut into bite-sized pieces**

**½ cup freshly grated Parmesan cheese or shredded vegan cheese of choice, optional**

**⅔ sheet (⅓ of 17.3-oz. pkg.) frozen puff pastry, thawed**

The secret ingredient in this spin on classic chicken divan is creamy, woodsy portobello mushroom soup. Cutting the puff pastry into equal portions before baking makes serving really easy. Asparagus can replace the broccoli, if desired.

**1.** Preheat oven to 425°F, and place oven rack in bottom third of oven. Coat 13- x 9-inch baking dish or oval casserole or gratin dish with cooking spray.

**2.** Place broccoli florets in microwave-safe casserole with lid, and add 3 Tbs. water. Cover, and microwave on high power 2 minutes. Stir, cover, and microwave 2 minutes more, or until broccoli is tender. Drain, and set aside.

**3.** Meanwhile, whisk together soup, mayonnaise, sherry, and poultry seasoning in large bowl. Season with salt and pepper, if desired. Add seitan and broccoli florets; stir to combine. Transfer broccoli-seitan mixture to prepared baking dish, and sprinkle with Parmesan cheese, if using.

**4.** Cut pastry into 6 equal squares. Place squares evenly over seitan mixture. (Filling does not need to be completely covered by squares.)

**5.** Bake 20 minutes, or until pastry is puffed and golden and filling is hot and bubbly.

## NUTRITION INFORMATION

| | |
|---|---|
| Calories: 404 | Cholesterol: 16 mg |
| Protein: 28 g | Sodium: 487 mg |
| Total Fat: 23 g | Fiber: 3 g |
| Saturated Fat: 4 g | Sugar: 2 g |
| Carbohydrates: 23 g | |

# TEMPEH PRIMER

An Indonesian staple made from partially cooked, fermented soybeans that are pressed into cakes, tempeh has a mild, nutty taste and absorbs flavors well. Tempeh should always be cooked before eating to avoid a bitter flavor. (Most commercial varieties are steamed prior to packaging, but benefit from brief cooking to enhance texture.) Tempeh should have few or no black spots, which appear when it is exposed to air. (You can still eat it with spots; the taste will just be stronger.) Flavored tempeh—often fermented with wild rice, vegetables, or herbs—is delicious on sandwiches or in recipes where the flavors complement the other ingredients.

## TO COOK TEMPEH:

**STEAM** strips, cubes, crumbles, or whole cakes of tempeh 10 to 20 minutes to tenderize. Steaming also enhances tempeh's texture before baking.

**SAUTÉ** tempeh cubes or crumbles in oil 3 to 7 minutes, or until browned. Use plenty of oil to lock in moisture and prevent sticking.

**SIMMER** crumbled tempeh in soups and stews where it soaks up the flavors of the liquid and foods around it.

**GRILL** tempeh strips—but marinate them first and brush well with oil to prevent the dry grill heat from making the tempeh brittle. The soaked-in marinade also "steams" the tempeh from the inside out.

# TEMPEH BACON

YIELD: MAKES 24
SLICES

**1 8-oz. pkg. tempeh,
sliced into 24 very
thin slices**

**¼ cup low-sodium
soy sauce**

**2 Tbs. apple cider
vinegar**

**1 tsp. light brown
sugar**

**½ tsp. ground cumin**

**½ tsp. ancho chile
powder**

**2 tsp. liquid smoke,
optional**

**1 Tbs. canola oil**

**1 tsp. smoked
paprika, optional**

This simple recipe can be assembled the night before then cooked off in the morning for a weekend breakfast or brunch. Or use it for a tempeh BLT. The tempeh strips can even be left marinating in the fridge 2 to 3 days. Just be sure to eat the bacon as soon as it's cooked—otherwise, it may lose its crispness.

**1.** Lay tempeh slices in 2 13- x 9-inch baking dishes. Bring soy sauce, vinegar, brown sugar, cumin, ancho chile powder, and ½ cup water to a boil in small saucepan. Boil 1 minute, then remove from heat, and stir in liquid smoke, if using. Pour over tempeh slices. Let cool, then cover and chill 2 hours, or overnight.

**2.** Preheat oven to 300°F. Line 2 baking sheets with parchment paper. Carefully transfer tempeh slices to prepared baking sheet, and discard marinade.

**3.** Brush slices with canola oil, and sprinkle with paprika, if desired. Bake 10 to 15 minutes, or until beginning to brown. Flip tempeh slices, brush with oil, and bake 5 to 7 minutes more, or until crisp and dark brown.

VEGAN

## NUTRITION INFORMATION

Calories: 24
Protein: 2 g
Total Fat: 1.5 g
Saturated Fat: 0.5 g
Carbohydrates: 1 g
Cholesterol: 0 mg
Sodium: 31 mg
Fiber: 0 g
Sugar: 0 g

# IRISH STEW

1 Tbs. olive oil

10 small frozen pearl
onions, thawed

1 medium carrot, cut
into ½-inch pieces
(⅔ cup)

1 Tbs. flour

4 oz. seitan, cut into
1-inch pieces

2 slices smoky
tempeh bacon, cut
into ½-inch pieces

1 clove garlic,
minced (1 tsp.)

1 tsp. fresh thyme,
chopped

1 cup stout beer

1 14-oz. can low-
sodium vegetable
broth

6 oz. butternut
squash, cut into
½-inch cubes (1 cup)

⅓ cup frozen shelled
edamame

This stew tastes even better as leftovers, once
the flavors have had a chance to develop.
Serve it with mashed potatoes for a deliciously
comforting meal.

**1.** Heat oil in saucepan over medium-high heat. Add
onions and carrot, and cook 5 minutes. Stir in flour,
and cook 2 minutes more. Add seitan, tempeh bacon,
garlic, and thyme, and cook 2 minutes.

**2.** Pour in beer, and bring mixture to a boil. Cook
3 minutes, stirring and scraping any bits that may be
stuck to bottom. Add vegetable broth and butternut
squash, and bring to a simmer. Reduce heat to
medium-low, and cook 20 minutes. Add edamame
and cook 10 minutes more. Season with salt and
pepper, and serve.

VEGAN

## NUTRITION INFORMATION

Calories: 308
Protein: 23 g
Total Fat: 8.5 g
Saturated Fat: 1 g
Carbohydrates: 36 g
Cholesterol: 0 mg
Sodium: 384 mg
Fiber: 6 g
Sugar: 7 g

# TEMPEH STRIPS
## WITH COLLARDS

Sweet and sticky with just a little kick, these sliced tempeh strips are briefly marinated, baked, then reglazed to trap in maximum flavor and tender texture.

**YIELD: SERVES 6**

**2 8-oz. pkg. tempeh, sliced into ½-inch strips**

**⅓ cup maple syrup**

**¼ cup orange juice**

**¼ cup safflower oil, divided**

**2 Tbs. ketchup**

**2 Tbs. Dijon mustard**

**1 Tbs. sriracha sauce**

**1 Tbs. low-sodium tamari**

**1 tsp. freshly ground black pepper**

**¼ tsp. ground cinnamon**

**2 cloves garlic, minced (2 tsp.)**

**2 12-oz. bunches collard greens, stems and ribs removed, leaves thinly sliced**

**2 cups frozen fire roasted corn, thawed**

**1.** Place tempeh strips in medium heat-proof bowl. Set aside.

**2.** Whisk together maple syrup, orange juice, 2 Tbs. oil, ketchup, mustard, sriracha, tamari, pepper, and cinnamon in medium saucepan. Bring to a simmer over medium heat, and cook 5 to 7 minutes, or until slightly thickened. Pour hot mixture over tempeh strips, cover, and let marinate 30 minutes, or overnight.

**3.** Preheat oven to 350°F. Line baking sheet with foil, and coat with cooking spray. Arrange marinated tempeh strips on prepared baking sheet; reserve marinade. Cover baking sheet tightly with foil, and bake 15 minutes. Remove foil, and flip tempeh pieces. Bake, uncovered, 5 minutes more, or until tempeh is slightly browned. Remove from oven, and brush tempeh with remaining glaze.

**4.** Meanwhile, heat remaining 2 Tbs. oil in large saucepan over medium-high heat. Add garlic, and cook 30 seconds. Add collard greens in two batches, wilting first batch before adding second. Stir in corn, and season with salt and pepper, if desired. Cook 5 to 7 minutes or until greens are tender, stirring occasionally. Serve topped with tempeh slices.

VEGAN

## NUTRITION INFORMATION

Calories: 370

Protein: 18 g

Total Fat: 19 g

Saturated Fat: 2 g

Carbohydrates: 37 g

Cholesterol: 0 mg

Sodium: 358 mg

Fiber: 5 g

Sugar: 17 g

# GLAZED MAPLE-MUSTARD TEMPEH BOURGIGNON

YIELD: SERVES 4

Shiitake mushrooms, marinated tempeh, and flavorings like herbes de Provence and balsamic vinegar make this updated classic a taste sensation.

**2 cups medium-bodied red wine, such as Pinot Noir**

**1 8-oz. pkg. tempeh, cut into 1-inch cubes**

**1 small onion, chopped (about 1 cup)**

**1 large carrot, peeled and cut into ½-inch dice (about 1 cup)**

**3 cloves garlic, peeled and chopped (about 1 Tbs.)**

**3 Tbs. olive oil, divided**

**½ tsp. herbes de Provence**

**1 bay leaf**

**1 Tbs. balsamic vinegar**

**2 Tbs. tomato paste**

**7 oz. sliced shiitake mushrooms (about 4 cups)**

**1 Tbs. chopped fresh parsley**

**1.** Combine wine, tempeh, onion, carrot, garlic, 1 Tbs. olive oil, herbes de Provence, and bay leaf in large bowl. Cover, and refrigerate 1 hour.

**2.** Strain vegetables and tempeh, and reserve wine.

**3.** Heat remaining oil in Dutch oven over medium-high heat. Add tempeh and vegetables, and cook 5 to 7 minutes, or until tempeh cubes are browned on all sides. Add vinegar, and quickly stir to coat evenly. Add tomato paste, and cook 1 minute. Stir in red wine marinade, scraping bottom of pot to release any stuck brown bits. Reduce heat to medium-low, cover, and simmer 30 minutes, or until carrots are tender, stirring occasionally. Add water if mixture seems too dry before carrots are fully cooked.

**4.** Add mushrooms and ¾ cup water, and simmer 10 minutes, or until tender. Remove bay leaf. Season with salt and pepper. Sprinkle with parsley, and serve over rice.

VEGAN

GLUTEN FREE

## NUTRITION INFORMATION

Calories: 269    Cholesterol: mg
Protein: 14 g    Sodium: 338 mg
Total Fat: 13 g    Fiber: 6 g
Saturated Fat: 2 g    Sugar: 9 g
Carbohydrates: 24 g

# GRILLABLE VEGGIE BURGERS

YIELD: MAKES 6
BURGERS

**4 oz. rigatoni pasta**

**½ cup red quinoa**

**7 oz. low-sodium
vegetable broth**

**1½ tsp. olive oil**

**¾ cup chopped
onion**

**9 cloves garlic, finely
chopped**

**1½ cups cooked
white beans, or 1 15-
oz. can white beans,
rinsed, drained,
and thoroughly
patted dry**

**½ cup steamed
broccoli**

**¼ cup plus 2 Tbs.
finely shredded
green cabbage**

**3 Tbs. finely
chopped red bell
pepper**

**2 Tbs. tomato sauce**

**6 Kalamata olives,
sliced**

**2 oil-packed sun-
dried tomatoes,
drained and finely
chopped**

**2 Tbs. canola oil for
oiling patties and
grill topper**

The secret "glue" that holds homemade veggie burgers together on an outdoor grill is overcooked pasta. A couple of other tips for success: Be sure to pat the beans dry before you add them to the patty mixture, and use a stainless-steel grill topper for a more stable grilling surface. Serve these mouthwatering miracles with your favorite burger buns and toppings.

**1.** Cook rigatoni in large pot of boiling salted water 19 minutes, or until very soft. Drain, measure out 1½ cups very tightly packed rigatoni, and set aside.

**2.** Bring quinoa and broth to a boil in saucepan. Cover, reduce heat to low, and cook 13 minutes, or until slightly undercooked; some of the white germ will have opened, but much of the quinoa will still have a slight bite. Drain, and set aside.

**3.** Heat oil in small saucepan over medium heat. Add onion, and cook 1 minute. Add garlic, and cook 1 minute more. Set aside.

**4.** Process rigatoni and white beans in food processor 1 minute, or until smooth and paste-like (it's OK if there are a few small bits of pasta still intact). Transfer mixture to large bowl. Stir in ¾ cup quinoa, broccoli, cabbage, bell pepper, tomato sauce, olives, sun-dried tomatoes, and onion-garlic mixture. Season with salt and pepper, if desired. Mash to combine. Form 6 ½-cup-sized patties. Brush tops of each patty with canola oil.

**5.** Heat grill to high heat. Brush grill topper with canola oil. Place each patty oiled-side down on grill topper. Set grill topper on grill, close grill cover, and cook 6 to 7 minutes. Brush each patty again with oil and carefully flip. Close grill, and grill 3 to 4 minutes more.

VEGAN

## NUTRITION INFORMATION

Calories: 276
Protein: 10 g
Total Fat: 9 g
Saturated Fat: 1 g
Carbohydrates: 41 g
Cholesterol: 0 mg
Sodium: 257 mg
Fiber: 6 g
Sugar: 3 g

# GREEK-STYLE LENTIL BURGERS

Take these veggie burgers to an omnivore cookout and your meat-eating friends will want to try them. They're such a delicious change from the usual barbecue fare.

## BURGERS

½ cup dried lentils

2 Tbs. olive oil, plus more for brushing patties

1 small onion, chopped (1 cup)

½ red bell pepper, diced (½ cup)

4 cloves garlic, minced (4 tsp.)

1 15-oz. can chickpeas, rinsed and drained

1 cup loosely packed parsley leaves

½ cup pitted Kalamata olives

2 large eggs

2 tsp. ground cumin

1 tsp. ground coriander

1 tsp. salt

½ tsp. ground black pepper

1 cup plain breadcrumbs

¾ cup grated carrots

½ tsp. baking powder

## TZATZIKI SAUCE

2 cups plain low-fat yogurt

1 medium cucumber, peeled, seeded, shredded, and drained

2 cloves garlic, minced (2 tsp.)

1 tsp. lemon zest

1 tsp. chopped fresh mint

1 tsp. chopped fresh parsley

1. To make Burgers: Cook lentils according to package directions. Drain.

2. Heat oil in skillet over medium heat. Add onion and bell pepper, and sauté 7 minutes. Stir in garlic.

3. Blend chickpeas, parsley, olives, eggs, cumin, coriander, salt, and pepper in food processor 2 minutes, or until smooth. Stir chickpea mixture, breadcrumbs, carrots, and baking powder into lentils. Shape into 8 patties. Layer patties between plastic wrap, and freeze.

4. To make Tzatziki Sauce: Combine all ingredients in small bowl.

5. Preheat grill to high. Brush frozen patties with oil, and cook 6 minutes on each side. Serve Burgers with Tzatziki Sauce.

## NUTRITION INFORMATION

| | |
|---|---|
| Calories: 262 | Cholesterol: 55 mg |
| Protein: 11 g | Sodium: 656 mg |
| Total Fat: 11 g | Fiber: 7 g |
| Saturated Fat: 2 g | Sugar: 5 g |
| Carbohydrates: 31 g | |

# TEMPEH-MUSHROOM BURGERS

YIELD: SERVES 8

Grated beet keeps these patties juicy and makes them look like "real" burgers.

**4 Tbs. light miso paste**

**2 8-oz. pkg. tempeh, grated**

**3 Tbs. canola oil, divided**

**½ cup gluten flour or vital wheat gluten**

**2 Tbs. guar gum**

**1 portobello mushroom, stemmed and grated (about ¾ cup)**

**1 small beet, grated (about ¾ cup)**

**1 small onion, grated (about ½ cup)**

**1 small carrot, grated (about ½ cup)**

**½ cup fresh or frozen corn kernels**

**½ medium green bell pepper, finely chopped (about ⅓ cup)**

**½ medium red bell pepper, finely chopped (about ⅓ cup)**

**2 cloves garlic, minced (about 2 tsp.)**

**1.** Preheat oven to 350°F. Coat baking sheet with cooking spray.

**2.** Dilute miso in ¼ cup water in bowl. Stir in tempeh and 1½ Tbs. oil. Stir in flour and guar gum.

**3.** Mound tempeh mixture on prepared baking sheet. Cover with foil, and bake 20 minutes, or until heated through.

**4.** Heat remaining 1½ Tbs. oil in skillet over medium heat. Add mushroom, beet, onion, carrot, corn, bell peppers, and garlic. Sauté 10 minutes, or until vegetables are tender.

**5.** Pulse vegetables and tempeh mixture in food processor 6 or 7 times or until just blended (do not overblend).

**6.** Shape tempeh mixture into 8 patties. Cover with plastic wrap, and refrigerate 4 hours, or overnight, to blend flavors.

**7.** Preheat grill to medium. Brush burgers and grill rack with oil. Grill 8 to 10 minutes per side.

VEGAN

## NUTRITION INFORMATION

Calories: 218    Cholesterol: 0 mg
Protein: 20 g    Sodium: 259 mg
Total Fat: 9 g    Fiber: 6 g
Saturated Fat: 1.5 g    Sugar: 3 g
Carbohydrates: 14 g

# BROCCOLI MEATBALLS
## WITH GARLIC-TOMATO SAUCE

Ground almonds and eggs hold these veggie-laced alternatives to traditional meatballs together. For appetizer-size meatballs, shape into 30 smaller rounds instead of 12, and bake 15 to 20 minutes.

**YIELD: SERVES 4**

MEATBALLS

**4 cups broccoli florets (1 large head)**

**1 cup raw almonds**

**¼ cup grated Parmesan cheese**

**¼ cup finely chopped fresh basil**

**¼ cup finely chopped fresh parsley**

**2 cloves garlic, minced (2 tsp.)**

**⅛ tsp. cayenne pepper**

**2 large eggs**

GARLIC-TOMATO SAUCE

**1 Tbs. olive oil**

**¼ cup diced white onion**

**1 large garlic clove, finely chopped**

**1 28-oz. can crushed tomatoes**

**1.** To make Meatballs: Preheat oven to 350°F. Line baking sheet with parchment paper.

**2.** Steam broccoli florets 10 minutes, or until tender and bright green. Cool.

**3.** Pulse almonds in food processor until finely ground. Transfer to large mixing bowl.

**4.** Pulse steamed broccoli in food processor until chopped. Transfer to bowl with ground almonds. Add Parmesan, basil, parsley, garlic, and cayenne. Season with salt and pepper, if desired.

**5.** Whisk eggs in small bowl, then stir eggs into broccoli mixture.

**6.** Shape mixture into 12 Meatballs by hand, pressing firmly to ensure Meatballs hold their shape. Place on prepared baking sheet, and bake 25 minutes, or until golden brown.

**7.** To make Garlic-Tomato Sauce: Heat oil in large saucepan over medium heat. Add onion and garlic, and cook 5 minutes, or until onion is soft. Add tomatoes and their juice, and cook 20 minutes, or until sauce thickens, stirring occasionally. Season with salt and pepper, if desired.

GLUTEN-FREE

## NUTRITION INFORMATION

Calories: 350
Protein: 18 g
Total Fat: 23 g
Saturated Fat: 3 g
Carbohydrates: 28 g
Cholesterol: 97 mg
Sodium: 503 mg
Fiber: 10 g
Sugar: 10 g

# PIZZAS & BREADS

High-protein breads and pizzas tend to be easier to find at the supermarket than they are to make in the kitchen. That's because commercial bakers have access to specialty ingredients and powerful kitchen tools that allow them to get a yeasty flavor and chewy texture from more than just wheat flour.

Still, there are some tricks you can try at home to kick up the protein and nutrients in homemade bread. Whole grain flours can be used for up to half of the all-purpose or bread flour called for in a recipe. Ethnic breads often call for the whole grains that are traditional diet staples in their native cultures. And nutrient-rich fillings, toppings, and accompaniments can help balance out the carb factor while making your daily bread (or pizza) even tastier!

# WHOLE-WHEAT FLAXSEED BREAD

YIELD: SERVES 8

**¾ cup water (at room temperature)**

**1 Tbs. molasses or honey**

**1 Tbs. olive oil, plus more for greasing bowl**

**4 Tbs. flaxseeds, divided**

**1⅓ cups whole wheat flour**

**⅔ cup bread flour or all-purpose flour**

**2 Tbs. nonfat dry milk powder**

**1½ tsp. yeast**

**1 tsp. salt**

**1 large egg white, beaten**

Flaxseeds give this fragrant whole-grain bread a nutty flavor and a richer nutritional profile. The flaxseeds also keep the bread moist and tender for several days. You can also bake the bread in a 1-lb. bread machine; just omit the shaping and scoring steps.

**1.** Stir together water, molasses, and oil in measuring cup until molasses dissolves. Set aside.

**2.** Grind 3 Tbs. flaxseeds to a powder in coffee grinder or mini-chopper. Place whole wheat flour, bread flour, ground flaxseeds, milk powder, yeast, and salt in food processor fitted with metal chopping blade; pulse several times to blend. With motor running, slowly add liquid through feed tube, and process until dough is smooth and pulls away from sides of work bowl. If dough seems too thick, adjust texture by adding 1 Tbs. water at a time. Process 1 minute.

**3.** Transfer dough to large bowl coated with oil. Turn dough to coat all sides with spray. Cover with plastic wrap, and let rise 1¼ to 1½ hours, or until dough has doubled in size.

**4.** Turn out onto lightly floured work surface, and shape into round or oval loaf. Place on baking sheet coated with cooking spray. Cover with plastic wrap coated with cooking spray. Let loaf rise 1 hour, or until almost doubled.

**5.** Preheat oven to 400°F. Brush loaf with egg white, and sprinkle with remaining 1 Tbs. whole flaxseeds. Score top of loaf with 4 ¼-inch-deep slashes using serrated knife. Bake bread 25 to 35 minutes, or until golden and hollow-sounding when tapped. Cool bread on wire rack.

## NUTRITION INFORMATION

Calories: 155
Protein: 5 g
Total Fat: 3 g
Saturated Fat: 0 g
Carbohydrates: 27 g
Cholesterol: 0 mg
Sodium: 229 mg
Fiber: 3 g
Sugar: 3 g

# FLAXSEEDS

Flaxseeds are high in healthy omega-3 fatty acids and offer a host of health benefits, from helping to lower cholesterol levels to reducing the risk of certain cancers. Ground seeds are the way to go—grinding makes them more digestible and unlocks the benefits. You can purchase preground flaxseed meal or make your own by pulverizing the seeds in a spice or coffee grinder. Then it's just a matter of adding a tablespoon or two of the nutty-flavored powder to a smoothie, sprinkling it over hot cereal, stirring them into yogurt, or adding them to oven-baked items such as veggie meatloaf, bread, and muffins.

# NO-KNEAD BREAD

No-knead bread was how people made bread thousands of years ago—before they discovered that by pulling, beating, stretching, stirring, or otherwise "kneading" wheat doughs they could speed up the gluten-developing process. Bakers experimented with the no-knead approach in the early 20th century, and versions of no-knead breads have been circulating in the United States for decades.

# NO-KNEAD HONEY-OAT BREAD

Fragrant, slightly dense, and pleasantly sweet, this loaf is great for toast—and sandwiches.

**YIELD: 16 SLICES (1 LOAF)**

**1 cup quick-cooking oats (not instant), divided**

**3½ cups unbleached bread flour or all-purpose flour, plus more as necessary, divided**

**1½ tsp. salt**

**1 tsp. rapid-rising, instant, or bread machine yeast**

**6 Tbs. honey**

**½ cup vegetable oil, plus more for brushing dough and oiling pan**

## NUTRITION INFORMATION

Calories: 179
Protein: 6 g
Total Fat: 5 g
Saturated Fat: <1 g
Carbohydrates: 29 g
Cholesterol: 0 mg
Sodium: 255 mg
Fiber: 2 g
Sugar: 7 g

**1.** Spread ¾ cup oats on microwave-safe plate. Microwave on high power 1½ to 2 minutes (stop to stir every 30 seconds), or until oats are fragrant and lightly toasted. Cool.

**2.** Combine 3¼ cups flour, salt, yeast, and toasted oats in separate bowl. Measure 1½ cups ice water, and combine with honey and oil in measuring cup. Vigorously stir honey mixture into flour mixture. (Dough should be slightly stiff; stir in just enough additional flour to stiffen dough slightly, if necessary.) Brush top of dough with oil. Cover bowl with plastic wrap, and let rise at room temperature 8 to 12 hours (first rise).

**3.** Vigorously stir dough, scraping down bowl sides. Stir in remaining ¼ cup flour. Stir in more flour if dough is at all soft, to have stiff but still stirrable dough. Oil 9- x 5-inch loaf pan, transfer dough to pan, and smooth surface with spatula or well-oiled fingertips. Press remaining ¼ cup oats on top of loaf. Cover with plastic wrap oiled on side facing dough.

**4.** Let dough rise 1¼ to 2½ hours at room temperature (second rise). Second rise alternatives: Let dough stand in turned-off microwave with 1 cup boiling water 45 minutes to 1½ hours for accelerated rise; for extended rise, refrigerate up to 48 hours, then set out at room temperature.

**5.** Preheat oven to 375°F. Remove plastic wrap, and bake loaf 30 to 35 minutes, or until top is well browned. Cover with foil, and bake 25 to 30 minutes more, or until skewer inserted in thickest part of loaf comes out with just a few particles. Bake 5 minutes more to ensure doneness. Cool on wire rack.

# CINNAMON-RAISIN ESSENE BREAD

YIELD: 12 SLICES

**2 cups wheat berries**

**¾ cup raisins**

**3 Tbs. cane or coconut sugar**

**2 Tbs. melted coconut oil or vegetable oil**

**1 Tbs. ground cinnamon**

**½ tsp. sea salt**

No yeast, no filler, no kneading, no rising time... Essene bread is the essence of easy, whole-grain goodness. The only thing that takes some time is the grain-sprouting process. But once you establish the right conditions with a large jar and some fresh water, Mother Nature does the rest of the work. Then, all you have to do is blend and bake. In this version, a hint of cinnamon-raisin sweetness turns a basic Essene bread recipe into a tasty breakfast option.

**1.** Place wheat berries in 2-quart wide-mouth jar, and cover with 4 cups lukewarm water. Cover jar mouth with cheesecloth held in place with rubber band, and set in cool, dark place to rehydrate for 12 hours, or overnight. Drain, rinse, and return wheat berries to jar. Lay jar on side so wheat berries spread in an even layer; cover mouth with cheesecloth, and store in cool, dark place 2 to 3 days to germinate, rinsing and draining wheat berries every 12 hours.

**2.** To make bread: Preheat oven to 250°F. Line baking sheet with parchment paper. Soak raisins in 1½ cups warm water in small bowl 5 minutes. Drain, and set aside.

**3.** Pulse sprouted wheat berries with sugar, oil, cinnamon, and salt in food processor until smooth, stopping frequently to scrape down sides. Transfer to bowl, and stir in raisins. (Dough should be slightly moist but not wet, and should hold together well.)

**4.** Pat dough into domed mound, and transfer to prepared baking sheet. Score top of loaf with large X using sharp knife. Bake 1 hour 45 minutes to 2 hours, or until knife inserted in center comes out clean. Cool completely before slicing. Store in refrigerator up to 1 week.

VEGAN

## NUTRITION INFORMATION

Calories: 228
Protein: 6 g
Total Fat: 4 g
Saturated Fat: 3 g
Carbohydrates: 47 g
Cholesterol: 0 mg
Sodium: 111 mg
Fiber: 2 g
Sugar: 12 g

# GLUTEN-FREE COUNTRY BREAD

YIELD: MAKES 1
LOAF (10 SLICES)

A good recipe for homemade bread is worth its weight in gold to gluten-intolerant bakers. This soft, chewy loaf fits the bill.

1 tsp. sugar

1 0.75-oz. pkg. yeast

1 cup brown rice flour

1 cup sunflower seeds

½ cup ground flaxseeds or flaxseed meal

½ cup potato starch

¼ cup soy flour

¼ cup tapioca flour or starch

1 Tbs. xanthan gum

1 tsp. salt

2 eggs

2 egg whites

½ cup soymilk or rice milk

¼ cup olive oil

¼ cup molasses

1 Tbs. apple cider vinegar

**1.** Coat 9- x 5-inch loaf pan with cooking spray. Combine sugar and ¼ cup warm water. Sprinkle yeast on top, then stir to combine. Set aside.

**2.** Whisk together rice flour, sunflower seeds, flaxseeds, potato starch, soy flour, tapioca flour, xanthan gum, and salt in large bowl. In separate bowl, whisk together eggs, egg whites, soymilk, oil, molasses, and vinegar.

**3.** Add dry ingredients to egg mixture, and beat with electric mixer on low speed 1 minute. Add yeast mixture, increase mixer speed to medium-high, and beat 3 minutes. Pour batter into prepared loaf pan; let rise 1 hour in warm place.

**4.** Preheat oven to 350°F. Bake loaf 45 to 55 minutes, or until deep golden brown (the outside will look very dark, but the inside will be soft and moist). Cool 10 minutes, then turn out onto cutting board, and slice.

GLUTEN-FREE

## NUTRITION INFORMATION

Calories: 315
Protein: 10 g
Total Fat: 16 g
Saturated Fat: 2 g
Carbohydrates: 38 g
Cholesterol: 42 mg
Sodium: 278 mg
Fiber: 5 g
Sugar: 6 g

# CHERRY TOMATO FOCACCIA

A basic focaccia dough is topped with nuts, cherry tomatoes, and aromatics for a bread option that's hearty enough to be served with a salad for a light lunch or supper.

**YIELD: SERVES 8**

TOPPING

**¼ cup shelled roasted pistachios**

**¼ cup olive oil**

**1 clove garlic, minced (1 tsp.)**

**½ tsp. finely chopped fresh rosemary**

**2 cups heirloom cherry tomatoes, halved**

FOCACCIA

**3½ cups bread flour**

**1 Tbs. sugar**

**2½ tsp. instant yeast**

**2 tsp. salt**

**Olive oil, for greasing baking sheet**

**1.** To make Topping: Pulse pistachios in food processor until ground, but with some larger pieces. Transfer to bowl, and stir in olive oil, garlic, and rosemary.

**2.** To make Focaccia: Stir together flour, sugar, yeast, salt, and 1¼ cups water in bowl. Knead dough in bowl 5 minutes. Cover bowl with towel, and let rise 1 hour, or until doubled in size.

**3.** Generously grease rimmed baking sheet with olive oil. Stretch dough into 12- x 11-inch rectangle in sheet pan. Let dough rise 1 hour.

**4.** Preheat oven to 450°F. Dimple dough with fingers. Whisk 2 Tbs. water into pistachio mixture, and brush onto dough. Press tomato halves cut-side up into dough. Bake 25 to 30 minutes, or until golden brown on top and bottom.

VEGAN

## NUTRITION INFORMATION

Calories: 329
Protein: 9 g
Total Fat: 11 g
Saturated Fat: 2 g
Carbohydrates: 48 g
Cholesterol: 0 mg
Sodium: 589 mg
Fiber: 3 g
Sugar: 3 g

# TARTE FLAMBÉE
## WITH HERB CHEESE & LENTILS

**YIELD: MAKES
12 SLICES**

**¼ cup all-purpose
flour**

**1 16-oz. pkg.
prepared pizza
dough, preferably
whole-wheat,
thawed if frozen**

**1 5.2-oz. pkg.
garlic-and-herb
spreadable cheese,
such as Boursin**

**1½ cups thinly sliced
shallots (3 large
shallots)**

**¾ cups cooked
lentils, preferably
black or French Puy
lentils**

In the Alsace region of France, this pizza-like dish
is traditionally made with crème fraîche and bacon
(lardons). We've lightened up this recipe by replacing
the crème fraîche with a French spreadable cheese
and the bacon with cooked lentils.

**1.** Preheat oven to 425°F. Coat two large baking sheets
with cooking spray.

**2.** Dust work surface with flour. Roll 1 pizza dough
to size of baking sheet. Transfer to prepared baking
sheet. Repeat with remaining dough and baking sheet.

**3.** Mix cheese with 2 Tbs. water in bowl until smooth.
Spread half of cheese on each pizza dough crust.
Sprinkle each with 1½ cups sliced shallots and ¾ cup
lentils. Bake 15 to 18 minutes, or until crust is golden
brown. Cool 5 minutes before slicing each tarte into
12 pieces.

## NUTRITION
## INFORMATION

Calories: 167
Protein: 4 g
Total Fat: 5 g
Saturated Fat: 2 g
Carbohydrates: 24 g
Cholesterol: 11 mg
Sodium: 377 mg
Fiber: 2 g
Sugar: 2 g

# PORTOBELLO MUSHROOM PIZZA
## WITH SPELT CRUST

YIELD: 8
SERVINGS

This pizza has a rich, flavorful, spelt crust that is similar to a whole-wheat crust. If you prefer a lighter crust, substitute ½ cup of oat flour for ½ cup of the spelt flour.

⅔ cup warm water

¼ tsp. active dry yeast

Pinch sugar

1½ cups spelt flour

½ tsp. salt

2½ Tbs. olive oil

2 or 3 portobello mushroom caps, thinly sliced

¾ cup prepared tomato sauce

1 cup shredded low-fat mozzarella cheese

**1.** Stir together water, yeast, and sugar in small bowl until yeast and sugar have dissolved. Let sit 5 minutes, or until foamy.

**2.** Pulse spelt flour and salt in food processor until combined. With machine running, add dissolved yeast mixture through feed tube and process until mixture is crumbly. Keep machine running, add 2 Tbs. oil and process just until dough forms a ball, adding 1 to 2 more Tbs. flour if dough is too sticky. Turn dough out onto lightly floured surface and knead briefly. Cover with plastic wrap, and let rise 45 minutes. Punch down dough, knead several times, then flatten into a circle. Using a floured rolling pin, roll dough out into a 12-inch circle. Transfer dough to pizza pan or baking sheet.

**3.** Preheat oven to 450°F. Heat remaining ½ Tbs. oil in skillet over medium-high heat. Add mushrooms and sauté 3 minutes. Remove mushrooms to paper towels with slotted spoon.

**4.** Spread pizza dough with tomato sauce, sprinkle evenly with cheese, and distribute mushrooms over cheese. Bake on lowest oven rack 20 to 25 minutes, or until cheese has melted and crust has turned golden brown.

NUTRITION INFORMATION

Calories: 184
Protein: 12 g
Total Fat: 7 g
Saturated Fat: 3 g
Carbohydrates: 21 g
Cholesterol: 19 mg
Sodium: 438 mg
Fiber: 5 g
Sugar: g

# WHITE PIZZA
## WITH BROCCOLI & MUSHROOMS

**YIELD: SERVES 6**

**2 Tbs. nonhydro-genated margarine or butter, divided**

**6 oz. mushrooms, sliced (2 cups)**

**8 oz. broccoli florets (3 cups)**

**1 Tbs. all-purpose flour**

**1 cup low-fat milk**

**2 cloves garlic, minced (2 tsp.)**

**¼ tsp. salt**

**½ cup shredded mozzarella, divided**

**¼ cup grated Parmesan, divided**

**1 13.8-oz. pkg. refrigerated pizza dough**

Paired with a two-cheese white sauce, broccoli makes a wonderful pizza topping. The secret to a crisp crust is preheating the baking stone or sheet. If you like extra-crispy pizza, prebake the dough 3 to 4 minutes before adding toppings.

**1.** Place pizza stone or baking sheet in center of oven, and heat to 425°F.

**2.** Melt 1½ tsp. margarine in skillet over medium-high heat. Add mushrooms, and cook 4 to 7 minutes, or until beginning to brown, stirring frequently. Add broccoli and ⅓ cup water. Cover tightly, and steam broccoli in skillet 3 to 4 minutes, or until tender.

**3.** Meanwhile, heat remaining 1½ Tbs. margarine in saucepan over medium-high heat. Add flour, and cook 2 minutes, or until pale golden, stirring constantly. Stir in milk, garlic, and salt. Cook 3 to 4 minutes, or until mixture thickens and begins to boil, stirring constantly. Remove from heat. Stir in ¼ cup mozzarella and 2 Tbs. Parmesan until sauce is smooth and cheese is melted.

**4.** Shape pizza dough according to package directions. Remove pizza stone from oven, and place dough on hot stone.

**5.** Spread white sauce over dough to within ½ inch of edge, and top with broccoli mixture. Sprinkle remaining mozzarella and Parmesan over top. Return to oven, and bake 18 to 20 minutes, or until edges of pizza are golden and center is hot and bubbly. Cool slightly before slicing and serving.

### NUTRITION INFORMATION

Calories: 275
Protein: 13 g
Total Fat: 9 g
Saturated Fat: 4 g
Carbohydrates: 38 g
Cholesterol: 10 mg
Sodium: 746 mg
Fiber: 3 g
Sugar: 7 g

# CHICKPEA & RED CABBAGE PITA PIZZAS

## WITH TOASTED CUMIN

Generous toppings make this a fork-and-knife pizza. Save leftover cabbage for sandwiches.

YIELD: SERVES 6

1½ Tbs. olive oil, divided

6 cups thinly sliced red cabbage

¼ cup balsamic vinegar

2 Tbs. honey

2 tsp. whole cumin seeds

1 large clove garlic, peeled

¼ tsp. salt

1 15-oz. can chickpeas, rinsed and drained, liquid reserved

½ tsp. ground black pepper

4 Tbs. chopped cilantro, divided

6 6-inch pita rounds (preferably not perforated)

4 oz. chilled soft fresh goat cheese, crumbled

**1.** Position rack just below center of oven. Place large rimmed baking sheet on rack, and preheat to 450°F.

**2.** Heat 1 Tbs. oil in large skillet over medium heat. Add cabbage, and toss to coat. Add vinegar and ¼ cup water. Bring to simmer. Cover, and cook 15 minutes, or until cabbage is just tender. Remove from heat, stir in honey, and season with salt and pepper, if desired.

**3.** Toast cumin in small skillet over medium heat 3 to 4 minutes, or until seeds get darker and very fragrant. Cool. Grind in spice grinder or coffee grinder.

**4.** Drop garlic and salt into food processor while running, and finely chop. Add 1¼ cups chickpeas, ¼ cup water or reserved chickpea liquid, 1½ tsp. cumin, and pepper. Blend to coarse purée. Transfer to bowl, and mix in 3 Tbs. cilantro.

**5.** Brush tops of pitas with remaining 1½ tsp. oil. Heat heavy skillet over high heat. Add 1 pita, oiled-side down, to skillet. Cook 2 minutes, or until crisp on bottom, pressing flat with spatula. Repeat with remaining pitas.

**6.** Spread chickpea purée on crisp side of each pita, leaving ½-inch border. Top each with ⅓ cup red cabbage, then dot with cheese. Press remaining ¼ cup whole chickpeas into topping. Sprinkle each pita with large pinch of remaining ½ tsp. cumin. Transfer pizzas to baking sheet with spatula, and bake 6 to 8 minutes, or until toppings are heated through. Sprinkle with remaining 1 Tbs. cilantro.

## NUTRITION INFORMATION

Calories: 369

Protein: 14 g

Total Fat: 9 g

Saturated Fat: 4 g

Carbohydrates: 58 g

Cholesterol: 9 mg

Sodium: 611 mg

Fiber: 6 g

Sugar: 13 g

# LENTIL-POTATO PIZ'AANS
## WITH BROCCOLI SLAW

A can of Indian-spiced lentil soup is the "sauce" on this potato-topped naan pizza.

**YIELD: MAKES 4 PIZZAS**

**3 tsp. vegetable oil or olive oil, divided**

**1 tsp. mango chutney**

**1 tsp. cider vinegar**

**2 cups broccoli slaw or grated broccoli stems and carrots**

**6 new or baby red-skinned potatoes, thinly sliced (1½ cups)**

**1 tsp. curry powder**

**1 15-oz. can Indian-spiced lentil soup**

**1 cup frozen peas**

**4 garlic or tandoori naan**

**1.** Preheat oven to 350°F.

**2.** Whisk 2 tsp. oil, chutney, and vinegar in medium bowl. Add broccoli slaw, and toss to coat. Season with salt and pepper, if desired. Set aside to marinate.

**3.** Toss potatoes with remaining 1 tsp. oil and curry powder in bowl; season with salt and pepper, if desired. Spread in single layer on baking sheet, and bake 5 to 6 minutes, or until beginning to brown on edges. Set aside. Increase oven temperature to 425°F.

**4.** Empty soup into strainer to strain off excess liquid. Transfer to bowl, and stir in peas.

**5.** Spread each naan with one-quarter of soup mixture, and top with potato slices. Place on baking sheet, and bake 10 to 12 minutes, or until naans are hot and crisp and potatoes on top are browned and tender.

**6.** Top hot pizzas with slaw mixture.

VEGAN

30 MINUTES OR LESS

## NUTRITION INFORMATION

Calories: 429
Protein: 17 g
Total Fat: 12 g
Saturated Fat: 2 g
Carbohydrates: 70 g
Cholesterol: 0 mg
Sodium: 752 mg
Fiber: 12 g
Sugar: 7 g

# DIPS, SAUCES & CONDIMENTS

Extra nutrients or empty calories? The choice is yours when it comes to dips, sauces, and condiments. The snack and meal extras that you use to amp up the flavor of foods can also prolong satisfaction levels when they contain a good dose of protein, fiber, vitamins, and minerals. And there's nothing like a dip or sauce served alongside some veggies for those times when you need a nibble but don't want a big serving of guilt to go along with it.

# HUMMUS-Y BEAN SPREADS

No chickpeas? No problem. Most hummus recipes can be made with any type of cooked beans or lentils. Just be sure to choose a legume that isn't too dark colored, which can make the blended hummus look gray or unappetizing.

# CLASSIC HUMMUS

**YIELD: SERVES 16**

**3 cups cooked chickpeas, or 2 15-oz. cans chickpeas, rinsed and drained, warmed**

**⅓ cup lemon juice**

**1 clove garlic**

**½ cup tahini**

Lightly flavored with tahini, this basic hummus is creamy-smooth. For a more full-bodied flavor, increase the tahini up to 1 cup. Stir the tahini well right before measuring—it separates when it sits.

Purée warm chickpeas, lemon juice, garlic, and ⅔ cup water in food processor 3 to 4 minutes, or until smooth, scraping down sides of bowl if necessary. Add tahini, and purée 2 minutes, or until mixture has consistency of soft cream cheese, adding 1 to 2 Tbs. water, if necessary. Season with salt and pepper, if desired.

### NUTRITION INFORMATION

| | |
|---|---|
| Calories: 95 | Cholesterol: 0 mg |
| Protein: 4 g | Sodium: 75 mg |
| Total Fat: 5 g | Fiber: 3 g |
| Saturated Fat: 0 g | Sugar: 2 g |
| Carbohydrates: 10 g | |

# FLAVORED HUMMUS

CLASSIC HUMMUS CAN BE DOCTORED UP WITH THE FOLLOWING FLAVORINGS (ADDED DURING THE LAST MINUTE OF BLENDING TIME) AND GARNISHED WITH TOPPINGS.

### PARSLEY HUMMUS
Blend in ½ cup chopped fresh parsley. Sprinkle with chopped parsley and Za'atar.

### SUN-DRIED TOMATO HUMMUS
Blend in ¼ cup sun-dried tomato pesto. Top with olive oil, chopped olives, and smoked paprika.

### ROASTED PEPPER HUMMUS
Blend in ¾ cup roasted red peppers. Garnish with smoked paprika and chopped parsley.

### SPICY HUMMUS
Blend in 1 Tbs. harissa (or 1 tsp. cayenne pepper mixed with 2 tsp. olive oil and ½ tsp. minced garlic). Garnish with 2 Tbs. olive oil, ¼ tsp. smoked paprika, and dash of chopped parsley.

### GREEN CHILE & CILANTRO HUMMUS
Blend in 3 to 5 Tbs. canned fire-roasted green chiles and ½ cup chopped cilantro. Garnish with olive oil, chopped green chiles, and chopped cilantro.

# EDAMAME PÂTÉ

YIELD: 4
SANDWICHES

The pâté (shown here on sandwiches) can also be spread on crackers or thinned with additional water and used as a dip.

**1¼ cups frozen shelled edamame, thawed**

**½ cup walnuts**

**⅓ cup mint leaves (packed)**

**1 green onion, chopped**

**½ tsp. salt**

**3 Tbs. lemon juice**

**8 slices whole-grain bread**

**2 cups arugula**

**4 jarred roasted red peppers, drained**

**2 small cucumbers, thinly sliced**

**1.** Purée edamame, walnuts, mint, green onion, and salt in food processor until finely chopped. With motor running, add lemon juice and 3 Tbs. water. Process until smooth.

**2.** Spread each of 4 bread slices with ⅓ cup pâté. Add ½ cup arugula, 1 roasted pepper, and cucumbers to each. Top with remaining bread slices.

VEGAN

GLUTEN-FREE

30 MINUTES OR LESS

## NUTRITION INFORMATION

Calories: 294
Protein: 14 g
Total Fat: 12 g
Saturated Fat: 1 g
Carbohydrates: 36 g
Cholesterol: ? mg
Sodium: 806 mg
Fiber: 9 g
Sugar: 7 g

# RICH & CREAMY CASHEW CHEESE

YIELD: MAKES
2 CUPS

2 cups raw unsalted
cashews, soaked
12–24 hours, and
drained

2 Tbs. nutritional
yeast

1 Tbs. lemon juice

2 tsp. white
balsamic vinegar

¼ tsp. granulated
onion powder

⅛ tsp. granulated
garlic powder

⅛ tsp. white pepper,
optional

This easy, spreadable, nut cheese is great on
its own and can be flavored to your tastes. Try
blending in ½ cup chopped parsley and chives;
2 Tbs. diced chipotles in adobo sauce; or 2 tsp.
dried herbs (oregano, basil, tarragon) in the
food processor after the base mixture has been
processed smooth.

Place cashews in bowl of food processor. Process
1 minute, or until rough paste forms. Add ½ cup water
and remaining ingredients. Process 3 to 5 minutes,
until smooth. Transfer to lidded container, and
refrigerate 12 hours to allow to thicken. Spread on
sandwiches, crackers, or pita.

VEGAN

GLUTEN-FREE

## NUTRITION INFORMATION

Calories: 82
Protein: 3 g
Total Fat: 6 g
Saturated Fat: 1 g
Carbohydrates: 5 g
Cholesterol: 0 mg
Sodium: 2 mg
Fiber: <1 g
Sugar: <1 g

# ROMESCO SAUCE

YIELD: MAKES
2 CUPS

This garlicky Spanish sauce is delicious over baked potatoes, veggie burgers, and roasted vegetables. You can also use it as an appetizer dip or a sandwich spread.

**1 large dried ancho chile**

**2 Tbs. olive oil, divided**

**½ cup chopped red onion**

**1 tsp. sweet paprika**

**1 pimiento (whole jarred sweet red pepper), drained and chopped**

**4 cloves garlic, minced (4 tsp.)**

**¼ cup low-sodium vegetable broth**

**1 15-oz. can diced tomatoes**

**1 slice whole-grain bread**

**¼ cup toasted sliced almonds**

**2½ tsp. sherry vinegar**

**1.** Place ancho chile in small bowl, and cover with boiling water. Soak 10 minutes, or until soft. Drain, remove stem and seeds, and thinly slice.

**2.** Heat 1 Tbs. oil in skillet over medium heat. Add onion, paprika, and ancho chile; sauté 6 minutes, or until onion turns golden. Add pimiento and garlic, then broth; cook 2 to 3 minutes.

**3.** Stir in tomatoes and their juice. Tear bread into small pieces, and add to skillet, along with almonds. Reduce heat to medium-low, and simmer 10 to 12 minutes.

**4.** Stir in vinegar and remaining 1 Tbs. oil. Season with salt and pepper, if desired. Transfer mixture to food processor, and pulse until chunky-smooth.

VEGAN

30 MINUTES OR LESS

## NUTRITION INFORMATION

Calories: 166
Protein: 4 g
Total Fat: 10 g
Saturated Fat: 1 g
Carbohydrates: 18 g
Cholesterol: 0 mg
Sodium: 206 mg
Fiber: 6 g
Sugar: 6 g

# PEANUT SAUCE FOR STEAMED VEGETABLES

YIELD: SERVES 8

**1 large bunch broccoli (1½ lb.), separated into florets, stems cut into spears**

**1 cup smooth peanut butter**

**¼ cup chopped cilantro**

**3 Tbs. sugar**

**2 Tbs. low-sodium soy sauce or tamari**

**2 tsp. cider vinegar**

**2 cloves garlic, minced (2 tsp.)**

This salty-sweet sauce is a great way to get kids to eat their veggies. We've given nutritional information with steamed broccoli, but the sauce can be served with any vegetable kids (or adults!) will eat.

**1.** Bring large pot of water to boil. Cook broccoli in water 2 to 3 minutes, or until bright green and tender. Drain, and rinse under cold water to cool. Shake, and pat dry.

**2.** Whisk peanut butter with 1 cup hot water in bowl. Stir in remaining ingredients. Season with salt. Place bowl in center of serving platter, and arrange broccoli around it.

`VEGAN`

`30 MINUTES OR LESS`

## NUTRITION INFORMATION

Calories: 212
Protein: 10 g
Total Fat: 10 g
Saturated Fat: 2 g
Carbohydrates: 32 g
Cholesterol: 0 mg
Sodium: 667 mg
Fiber: 8 g
Sugar: 20 g

# INDONESIAN PEANUT SAUCE

YIELD: MAKES 1½
CUPS

Toss this sauce with noodles, or serve as a dip for grilled tofu or tempeh skewers or fresh vegetables—you can even thin it with water for a salad dressing. The sauce will keep up to a week in the fridge.

**2 tsp. peanut oil**

**1 large shallot, minced (¼ cup)**

**1 clove garlic, minced (1 tsp.)**

**¾ tsp. red pepper flakes, or to taste**

**½ cup creamy peanut butter**

**½ cup light coconut milk**

**1 Tbs. low-sodium soy sauce**

**2 tsp. dark brown sugar**

**2 tsp. fresh lime juice**

Heat oil in saucepan over medium-low heat. Sauté shallot in oil 2 minutes, or until beginning to soften. Add garlic and red pepper flakes, and sauté 1 minute more, or until just fragrant. Whisk in peanut butter, coconut milk, soy sauce, brown sugar, and ½ cup water until smooth, and bring to a boil. Reduce heat to medium-low, and simmer 5 minutes. Stir in lime juice. Serve hot, or at room temperature.

VEGAN

30 MINUTES OR LESS

## NUTRITION INFORMATION

Calories: 169
Protein: 6 g
Total Fat: 14 g
Saturated Fat: 4 g
Carbohydrates: 8 g
Cholesterol: 0 mg
Sodium: 251 mg
Fiber: 2 g
Sugar: 4 g

# TEMPEH BOLOGNESE SAUCE

YIELD: 6 SERVINGS

Crumbled tempeh adds meaty texture to this classic pasta sauce that's ready in under 30 minutes and freezes beautifully.

**8 oz. whole-grain tempeh**

**2 Tbs. olive oil**

**1 medium onion, finely chopped**

**2 cloves garlic, minced**

**1 Tbs. soy sauce or tamari**

**1 28-oz. can crushed tomatoes**

**1 cup tomato puree**

**2 Tbs. chopped fresh basil or 2 tsp. dried**

**2 Tbs. chopped fresh parsley**

**2 tsp. dried oregano**

**1 small bay leaf**

**1.** Crumble tempeh into fine pieces using your hands. Set aside.

**2.** Heat oil in large saucepan over medium heat. Add onion and cook 5 to 7 minutes, or until golden, stirring often. Add garlic and sauté 15 seconds. Stir in tempeh, 1 cup water, and tamari. Bring to a boil. Reduce heat, cover, and simmer 5 minutes. Remove cover and simmer until liquid is reduced and tempeh begins to sizzle.

**3.** Add remaining ingredients to tempeh mixture and mix well. Cover, and simmer 10 minutes. Season with salt and pepper, if desired.

VEGAN

30 MINUTES OR LESS

GLUTEN-FREE

## NUTRITION INFORMATION

Calories: 181
Protein: 10 g
Total Fat: 7 g
Saturated Fat: 1 g
Carbohydrates: 24 g
Cholesterol: mg
Sodium: 358 mg
Fiber: 6 g
Sugar: g

# DESSERTS

Julia Child once said, "Fat gives things flavor." That is especially true for desserts, where high-fat ingredients are used (often liberally) to impart a richness and a delicate texture. The trick, then, is to find lower-fat, higher-nutrient substitutes that can stand in for high-fat items without sacrificing any of the decadent deliciousness we all long for in dessert.

The dessert ingredient superstars include some familiar foods elsewhere in this book: Greek yogurt, tofu, nuts, and whole grains put a healthy spin on cakes, pies, cookies, and creamy desserts. They all clock in under 400 calories, too, which means you can indulge (and in some cases enjoy seconds) without overdoing it or blowing a healthy eating regime.

# LABNEH

Also known as yogurt cheese, labneh is a Middle Eastern strained plain yogurt. Make your own by draining plain Greek yogurt in a strainer placed over a bowl for several hours.

# LABNEH TART
## WITH HONEY-CRANBERRY TOPPING

This naturally sweetened tart offers a tasty alternative to holiday pies and desserts and shows how thickened yogurt can be used as a dessert filling.

YIELD: SERVES 10

¼ cup plus 1 tsp. melted coconut oil, divided

1¼ cups rolled oats

1¼ cups unsweetened coconut

¼ cup oat flour, sifted

¼ cup brown rice flour

¼ tsp. sea salt

5 Tbs. maple syrup

2 tsp. vanilla extract

½ cup fresh or frozen cranberries

8 Tbs. honey, divided

1½ cups labneh

1 vanilla bean

**1.** Preheat oven to 375°F. Brush 9-inch springform pan with 1 tsp. oil. Set aside.

**2.** Blend oats, coconut, oat flour, rice flour, and salt in food processor until coarsely ground, and transfer to bowl. Stir in remaining ¼ cup oil, syrup, and vanilla.

**3.** Press crust into bottom of prepared pan. (Do not press up sides.) Bake 25 minutes, or until edges begin to brown.

**4.** Meanwhile, bring cranberries and 6 Tbs. honey to a simmer in medium saucepan. Reduce heat to medium, and cook 3 minutes, or until cranberries burst, stirring occasionally. Transfer to bowl, and set aside.

**5.** Place labneh in bowl. Scrape in seeds from vanilla bean, then whisk in remaining 2 Tbs. honey. Spread labneh mixture over baked crust, and drizzle with cranberry mixture. Serve warm or chilled.

GLUTEN-FREE

### NUTRITION INFORMATION

Calories: 355
Protein: 5 g
Total Fat: 19 g
Saturated Fat: 15 g
Carbohydrates: 37 g
Cholesterol: 24 mg
Sodium: 54 mg
Fiber: 3 g
Sugar: 22 g

# CHERRY-PISTACHIO CRISPS

YIELD: SERVES 8

Deep-red cherries bubbling under a sweet, fragrant, pistachio-flecked topping make individual crisps especially festive. Serve warm topped with ice cream, whipped cream, or Greek yogurt and a sprinkle of chopped pistachios.

**2 10-oz. bags frozen sweet cherries**

**3 Tbs. maple syrup, divided**

**2 tsp. arrowroot powder**

**1 tsp. grated orange zest**

**3 tsp. vanilla extract, divided**

**½ tsp. ground cinnamon**

**⅛ tsp. almond extract**

**1 cup old-fashioned rolled oats**

**⅓ cup unsweetened shredded dried coconut**

**⅓ cup almond meal**

**¼ cup coconut sugar**

**¼ cup gluten-free oat flour, sifted**

**¼ tsp. sea salt**

**¼ cup melted coconut oil**

**½ cup raw pistachios, roughly chopped, plus more for garnish**

**1.** Preheat oven to 375°F. Arrange 8 ½-cup ramekins on a baking sheet.

**2.** Toss together cherries, 2 Tbs. maple syrup, arrowroot powder, orange zest, 2 tsp. vanilla, cinnamon, and almond extract in medium bowl. Fill each ramekin with generous ⅓ cup cherry mixture, and set aside.

**3.** Toss together oats, coconut, almond meal, coconut sugar, oat flour, and salt in medium bowl. Stir in oil, remaining 1 Tbs. maple syrup, and remaining 1 tsp. vanilla. Add pistachios, and stir until combined. Top each ramekin with ¼ cup pistachio mixture.

**4.** Bake 20 to 25 minutes, or until crisps bubble around edges and tops are golden. Garnish with more pistachios, if desired.

VEGAN

GLUTEN-FREE

30 MINUTES OR LESS

## NUTRITION INFORMATION

Calories: 300
Protein: 5 g
Total Fat: 15 g
Saturated Fat: 9 g
Carbohydrates: 37 g
Cholesterol: 0 mg
Sodium: 67 mg
Fiber: 5 g
Sugar: 23 g

# CHOCOLATE-CHERRY QUINOA MUFFINS

YIELD: MAKES 12 MUFFINS

1⅔ cups all-purpose flour

⅔ cup unsweetened cocoa powder

1½ tsp. baking powder

½ tsp. salt

2 large eggs

1¼ cups light brown sugar

1 tsp. vanilla extract

⅓ cup vegetable oil

⅓ cup low-fat sour cream

1 Tbs. instant espresso granules, dissolved in 1 Tbs. hot water

1 cup finely grated zucchini

1 cup cooked quinoa

2 cups fresh or frozen pitted sweet cherries, halved

A cup of grated zucchini keeps lightly sweet muffins moist and tender. You can swap other seasonal fruits for the cherries throughout the year—the muffins are especially good with diced pears in fall.

**1.** Preheat oven to 350°F. Coat 12-cup muffin pan with cooking spray.

**2.** Whisk together flour, cocoa powder, baking powder, and salt in medium bowl.

**3.** Beat eggs and brown sugar in large bowl with electric mixer on medium speed 1 minute, or until smooth. Add vanilla, oil, sour cream, and espresso; beat 1 minute more. With mixer running on very low speed, gradually add flour mixture, beating just until combined. Add zucchini and quinoa, and mix until just combined. Fold in cherries. Spoon batter into muffin cups (they will be very full).

**4.** Bake 26 to 28 minutes, or until toothpick inserted in center comes out clean. Cool in pan 10 minutes, then transfer to cooling rack to cool completely. Wrap in plastic, and store at room temperature or in freezer.

## NUTRITION INFORMATION

Calories: 274
Protein: 5 g
Total Fat: 9 g
Saturated Fat: 1 g
Carbohydrates: 47 g
Cholesterol: 32 mg
Sodium: 197 mg
Fiber: 3 g
Sugar: 27 g

# FRESH BERRY TART
## WITH TOASTED NUT CRUST

A crumbly homemade nut crust sets this tart apart from other berry pies. It can be made up to three days ahead and refrigerated until ready to use.

### CRUST

¼ cup each almonds, pecans, and hazelnuts

¾ cup whole-wheat flour

¼ cup sugar

¼ tsp. salt

6 Tbs. chilled unsalted butter, diced

1 large egg yolk

### FILLING

½ cup light sour cream

½ cup nonfat plain Greek yogurt

2 Tbs. light brown sugar

1 tsp. vanilla extract

¼ tsp. grated orange zest

1 cup blueberries

1 cup raspberries

1 Tbs. orange juice

**1.** To make Crust: Preheat oven to 350°F. Coat 9-inch tart pan with cooking spray. Spread nuts on baking sheet, and toast in oven 12 to 15 minutes, or until browned.

**2.** Pulse nuts, flour, sugar, and salt in food processor until nuts are ground to powder. Add butter, and pulse until mixture resembles coarse meal. Add egg yolk, and pulse until moist clumps form. Press dough into bottom and sides of prepared pan, about ¼-inch thick, and pierce with fork. Freeze 30 minutes.

**3.** Adjust oven temperature to 400°F. Bake Crust 12 to 14 minutes, or until golden. Cool.

**4.** To make Filling: Whisk together sour cream, yogurt, brown sugar, vanilla, and orange zest in small bowl. Toss berries with orange juice in separate bowl.

**5.** Spread sour cream mixture in Crust with spatula. Spoon berries over top a little at a time, until sour cream mixture is evenly covered. Refrigerate 30 to 60 minutes before serving.

### NUTRITION INFORMATION

Calories: 288
Protein: 6 g
Total Fat: 19 g
Saturated Fat: 9 g
Carbohydrates: 26 g
Cholesterol: 58 mg
Sodium: 87 mg
Fiber: 4 g
Sugar: 13 g

# TOFU CRÈME AU CHOCOLAT

**4 oz. dark chocolate, broken into pieces**

**1 Tbs. Earth Balance Original Buttery Spread**

**1 14-oz. pkg. silken tofu, drained**

**¼ cup dark brown sugar**

**1¼ tsp. vanilla extract**

**⅛ tsp. salt**

We've given this dessert its French name to highlight how decadent it is—a chocolate pudding for grown-ups as well as kids! It also makes an incredible pie filling. Be sure to get the melted chocolate very hot (without burning) so it will blend smoothly into the tofu. If it does separate from the tofu base, simply warm the mixture in the microwave 1 minute and whisk until smooth.

**1.** Melt chocolate in microwave on medium power or in double boiler. Stir in buttery spread until no lumps remain.

**2.** Blend tofu, brown sugar, vanilla, and salt in blender or food processor 1 to 2 minutes, or until smooth and creamy.

**3.** Add chocolate to tofu mixture, and blend 30 seconds, or until smooth and creamy. Transfer to bowl, cover, and refrigerate 2 hours, or until set.

## NUTRITION INFORMATION

Calories: 146
Protein: 3 g
Total Fat: 8 g
Saturated Fat: 4 g
Carbohydrates: 15 g
Cholesterol: 0 mg
Sodium: 56 mg
Fiber: 1 g
Sugar: 12 g

# CHOCOLATE SWEET POTATO TORTE

YIELD: SERVES 12

Puréed sweet potato, cocoa, almond flour, and eggs yield a dense, fudgy cake perfect for chocolate lovers.

**1 cup packed cooked, mashed orange-fleshed sweet potato**

**1½ cups sugar, divided**

**1 cup almond flour**

**½ cup unsweetened dark-chocolate cocoa powder**

**⅛ tsp. salt**

**4 large eggs**

**2 oz. bittersweet chocolate**

**2 Tbs. nonfat milk or vegetable milk**

**1.** Preheat oven to 375°F. Coat 9-inch springform pan with cooking spray.

**2.** Blend sweet potato, 1 cup sugar, almond flour, cocoa, and salt in food processor 30 seconds, or until smooth, scraping bowl as necessary.

**3.** Separate 3 eggs, placing whites in bowl of electric mixer. Add 3 yolks and remaining whole egg to sweet potato mixture; pulse to combine. Transfer sweet potato mixture to large bowl.

**4.** Beat egg whites with electric mixer at high speed until soft peaks form. Add remaining ½ cup sugar; beat 2 minutes more, or until stiff, glossy peaks form.

**5.** Fold one-third egg white mixture into sweet potato mixture with spatula. Gently fold in remaining whites. Pour batter into prepared pan. Bake 45 minutes, or until toothpick inserted in center comes out clean. Cool 10 minutes in pan on wire rack. Remove springform sides; cool completely.

**6.** Melt chocolate in small saucepan over medium-low heat. Stir in milk. Spread chocolate mixture over top of cake. Let stand until chocolate sets.

GLUTEN-FREE

## NUTRITION INFORMATION
Calories: 227
Protein: 6 g
Total Fat: 9 g
Saturated Fat: 2 g
Carbohydrates: 37 g
Cholesterol: 71 mg
Sodium: 61 mg
Fiber: 3 g
Sugar: 29 g

# GLAZED CHOCOLATE AVOCADO CUPCAKES

**YIELD: MAKES 12 CUPCAKES**

Avocado replaces the eggs and most of the oil in a rich, chocolatey batter that turns out supermoist baked goodies.

## CUPCAKES

**1½ cups all-purpose flour**

**¾ cup unsweetened cocoa powder**

**1 tsp. baking powder**

**¾ tsp. baking soda**

**¾ tsp. salt**

**1 avocado, pitted and peeled**

**1 cup pure maple syrup**

**¾ cup plain soymilk**

**⅓ cup canola oil**

**2 tsp. vanilla extract**

## GLAZE

**¼ block soft silken tofu (from 14-oz. container), drained and patted dry**

**3 Tbs. pure maple syrup**

**½ tsp. vanilla extract**

**⅛ tsp. salt**

**4 oz. semisweet vegan chocolate, melted**

**1.** To make Cupcakes: Preheat oven to 350°F. Line 12-cup muffin pan with paper liners. Whisk together flour, cocoa powder, baking powder, baking soda, and salt in bowl. Purée avocado in food processor until smooth. Add maple syrup, soymilk, oil, and vanilla, and blend until creamy. Whisk avocado mixture into flour mixture.

**2.** Spoon batter into prepared cupcake cups. Bake 25 minutes, or until toothpick inserted into center comes out with some crumbs attached. Cool.

**3.** To make Glaze: Blend tofu, maple syrup, vanilla, and salt in food processor until smooth. Add chocolate to tofu mixture and blend until smooth. Transfer to bowl. Dip tops of Cupcakes into Glaze, pulling straight up from Glaze to form peaks.

VEGAN

## NUTRITION INFORMATION

Calories: 287
Protein: 5 g
Total Fat: 12.5 g
Saturated Fat: 3 g
Carbohydrates: 44 g
Cholesterol: 0 mg
Sodium: 304 mg
Fiber: 4 g
Sugar: 24 g

# RAW CHOCOLATE MOUSSE

YIELD: SERVES 4

Avocados give this luscious dessert its rich, creamy texture. The key is to use avocados that are neither underripe nor overripe, both of which have superstrong avocado flavor.

**3 Hass avocados (2 cups mashed)**

**¼ cup plus 3 Tbs. raw agave nectar**

**¼ cup plus 2 Tbs. raw cocoa powder**

**3 Tbs. raw almond butter**

**1 tsp. lemon juice**

**½ tsp. flavored extract such as mint, cherry, orange, almond, hazelnut, or coffee, optional**

Purée all ingredients in food processor 3 to 4 minutes, or until smooth and creamy, scraping down sides of bowl occasionally. Transfer to bowls, and serve immediately.

VEGAN

GLUTEN-FREE

30 MINUTES OR LESS

## NUTRITION INFORMATION

Calories: 370
Protein: 5 g
Total Fat: 24 g
Saturated Fat: 4 g
Carbohydrates: 44 g
Cholesterol: 0 mg
Sodium: 11 mg
Fiber: 10 g
Sugar: 29 g

# PEANUT BUTTER CHOCOLATE CHIP COOKIES

Good luck eating just one of these tender, chewy chocolate chip cookies.

YIELD: MAKES 24 COOKIES

1½ cups crunchy peanut butter

2¼ cups spelt or all-purpose flour

1 tsp. baking soda

1 tsp. salt

1½ cups maple syrup

2 tsp. vanilla extract

1½ cups vegan chocolate chips

**1.** Preheat oven to 375°F. Coat baking sheets with cooking spray or line with parchment paper. Spoon peanut butter into microwave-safe bowl, and heat on high power 30 to 45 seconds, or until melted, stirring once or twice.

**2.** Combine flour, baking soda, and salt in large bowl. Stir in peanut butter, maple syrup, and vanilla until blended. Fold in chocolate chips.

**3.** Drop 2 Tbs. dough for each cookie onto prepared baking sheet, and flatten slightly. Bake 15 to 17 minutes, or until golden brown. Cool 5 minutes, then transfer to wire rack to cool completely.

VEGAN

## NUTRITION INFORMATION

Calories: 237
Protein: 6 g
Total Fat: 11 g
Saturated Fat: 3 g
Carbohydrates: 31 g
Cholesterol: 0 mg
Sodium: 238 mg
Fiber: 2 g
Sugar: 19 g

# BANANA-MAPLE CASHEW PUDDING

YIELD: SERVES 4

**2 bananas, cut into chunks**

**1½ cups Cashew Cream**

**3 Tbs. pure maple syrup**

**1 Tbs. orange juice**

**1 pinch salt**

Dress up this quick dessert as shown with cashew pieces and caramelized banana slices. To prepare bananas, sprinkle with maple sugar and sauté 2 to 3 minutes over medium-high heat, or until browned and glistening.

Blend all ingredients in blender or food processor until smooth.

VEGAN

GLUTEN-FREE

## NUTRITION INFORMATION

Calories: 246
Protein: 6 g
Total Fat: 12 g
Saturated Fat: 2 g
Carbohydrates: 30 g
Cholesterol: 0 mg
Sodium: 42 mg
Fiber: 2 g
Sugar: 19 g

# CASHEW CREAM

YIELD: MAKES
3 CUPS

**2 cups raw cashews**

**8 cups boiling water**

For raw and vegan baking recipes, cashew cream can be used as a substitute for cream cheese, cream, and sour cream. Here's how to make a 3-cup batch, which will keep in the fridge for up to one week.

Cover cashews with boiling water in large bowl. Cover with clean kitchen towel, and let stand 6 to 8 hours. Drain cashews, then blend in blender with ⅓ to ½ cup cold water 5 minutes, or until smooth and thick, like sour cream.

VEGAN

GLUTEN-FREE

## NUTRITION INFORMATION

Calories: 53
Protein: 2 g
Total Fat: 4 g
Saturated Fat: <1 g
Carbohydrates: 3 g
Cholesterol: 0 mg
Sodium: 2 mg
Fiber: <1 g
Sugar: <1 g

# RAW CASHEW CHEESECAKE

**YIELD: SERVES 12**

This dairy-free, no-bake dessert is made with a cashew "cream cheese" that is sweetened with agave nectar, then chilled atop a macadamia nut crust.

**2 cups macadamia nuts**

**1½ cups cashews**

**½ cup pitted Medjool dates**

**¼ cup dried coconut**

**6 Tbs. coconut oil, melted (gently warmed)**

**¼ cup lime juice**

**¼ cup raw agave nectar**

**½ sun-dried vanilla bean**

**3 cups mixed berries, such as blueberries and raspberries, optional**

**1.** Place macadamia nuts in large bowl, and cover with cold water. Place cashews in separate bowl, and cover with cold water. Soak nuts 4 hours, then rinse, drain, and set aside.

**2.** Pulse macadamia nuts and dates in food processor to a sticky crumb-like consistency. Sprinkle dried coconut on bottom of 8-inch pie pan. Press macadamia nut mixture onto coconut to make crust.

**3.** Place cashews, coconut oil, lime juice, agave nectar, and 6 Tbs. water in bowl of food processor. Scrape seeds from vanilla bean into food processor bowl, and purée until smooth. Pour mixture onto crust, and freeze 1 to 2 hours, or until firm. Remove from freezer, slice while frozen, and transfer to serving platter. Defrost in fridge 1 hour, or on countertop 30 minutes; top with berries, if desired; and serve.

VEGAN

GLUTEN-FREE

## NUTRITION INFORMATION

Calories: 359
Protein: 5 g
Total Fat: 28.5 g
Saturated Fat: 9.5 g
Carbohydrates: 24 g
Cholesterol: 0 mg
Sodium: 7 mg
Fiber: 4 g
Sugar: 14 g

# AGAVE NECTAR

Agave nectar is a sweetener derived from the agave plant, which is grown and harvested primarily in Mexico. In the same way maple syrup is harvested from trees, the liquid syrup is extracted from the cactus-like plant's core, then heated to change the complex carbohydrates into simple sugars before being bottled and sold. In recipes calling for honey, it can be used as a foolproof substitute in equal measure. (1 cup agave = 1 cup honey.) Use slightly less agave when using it to replace sugar—½ cup agave for every cup of sugar—and decrease the liquid in the recipe by ¼ cup and the cooking temperature by 25 degrees. (Agave is more sensitive to heat and burns easier than sugar.)

# INDEX

# ABOUT MARY MARGARET CHAPPELL

Mary Margaret Chappell is the former food editor of *Vegetarian Times*. She lives in Cancale, France.

# ABOUT *VEGETARIAN TIMES*

For over 40 years, *Vegetarian Times* has been at the forefront of the healthy living movement, providing delicious recipes, expert wellness information and environmentally sound lifestyle solutions to a wide variety of individuals. Our goal is to remain a trusted resource for our faithful readers and to reach out to the new generation of full-time vegetarians and flexitarians who find themselves increasingly drawn to the health-conscious, eco-friendly, "green" lifestyle we have always promoted.

# ACKNOWLEDGMENTS

Passionate editors, talented recipe developers, creative photographers, and clever food stylists all contributed to this book and made it the beautiful work that it is.

Elizabeth Turner, Daphna Shalev, Scott Hyers, Amy Spitalnick, Jolia Sidona Allen, Don Rice, and Tami Fertig made up the team that turned typed-out recipes into the gorgeous creations on these pages as the *Vegetarian Times* editorial staff. Fiona Kennedy and Abigail Wolfe prepared and reworked each dish as recipe testers, providing their invaluable input on how a dish should be made or could be improved. Allison Ildefonso supplied invaluable editorial support on a tight deadline—while taking midterms, no less!

AIM Media Healthy Living Group General Managers past and present, Pat Fox and Kim Paulsen continue to champion the *Vegetarian Times* brand through projects like this one.

And finally, special thanks go out to *Vegetarian Times* readers, social media followers, and website visitors over the years. Their comments, insights, and commitment to healthy, humane eating habits have made *Vegetarian Times* the largest and most trusted source of vegetarian recipes in the world.